Hell, Yes, I'd Do it All Again

by

T. Fred Harvey

Hell, Yes, I'd Do it All Again

Copyright 2012
by
T. Fred Harvey
Front cover design by Renny James

ISBN 978-1-934335-43-7

Special Delivery Books
46561 State Highway 118
Alpine, Texas 79830

Printed in the United States of America

Dedicated to the memory of my daughter
Mary Lou Harvey Sauriol

Foreword

During my forty-three years as an educator, I have had the privilege and pleasure of reading a great number of creative writing projects. I marveled over the years at how some students developed a piece of writing entertained, mystified and/or inspired me. Although I never had Fred (Sonny as his family calls him) as one of my students, I wish I had. His stories about his life impressed me. As I read the first one, I caught myself reading it as a teacher and looking for the six traits of writing I had taught students for years. Of those traits, the two most challenging for my students included voice (the ability to create feelings and emotions which capture a readers interest) and word choice (finding and using just the right words to help a reader visualize and make a story come to life). Fred has mastered both of these traits in his well–written personal stories.

Hell, Yes, I'd Do It Again tells of a period in history that occurred before my birth or during my early youth, therefore I can't personally relate to the period. Yet, the stories of his early life in West Texas sent my emotions on a roller coaster ride. I laughed at some of his mischievous, childish antics. I grew angry when, because of his cleverness, a woman accused him of cheating during an Easter egg hunt. I cheered at his mother's determination to overcome difficult circumstances to get a weapon to her son before he left for the battlefield. I cried with him when a best friend died. My emotions soared again as I read of his WWII experiences. I shudder at how, as an 18-year-old, his youthful innocence and desire to see action drove him to quit high school and join the Marines. I felt fear, anxiety and pride as I read how he grew, matured and changed into a man. I felt his pain as he suffered a life-threatening injury trying to save the lives of his buddies. I felt his frustration as he struggled to cope with the long recovery and life-altering circumstances. I shed tears of disappointment and joy through his lifetime of romantic encounters. All the emotions I experienced while reading *Hell, Yes, I'd Do It Again,* inspired and challenged me to seize the moments as they come, hold on to them, learn from them and never give up.

I heartily recommend reading *Hell, Yes, I'd Do It Again.* As you read, I hope you will see life through Fred's eyes and feel his heartache, pain, fears, disappointments, joy, hope and passion for life. May Fred's words come to life and touch your heart as they did mine.

Nina Maddux
Parsons, Kansas

Acknowledgments

My eternal love and thanks to Billie Ford Harvey, my wife of thirty years, who filled the void during my years of Godlessness. This fine lady reared our children Mary Lou and Charles in God's Image. Mary Lou resides with her Lord in Heaven and Charles works for his Lord Jesus through the Bell Vue Church of Christ in Fort Collins, Colorado.

This litany of life's yarns would never have happened had not Iris Johnson Parchen implored me to write this book. Now that it's finally done, thanks, Iris.

I coached for forty-five years in the image of Doctor M. O. Juel. Following his coaching methods I developed my philosophies. People might never see me as a great coach, but through him, I feel I proved myself a successful mentor.

I served in the Marine Corps with a great guy named Peter J. C. Adam. Peter convinced me that I needed to attend college when injuries cut my career in the Corps short, and his advice proved to be my salvation. Then in the fall of 1945 a young lady I remember only as Babe came into my life. I met Babe (her surname has faded with time) in New Orleans. She came from either Biloxi or Gulfport, Mississippi. I tried for twenty years to find her, as she played a very important part in my life. At this late date, I thank her.

Lois Glass Webb and Jim Webb, a writing team residing in Ruidoso, New Mexico have given me invaluable help in getting this manuscript ready. Jim's advice on the publishing game served

3

as a wake-up call. One shouldn't hop into the complex, tricky business of publishing without advice. Lois, author of *The Judge's Daughter,* has given me big, big help in the art of writing. What a wonderful couple.

A special thanks to Emily Allen of Llano, Texas who gave up vacation time to help me bring this manuscript together. Until she came along, I had come to a complete standstill on this project. Her editing and computer skills helped set me free.

Of course I cannot leave out Harry Eskew, a longtime friend and buddy who helped and encouraged me along the way to get this ready to print.

I would be remiss if I did not include five members of the Hill Country Writers Club as they accorded me encouragement and advice along the way. This group includes Jean Townsend, Emma Harris, Ursula Kramer, Iris Adams, and a special thanks to Polly Olson who spent countless hours correcting my spelling and grammar. Thanks, ladies, for sharing your time with me.

Preface

When I sat down to take on this project, it did not take me long to realize I knew very little about the art of writing. Heck, when I dropped out of high school in the year 1942 to join the Marine Corps, I lagged behind by two courses in English. I never caught up. No one has ever accused me of being a grammarian or a colorist with words, so you can take this preface as a warning: what you see is what you read. When I had done several chapters, I sent them to a professional editor to get a cost estimate. The answer: "I wouldn't touch this thing for less than $4,000!" (Notice she put one of these things "!" in her answer. I figured this meant we couldn't do business.) Now, I've played lots of poker so I know when to fold. At the numbers she quoted, I folded like a greasy taco. I didn't like the odds for recouping a return on my investment.

Being a bit contrary and big-time in stubbornness, I've decided to go ahead with this project. But, I need your help in the usage and grammar department. Since you need to abet the crimes I lay on the King's English, I have put at your disposal a bunch of these things: (, " ; : ' . ? ( ) * /!). Now, you put them where you think they are needed. This computer pretty well takes care of the spelling, so don't concern yourselves about this phase.

All the literary pundits I've talked to have said, "Harv, to write your life's story, write it like it was and, above all, write in your own words." I've done just that, but in doing so, some profanity crept into the text. It's not my intention to offend anyone so, with the above-mentioned do-dads, I have thrown in a few bleeps to cover the profane. Radio and TV get around the bad words by slipping in a bleep when an offensive word slithers in. Along my way, many four-letter words slipped in. Dang, I can't communicate without using some of these baddies. So, when you come to a word you deem offensive, just pinch-hit one of these bleep, bleep, bleeps that I've provided. Ain't this accommodating?

During my span of years, many people and events have come into my life. With these numbers, it proved impossible to mention them all. I have taken the liberty of taking two or more people and making them into a composite of oneness. I've also changed some names so as not to embarrass or alienate anyone.

Events and people, like threads, have interwoven to form the fabric of my memories. I can't cause, nor can I create. I can only write of what I've done, seen, and felt. I feel that to use real life as raw material for writing, one must have lived it. Expect no sophisticated lines or thoughts. That which you read comes from my arsenal of memories.

So, let's get on with it!

Chapter 1

I Fought the Lord and the Lord Won

As a child, my cultivation in the area of religious persuasion verged on nonexistent. However, at home I encountered a semblance of religion through a large, but old family Bible. During those early years, the written words of this old volume did not register in my young mind, but the inky, black graphic arts imagery portraying various events of the Old Testament certainly did. Scenes depicting events such as snakes in the Garden of Eden, the blazing destruction of Sodom and Gomorrah, sword-wielding archangels and David and his slingshot made deep impressions on my young psyche. Those images put the fear of God in me at an early age. This, I gather, ingrained a semblance of belief within me.

Prior to the Great Depression, the Harvey family had modest means, but we got along quite comfortably. My father owned and operated a small construction company that did very well during the good times of the Roaring Twenties. But, when the hard times hit, they really hammered the eleven-member Harvey family.

My dad lost his small business. Soon afterwards, the bank foreclosed on our home, located on the outskirts of Abilene, a small West Texas town. This compelled the family to relocate in the town proper. We moved into a large, but cheap rental house. Here I fell in with a couple of kids who, for some reason, attended church. They invited me to go to church with them. I accepted and found myself in a house of God for the first time. Heck, I went all out. I attended Sunday school and worship service, returned on Sunday night, and even went in on Wednesday nights for some kind of meeting, as I didn't have any other place to go. Also, they had some events they called potluck suppers. Of course, I didn't miss any of these potlucks, as there I played my best game. I didn't learn the rules of potluck 'til years later. No one told me that you needed to bring a pot. Hey! I thought of all that grub as just a gift. After all, we ate in God's house.

Then along came Easter. The other kids began to talk about this holy event a good week in advance, not why we celebrated, but rather the egg hunt that it included. They held this game on the Saturday prior to Easter Sunday. During the days leading up to this big, big event, I went into a state of wild anticipation. I could hardly wait.

Ultimately, the big day arrived. I arrived at the church an hour prior to the set time for this big event. Soon folks, some moms included, began to arrive. Right quick-like I noted that this was a dress-up affair. The marked contrast between those kids' apparel, and the garb that adorned this waif's frame, seemed readily apparent. They decked themselves out in affluent finery. All the little girls wore colorful garb, complete with ribbons and bows. Their heads bore wide-brimmed straw hats that highlighted their pretty dresses. The boys, too, wore their best togs, including some suits, complete with vests and caps. All this pomp and circumstance awed me.

In rank contrast, there I stood, shoeless, clad in a faded, tattered shirt and shapeless, baggy pants. I gave little thought to the contrast in our dress, but I really worried about the baskets each of them carried; woven of green straw and filled with green artificial grass. I figured I needed a basket to compete. So, I lit a shuck for the house. At full gallop, fired by a sense of urgency, I arrived home sudden-like. By this time, I had already made up my mind as to how to devise a basket of sorts. The plan was simple. I found an empty three-pound coffee tin. I punched two holes with a hammer and a nail, near its upper rim. Into these holes, I stuck a piece of baling wire to fashion a bail or handle. I pulled some green grass from the yard. Again, at that same full gallop, I headed back to the church.

I made it in time. I could see the hiding party still stashing the eggs on a big, weedy vacant lot adjacent to the church. Once they hid all the eggs, they herded us youngsters outside and placed us on a line drawn in the dirt. To my dismay, all the moms stood in the alignment, holding their sweet young things in tow. Man, I didn't go for this team stuff. To counter this development, I needed to resort to speed and canniness. Of course, I had the mother of all motivators going for me: hunger. The others saw this as just a game. I saw it as dead serious.

The good Pastor, serving as the starter, got us in the ready position. Then, he announced a prize for the person who found the most eggs and that many of the wrapped eggs had money hidden in them.

To top this, he added, "There's a golden egg out there in hiding and the finder of this special egg will receive a prize of one dollar. Now, when I blow this whistle, you go." To me that whistle meant *sic 'em*!

When that whistle sounded, I came off'n that taw line like a hungry wolf. Why, I had already found three eggs before some of the others got off the starting line. I moved through that field of scrub mesquite and wild grass faster than a minnow can swim across a dipper. That three-pound coffee can quickly runneth over. My trouser pockets turned into receptacles. When I'd filled those, I tucked in my shirttails and my shirt served as a bag of sorts.

When the takings slimmed down, I let up. Some of the kids cried. They couldn't find any, poor things. Many mothers had left the sidelines and lead their youngsters about, searching for culls. Many moms, I felt, looked at me with disdain. From the sidelines they had, no doubt, observed my mad dash through the finding

9

field.

Back in the auditorium, the counting began. When it finished, I had won overwhelmingly with a total of thirty-two eggs. Among them sat the golden egg worth one big buck. Oh boy! I stood in a state of out-right elation. But, my happiness proved short lived, for out of an assemblage of moms, a very large lady stepped up and, in a loud shout, she said, "Listen, everybody!" When she got everyone's attention she pointed at me and declared, "That little scamp cheated. He watched as the Easter eggs were being hidden." All eyes turned toward me. No words can begin to portray the utter devastation and gut-searing embarrassment I felt. Everyone looked at me in stunned silence. Jeering and catcalls began. I couldn't catch my breath. Tears welled into my eyes. Checking back audible sobs, I ran blindly down the aisle and out the door, emitting cries of anguish as I raced homeward.

To my relief, the yard stood empty. I scrambled through an opening that led under the house. There I remained until my mother beckoned me at dusk. The somber light hid my red, swollen eyes. My dreams of sharing the eggs of Easter with my sisters had died. I've often wondered who the prize money might have gone to. I guess the big lady deserved it because she might have had a claim to it. A nobody found it. I didn't set foot in another church for six years.

In 1935, we moved to Odessa, an oil boomtown in West Texas. Here, again, I fell in with a churchgoing friend. For several weeks, he got after me to attend Sunday school and worship services with him. I finally and reluctantly accepted his invitation.

One Sunday morning, I put on a clean shirt, drew on my only decent pair of pants and plastered my hair down with highly perfumed, oily brilliantine. Shoes? Heck, I never wore shoes this time of the year, summer, mainly 'cause I'd already worn out that year's pair. I could only hope for shoes by the time winter set in.

A large, buxom lady met us at the church door. She loomed over me, barring my entry. With a menacing glare, she gave me the old once over. With a pointed finger, she allowed, "Young man, you go right home and put on your shoes before you come in." Stunned and hurt, I backed away and did an about-face. I ran home, shedding bitter tears. Of course, my faith went back into a long hibernation.

In the early part of 1941 just six of us kids remained at home. My three older sisters had married and left the nest. Times grew a little bit better at the Harvey house, as my dad worked every day. During this period, I saw very little of him, as I had school and sports the year 'round and he spent less time at home. By the time he got in, if he came home at all, I'd gone to bed. My father never talked much to his kids. In fact, I can't recall a moment when he and I ever indulged in any meaningful dialogue. He never talked to me about sports, hunting, fishing or asked how I did in school. In short, we never had any semblance of a warm father-son relationship. One time I heard my mother say to him, "Bud, you ought to spend some time with Sonny, telling him the things a boy should know." He replied with a grunt.

One night I came in from an out-of-town track meet. As usual, I came into the house through the kitchen door. There at the kitchen table, to a minor surprise, sat my dad with Mom. If there had been an on-going conversation, it ceased when I opened the door. As I entered, he got up and silently went into their bedroom just off the kitchen.

I greeted Mom cheerfully as usual. She avoided my eyes and wiped her own with her apron. I noted, with concern, a puffy redness about them. She got up and went to the oven and brought out a baked potato and a big bowl of pinto beans. Thanking her, I dug in. In silence, she entered that same bedroom. My thoughts centered wholly on the food.

Without preamble, I heard a loud, beseechingly desperate cry come through the closed door, "No, no Jessie, not that!" With a gasp, I spewed a mouth-full of food, knocked over the small table and went through that door without benefit of the knob. In the dimly lit bedroom, I viewed a scene of heart-choking horror, a picture forever etched in my memory. My father desperately grappled for the pistol my mother tried to bring down on herself or him. Without wavering or hesitation, I lunged at her with all the force I could muster. I caught her with a fist to the side of the head. She sagged at the knees, dropped the pistol and fell forward. Inert, she lay face down on the floor. I was horrified by what I had done. My father staggered back and slumped, whimpering, into a corner. I headed to the bathroom and came out with a bath towel sopping wet with cold water. I applied it to her suffering face until she came around.

Unsteadily, I helped her to her feet and then seated her on the side of the bed. All the while, Dad remained in the corner, too shaken to get up or offer any assistance. Sobbing, I cried, "Why, Mother? Why, why?"

With a clear, steady voice she said, "Your daddy does not love us any more. He has another woman."

I picked up the pistol, unloaded and stuck it inside my belt. I asked my father to leave. He complied. Then to my mother, "Where did you get this pistol?"

She replied, "I borrowed it from Mr. Thomas." He lived next-door.

"I will take it to him."

He answered my knock. I handed him the big six-shooter. In a stern, calm voice I said, "Mr. Thomas, here is your gun, and don't you ever loan it to a member of my family again!"

"Why? What happened?"

"It's none of your damned business!"

Returning, I asked my mother to forgive me for hitting her, adding that I had reacted out of fear of what could have happened. She gave me a reassuring hug and told me that I had done the right thing. All was forgiven.

We talked late into the night. We decided not to mention the events of the evening to the rest of the family. My younger brother and sisters had not witnessed the sorrowful drama which had played out that night. Yet, that sad, sad event forever shaped all our lives.

A long and endless night lay ahead for me. I spent those sleepless hours in prayer to God asking that he see fit to hold the family in his hands and bring my father back to us. He did not act on my prayers. This proved a defining event in my young life. I went through that door to my mother as a fifteen-year-old boy and stepped into a man's world.

Several weeks later, I attended the divorce proceedings with my mother. And I remember it well. My father made no attempt to speak to us so we did not talk to him.

The judge called him forward and said, "Mr. Harvey, I'm granting you a divorce. The six minor children will remain with their mother. You will pay child support to Mrs. Harvey each month in the amount of forty-two dollars. The first payment is due at this time."

My dad brought out his wallet and counted out forty-two dollars and handed it to the court clerk and walked out. For six kids, that amounted to seven dollars a month to feed and clothe each one.

That proved to be the last red cent that Mother ever received from him. From time to time, we did go before the judge and the sheriff, asking for help in collecting the support money.

They always said, "Jessie, when we see Bud, he tells us he is broke. We can arrest him and throw him in jail, but there again, if he is in jail he can't work. Without working, he can't make payments."

We opted for arrest and jail. It never happened.

At this point in my life, I had begun to look at God in the same light as Santa Claus and the Easter Bunny, a figment of one's imagination. At that early age, I became agnostic in my beliefs. I never shared this apprehension with anyone.

During War II, I served with the Marine Corps, fighting its

way through the Solomon Islands. There the apprehensions of agnosticism gave way to total atheism. How could a loving and merciful God, if he existed, let men lay so much carnage, butchery and heartbreak on each other? Someone coined this phrase during that war, "There are no atheists in foxholes." Wrong!

In the latter part of WWII, the Marine Corps invaded the small volcanic island of Iwo Jima. There I saw mankind really get on with it, man's inhumanity to man.

We took heavy casualties around the clock for the first several days on the island. It proved impossible to determine the locations of the defenders' lines. The brass figured that a night reconnaissance patrol could find some answers.

At midnight, my platoon sergeant awakened me and told me I'd be the third member of a three-man reconnaissance patrol scheduled to scout enemy lines at 0100. We received our orders at the battalion command post with instructions to return before daylight.

We went through the wire (the barbed wire that protected our positions) promptly at 0100. Since our assignment involved reconnoitering, we needed to avoid contact with the enemy if at all possible. The brass expected us to ingress their positions, gather information and get out. Utilizing stealth, we penetrated several hundred yards into their zone and soon found ourselves surrounded by unsuspecting Japs. Man! They were everywhere, like fleas on a dog's rump. They went in and out of caves and holes, busily setting up gun positions, moving ammunition, laughing, talking and doing all those things that troops do. Noting that most of them did not wear their helmets, I suggested to the other two that we take off our helmets. The silhouettes of our headgear made us standout. They had no idea that we moved amongst them. Of course, we were scared out of our wits. I'm sure they saw us but paid us no heed, since in the dark we looked like their own.

Without stealth we walked, outwardly casual-like through the area, veering only enough to avoid getting too close to any groups or individuals. We made slow but deliberate progress. The zigzagging course we took to avoid Jap positions took a lot of time. I thought my pounding heart might give us away.

After a couple of hours, gray streaks began to slash the eastern night sky, heralding the coming of a new day. All too soon, those whispers of light began to give way to a full-blown dawn. Time had run out on us, and we found ourselves in real trouble. Caution gave way to a controlled sense of desperation. To our good luck, most of the enemy had returned to their posts below ground. We didn't know how far we stood from our lines. I brought up the rear when we took off in a low-moving dogtrot. We had not gone far when, from within yards of my five o'clock position, I heard the bolt action on a machine gun declaring the operator had braced it for firing. I'd heard this harbinger of death before. It stood as one of the hard lessons I had learned in the jungles during the Solomon Islands campaigns. I recognized the telling sound of a Nambu, a Japanese light machine-gun. This deadly weapon could spit out a clip of twenty cartridges in less than two heartbeats. Damn, I hated that nasty little twenty-five-caliber weapon.

At that first metallic sound I shouted, "Hit the deck!" I landed on the ground at the same instant that a short burst of gunfire ripped the air just inches above my head. I lay so flat on the deck that I could have crawled under a snake's belly. For Joe, the guy in front of me, luck had played out. He had taken one or more slugs in the back. The other man ran helter-skelter toward our lines. His headlong dash grabbed the attention of the Nambu and it continued to spit short bursts at the hustling Marine. While this happened, the adrenaline and sense of reasoning within me worked in tandem, each feeding on the other. My situation was critical. I lay in the Jap's back yard, my position exposed with only my pistol to defend myself. I took a quick peek at the inert body, seven or eight yards ahead of me. Seeing no movement, I reckoned Joe had bought the farm. He carried an M-1 rifle. To survive this untenable fix, I needed that rifle and a position of concealment. I knew that

15

the Nambu's clip held twenty cartridges and the gunner fired in short bursts of three to four bullets. I figured he had only a burst or two left. He had one.

When the clip played out, it ejected. Its sharp, tinny sound signaled me to move, and move I did. I came out of that prone position like a bolt of lighting. Man, in that span of eight yards I could have beaten Jesse Owens. I kept my plan simple: I'd race by, pick up the rifle on a dead run and try to make it to a line of boulders about twenty yards beyond. Damn! On about the third step I saw Joe move slightly. The plan changed. I opted to take him instead. When I got there, I grabbed the back of his collar. Utter panic poured raw adrenaline into my engines. I could never have dragged him that far and fast otherwise. The rocks as a safe haven no longer stood as an option, we couldn't make it that far. Out of gut-wrenching terror, I reacted on impulse, not rooted in thought or reasoning. With Joe in tow, we moved into a slight depression in the volcanic ash. No more than a shallow dip, it had to do duty as a shelter for the time being. What a poor place to defend and it offered very little in the way of protection, but nothing else showed any more promise. By instinct, I hit the deck. My timing proved perfect. The rattling peal of gunfire passed within inches of our heads. Well, I figured, we were safe for the time being. Then problems began to escalate faster than I could resolve them.

All this had happened in a matter of seconds. Joe began to come out of his stunned state, but in a great deal of pain and not cognizant of our situation. I wanted to tend to his back wounds, but he tried to get up. I had to use all my strength to hold him down, but I couldn't use my body weight on him, as that lifted me into the line of fire of the Nambu. I had to work on him from a prone position, which was awkward as hell.

To my horror and dismay, the gaping gash on his back stood as the lesser of the problems we faced. A second, more dire and life threatening problem for both of us presented itself. Joe had a thermite grenade attached to the backside of his cartridge belt and its detonating device had taken a glancing hit from a 25-caliber bullet. Now, a thermite grenade stands as one of the more ignoble tools of war. It does not explode like a conventional grenade, but rather detonates where it lands and burns like an acetylene torch. It melts anything it comes in contact with. Scared half to death again, I wondered what happens when you're scared half to death twice? I soon learned.

I saw that the damaged detonating device of the grenade lay in such an unstable posture that a wrong move could spell disaster for the two of us. I gave some hard thought to the best way to get this thing off his belt and out of our hole. He began to move and scramble with intent purpose.

"Hey! What the devil are you trying to do?"

"I've got to get up!"

"What for? You'll get yourself killed! That Nambu will chew you up!" I dared not tell him about the thermite grenade, fearing it might cause further panic. Such grenades are literally very small incendiary bombs.

"I've got to pray to God and to my mother. Let me up now."

It turned into a flat-out desperate struggle. Using my body weight to hold him down wasn't an option. That put me into the line of fire and atop that volatile grenade. My valor ebbed fast. I took this developing situation quite seriously. Out of utter desperation, I whipped out my pistol and put its business end in his pain-stricken face. At this point, I broke all ties with God and the tenuous beliefs that lingered within me. Not given to the liberal use of the profane, in this stressful moment, however, I cut loose and shouted blasphemous maledictions for God, my injured comrade, and the notorious Nambu to hear. The gun in my tormented buddy's face, he heard me shout, "You son-of-a-bitch, lie still and shut up or I'm going to blow your frigging head off. There's nobody on this whole damned earth going to get you outta this hang-up but old Fred Harvey. Not even your damned God or your mother can help you. Prayer ain't getting us outta this fix. You got

of battle, about 13:00, I heard my name called. Damn! The voice of Bull Fisher, my platoon sergeant, boomed over the other noise. He had brought in a combat patrol to find us.

I answered, "Sarge, we're just beyond that ridge of boulders in front of you. You better take positions behind them. We're in the firing line of a Nambu! They've zeroed in on us. I figure they're using us for bait. I heard them talking up and down the line on both sides. That ain't all! Our guys are dropping mortar rounds in this area!

He yelled, "We took care of that. Hold on. We'll move into those rocks and get you outta there. Are either of you hurt?"

"Joe's bad hit, lost lots of blood, but I think he is going to be okay. You guys be careful! We're protected for the time being!"

The platoon quickly moved into positions behind the boulders. Then Bull called out, "Harv, we're set, can you show us 'bout where you're located?"

"I'll hold up a hand and then throw a grenade in the general area where the Nambu is located."

"We see you. Now, throw!" I did and the Nambu answered, giving away its position. The platoon laid down a withering barrage of small arms fire, putting the Nambu company out of business. Peter Adam got to me first along with several other guys. He directed them to put Joe on the stretcher and sent them on their way. He said, "Let's get out of here. I'll cover you." I got set to make a run for it, but as an after–thought, I told Pete that I wanted to pick up Joe's rifle. I took one last look at the shallow defilade in the sands of Iwo Jima. What a lifesaver, the dearest plot of ground that I ever occupied! Joe and I owed our lives to it.

In a state of rage, Pete said, "We would have found you sooner, but Ski came back a blithering idiot. He refused to go back to show us the way to you guys. He reported you dead. Some of the guys wanted to shoot him. The Bull sent him under guard to be taken off the island."

The hours seemed endless, forever etching that long,

memorable day in my mind. It marked my absolute separation from God, a cleavage that lasted for eighteen years.

Then along came David.

After the war, I went into teaching and coaching on the high school level. I spent my first ten years as an assistant coach. In the early 1960s, Eastwood High, a brand new school located in the far West Texas city of El Paso offered me the position as head football coach. The school opened with a student body comprised of seventh, eighth, and ninth graders, with an additional grade added each year until it grew to include a four-year high school.

That summer, prior to the fall opening of Eastwood, I spent a great deal of time at the gymnasium, getting the new football equipment marked and put in order. One torrid, hot afternoon a knock came to my office door.

"Come in." In walked a slightly built, clean-cut kid. Confidently, he walked up to my desk and pushed his right hand to me. I stood to accept it. His touch produced a manly, firm grip that impressed me.

"Coach Harvey, my name is David Hayes. I'm going to be your quarterback." His self-assured, brash manner sort of took me aback.

While looking him over, I said to myself, "Yeah, if I have to depend on a boy who can barely reach across this desk, I'm in real trouble." I soon realized, however, that this kid possessed one of the primary prerequisites of a quarterback: self-confidence. This characteristic alone served to make him at least someone to consider as a candidate for that all-important position.

I found David's leadership qualities readily apparent. Within a week of that first meeting, he had rounded up 15 to 20 prospects. He had them working out in 101-degree heat. By rule, I couldn't meet with them until the first week of August. David dropped by each morning and I suggested a few drills he could use during those hot, hot days. They finished up each day with a lively touch-pass football game. Of course, I slipped around and observed these events from afar. I liked what I saw.

Thanks to David's leadership and the team's enthusiasm, the entire group reached excellent physical condition by the time official practice started. August found us ready.

As a new facility Eastwood did not have a practice field. An elementary school about a half mile up the road had a large grassed area. Problem solved. A bus and driver transported the team up and back each day. This worked out well.

I left school early and proceeded to the elementary school and got the field equipment in place. With this done, we got right into the workout when the team arrived. Bill Crow, my assistant coach, stayed in the gym and got the team suited up and on the bus. He remained in the dressing room and treated players with ouches, then brought them to the field in his car. Clearly we had things organized.

About the second week, things went wrong. On this particular day, I walked out to meet the bus as usual. Alarmed at the sight of a black and white police cruiser trailing the bus, with lights a-flashing, I watched warily as both came to a stop in the parking lot. The boys began to empty the bus slowly, sans their usual banter and enthusiasm. A visibly disturbed police officer proceeded in my direction saying, "Coach, we have a situation here."

"What's the problem, Officer?"

"You have some wise guys who think it's a sport to moon a police officer along with any others who might be looking on."

"All right, you guys line up." I then went to my car and brought forth my paddle. None of them had seen my paddle before, an ominous-looking item made from a 36-inch baseball bat. With its business end planed down to a quarter-inch thickness, the bat brought forth an audible gasp from the assemblage.

I asked the officer, "Do you want to take them down to the station or do you want me to handle it here?"

He looked at the board, "I think I'd rather see you handle it here and now."

"Okay. You people that showed your butts, step forth!"

Nobody moved. "All right, I'm going to stand here until the guilty are men enough to step forth to take what's coming to 'em."

After a short delay, one player, David, stepped forward. No others made a move.

The officer said, "More than one was in on it. In fact nearly all the windows on my side of the bus were filled with shiny butts."

"Sir, I was the only one," David asserted. The officer only shook his head.

David repeated, "Coach, I was the only one." I glared into each face in the lineup. Three boys could not look me in the eye. I shook my head in disgust.

To David I said, "Grab your ankles." Then with a heavy heart, I applied three brisk swats to the plucky young man's posterior. The officer shook David's hand, glared at the others and left.

That night I got a call from Bill Hayes, David's father, saying that he had received several calls from parents each condemning my actions. David had not mentioned the paddling to him. Talking it over with his son, he had found that David had no complaints about the episode.

In closing, Mr. Hayes added, "Coach, I want you to know that you have the full support of the Hayes family in your methods and coaching philosophies. I think we're going to have a great season."

The next morning three boys turned in their equipment. That afternoon, as usual, I waited for the bus. It arrived, but empty. Damn! What now?

"Where is the team?" I asked the driver.

He pointed back up the street, "Ya know, Coach, that boy you whacked yesterday told me to leave and said he'd see that the team got here. I guess they walked."

In wonder, I trotted out to the street and there they were, more than a quarter-mile up the road, leap-frogging at a dead run. They arrived, gasping for breath, and assembled before me. Three youngsters stepped forward.

One said, "Coach, we've got three swats a-coming." I complied.

To a man, their teammates whooped it up and patted them on the back. I saw character and leadership in this band of troopers. I coached football for forty-five years and coached some great teams, but these boys still stand as the greatest and most memorable of them all.

That first season the team went through the schedule undefeated, due, in no small part, to fine athletes and superb team leadership. David served as one of those chieftains. As a passer, at quarterback, David reached about a three on a scale of ten. Since David did not have a strong passing arm, we didn't throw the ball much. Our passing game consisted of a couple of sprint-out passes and a run or throw option play. Unfortunately, David also proved slow afoot so he didn't threaten opponents in the running department. Somehow, however, he could take the team to the Land of Six, the end zone, and did it often.

That first year we operated like a well-oiled, fine-tuned machine. We waltzed right through the season and went into the championship game against Burges undefeated. Man, what a tough game. Both teams fielded great defenses, but neither could score. We could move the ball fairly well, but just could not score. The game looked like two dogs in a tug-of–war with a rib bone.

David called the plays on the field. Going into the fourth quarter, he had thrown nary a pass. Consequently, our opponent's defense disregarded the air lanes and threw up virtually an eleven-man front, almost impossible to run against. Early in that fourth quarter with the ball on our own forty-five yard line, I grabbed a sub and sent him in with instructions for David to throw the ball. The rollout pass lane stood wide open. David called a play, but an off-tackle run instead of the pass. Thinking the sub had made a mistake, I called on another sub to take in the same information. I got in the first sub's face, and berated him for not taking in the right message. He stammered, "Coach, I told David to call the pass play!" I cooled and stood back to watch the pass play.

I'll be damned, another running play. Now this ol' coach really had the steam rising.

I seized the back-up quarterback by his facemask and yelled, "Get in there for David and run a sprint-out pass!"

He trotted out and David tottered in and seated himself at the far end of the bench. Dang! Was this kid tired? No way. I didn't know of a more splendidly conditioned athlete than David. This had me concerned, but my anger kept me from going to him.

To my dismay, the ball was fumbled on the snap. Luckily, we recovered. Fourth down on our own forty-yard line. Time to punt. Wesley Price, one of our team captains, called a time out. The big tackle trotted toward me.

I thought, what tha hell is going on now?

Wes, looking me in the eye, declared, "Coach, we need David!"

"Price, you got me down for dumber than I really am." That's as far as I got.

"Coach Harvey, the team wants David," he persisted.

Out of frustration I shouted, "Take him!"

This big ol' kid raced to the end of the bench, jerked David to his feet and literally dragged him to an anxiously awaiting huddle where they welcomed him like money. With fourth down and twelve yards of tough grass for a first down, I expected to see the team come out in a punt formation. Instead, I saw a running formation. Damn!

On the snap of the ball, the linemen exploded off that line-of-scrimmage and bowled their assignments over like ten-pins. John Josey, a little halfback, took the ball from David and was convoyed, by what looked like the whole student body. Around the right end they went. When the dust settled, we had a first down. From then on, plays followed a classic example of five yards and a cloud of dust. Not pretty, but devastatingly effective. The team responded to David's leadership. He had them so fired up they could have whooped up on Russia. With ball control and a stout defense, the team went on to win the championship game.

When the game ended, all pandemonium broke loose. Fans poured onto the field to join the celebration of victory. In a state of absolute elation, my chest swelled with pride for the team. They had performed magnificently.

In my euphoria, I looked beyond the mingling, noisy crowd to see the team on the far end of the field, still at the spot where the game ended. I headed toward them. They moved in my direction with David in tow. Something was wrong. Two teammates, each holding one of his hands, led David toward me. As they neared, Wes visibly shaken, said, "Coach, David can't see very well!"

"What do you mean?"

"Everything is just a blur to him!"

I looked into his eyes and saw the hemorrhaging. "How do they feel, Dave?"

"They feel real bad, like something is in them."

To no one in particular I said, "Go find Doctor Droutsas." Three kids broke for the crowd and returned in short order with the MD in tow.

He took one glance and ordered, "Someone find his parents and have them follow the ambulance. I'm taking him to the hospital right now. It looks like he might have real problems." I told the doctor I'd take care of things here and follow as soon as I could.

The team assembled around me and dropped to one knee. Ironically, this field shortly before the scene of wild exhilaration, now bathed in despair. Gloom had shattered the moment.

Wesley told the story. "The night before the first game of the season, I invited several of the guys to spend the night at my house. My mom fixed a big meal. After dinner, we played games, but mostly talked football. We won that first game so we then made it a custom that prior to every game the same bunch spent the night at my house. We thought it brought good luck. Last night we got into a big pillow fight. It got pretty rough. Dave got hit hard in the face a couple of times. After the fight, he complained about his eyes hurting him. They were real red. Later he said a blur had developed in his right eye. The next morning he had limited vision in that eye and the other one had begun to blur. He told us not to tell anyone about the problem and assured us it would clear up."

As they had promised, no one knew of the problem except a few team members. Wes continued, "During the game, David got hit a couple of times and the condition grew worse. I told him to tell you, but he wouldn't hear of it. He told us he could finish the game. He could not see well enough to throw the ball, but he could see well enough to hand the ball off and the line had to do the rest. That's the story." With tears welling in his eyes he added, "Did we do wrong, Coach?" Emotion choked me, so I could only reach over and touch his chest. One of the team captains offered up a prayer. Worried like the whole team, I told them I needed to head right to the hospital and would call the captains just as soon as I found out anything.

At the hospital, I met with the team doctor and an eye specialist he had called in. A visibly shaken Mr. and Mrs. Hayes had heard the astonishing story from David during the ride downtown. We anxiously fixed our gaze on the ophthalmologist. He told us of a procedure, relatively new, which incorporated the use of a laser beam to repair damaged retinas.

All this took place nearly forty-five years ago when virtually no one had ever heard of laser techniques in the medical field. The specialist also told us that he had spoken on the phone with the very best eye surgeon in the state. That doctor said he'd fly into El Paso the next day, a Sunday, to evaluate David's condition. He planned to operate on Monday if he thought he should.

The doctors had heavily sedated David and allowed him no visitors except family. I saw him through an open door. To prevent further damage, they strapped his hands and arms to the bed rails and immobilized his head with leaden bags. His mom and dad

eyes that day after the game. They bandaged my eyes and put me to bed. My hands were strapped to the bed. The nurse then gave me a shot and while I was talking to my mom and dad everything got fuzzy. The next thing I remember, my mom was talking to me and told me that everything was going to be all right." He had slept the whole night through unaware of my presence.

The David Hayes story does not end here. Though David no longer participated in football, he and I remained close during his subsequent years in high school. He frequently dropped by my office just to talk and pass the time of day. I viewed those moments as prime time. One day he said, "Coach, I've taken up the guitar and really like music." That made me glad and I told him so.

"Move over, Elvis. David is a-coming!"

"No kidding, Coach, I think I'll be pretty good at playing the guitar."

"David, whatever you undertake, you'll be a success. You have the drive and capacity to succeed at most anything. In my book I've got you down as a real winner."

Several months later, there came a knock at my door late one night. I opened it to find David.

"Come in, Dave. What brings you out this late at night?"

"Coach, I want to ask you a question."

"Shoot. I may not know the answer, but I'll make you think I do. Lay it on me."

He began, "Coach, I told you that I was learning to play the guitar. Now, I've gotten some of the guys together and we are going to form a rock and roll band. We plan to play at school dances and things like that."

"That's great, but I can't sing or play. So what is your question?"

He stammered, "Coach, would you be disappointed in me if I let my hair grow like a hippy?" In the early 60s, just about every coach in the country abhorred the long-haired kid. Shoulder-length hair stood as a logo of anti-war groups, the drug culture and anyone against the establishment. Unfortunately, it became the coiffure of the times. The good kids adopted this fad and it just wasn't going away. No telling how many athletes we coaches shucked because we rebuked the tides of change wrought by the hellion times of the 60s. I admit to rabidly supporting the ban on long hair. Such feelings existed not just with football coaches, but extended to nearly all sports and their mentors.

With David's words, all my prejudices and biases faded completely in no longer a time than two beats of the heart. They say that time is nature's way of keeping everything from happening at once, but this happened in an instant. I asked myself, "What difference does it make? Long hair, the clothes he wears or the beat he dances to have no relevance to the making of a young man."

"David," I said, "you're one of the finest young men I know. The length of your hair or the music you make will never change how I feel toward you. The heartbeat of football was taken from you, but the game of life burns brightly within you. Now, go out there and give to music what you gave to football. You will do well."

He did just that. I attended a couple of his gigs and liked what I heard. I changed the rule on long hair. From then on I never made a big deal on the length of a boy's hair. I just said, "Wear it in a style so that I can see your eyeballs when I talk to you." Ya know, most all these guys did wear their hair a bit longer, but they always kept it well trimmed.

David had touched my life once again, all to make me a better man and father. I did not tell this story until ten years later.

One night at a football banquet, I had a typed speech in hand. As parents, fans, cheerleaders and players filed into the banquet room I stood at the door, greeting each as they passed.

One mother came up to me and said, "Coach, I want you and your staff to know that you have had a great influence on my son. You changed his whole life. My husband and I thank you."

As I sat picking at my food, deep in thought, a realization hit me. This coaching involves a two-way street. Sure, we influence lots of young persons, but I'll bet some student has, at one time or another, touched every coach who has come down the pike and helped them become a better man or woman. I shucked the prepared speech and told the David Hayes story.

David graduated and married a wonderful young lady. A couple of springs later as I coached baseball, I looked up and at the curb, near the diamond, sat David on the fender of his car. I called the team in and told them to take the day off, as a very special person had come here to see me. Surprised, but asking no questions, they beat it to the dressing room.

As I approached Dave, he laughed and said, "Coach, you're getting big and easy in your old age. I didn't think I'd live to see or hear of you giving a team off time."

"Hey, it's not every day that I have such a distinguished character as David Hayes come to see me. How're you doing, son?"

We sat on the grass and talked for nearly an hour. He finally stopped short and said, "Coach, I've set a new goal for myself. I want to make a million dollars before I'm twenty-five."

"That's a lot of money, Dave. Why?"

"It's the challenge more than anything, Coach."

"Now, just how do you propose to make a million bucks in so short a time?"

"To start with, I'm taking over a Volkswagen agency in New Mexico. My wife and I are leaving tomorrow and I wanted to say goodbye before I left."

"David Hayes, with your drive and ambition you'll do well. Good luck."

I offered my hand but he opted for a warm hug. We backed off, looked into each other's glistening eyes, he turned, got into his car and drove up the street. I watched until he faded from sight. A part of me went with him.

Several years later, while living in Korea, I received a letter from a friend with an enclosed newspaper clipping from the obit page: "David Hayes, age 25, passed away."

David has moved on, but the thoughts and memories of him linger on and on in my heart. I regret that I never told him that I loved him or told him *The David Hayes Story*. Somehow, I think he might know.

        The President of the United States takes pleas-
ure in presenting the SILVER STAR MEDAL to

        PRIVATE FIRST CLASS THIELE F. HARVEY, JR.,
            UNITED STATES MARINE CORPS,

for service as set forth in the following

CITATION:

        "For conspicuous gallantry and intrepidity
while serving with Company C, First Battalion,
Twenty-sixth Marines, Fifth Marine Division, in
action against enemy Japanese forces on Iwo Jima,
Volcano Islands, 20 February 1945. When his
three-man patrol which was sent out to establish
contact with the adjoining company was ambushed
by heavy fire from an enemy machine gun and one
of the men was seriously wounded, Private First
Class Harvey dragged the fallen Marine under
heavy fire to the shelter of a near-by hole.
Remaining with the wounded man while his companion went for aid, he held off the hostile forces
with his rifle and hand grenades until the arrival of the rescue party. Then, exposing himself to enemy fire and directing accurate heavy
fire on the Japanese position, he successfully
covered the evacuation of the casualty. By his
initiative, courage and unselfish devotion to
duty, he undoubtedly saved the life of his comrade and upheld the highest traditions of the
United States Naval Service."

                        For the President,

                        John L. Sullivan
                        Secretary of the Navy.

                        John L. Sullivan
                        Secretary of the Navy.

Chapter 2

The Angel of Quetzaltenango

My continuing passion for adventure had drawn me to this alien land, Guatemala, in far-off Central America. I was in the country only a few days when one fine morning I felt a need to get out and do some exploring. After a leisurely breakfast with my host family, they furnished me with a list of places to see with routes to follow. Excusing myself, I placed a bottle of red wine, along with a chunk of cheese and a couple of cold tamales, in a small backpack. Ready to go, the Lopez family ushered me to their front gate. When I stepped into the street that sunlit morning, I found myself in a world of tropical beauty. They pointed me in an easterly direction. I tipped my cap to them and took off at a brisk pace. I saw this shaping up as a great day. Little did I realize that this very special day might reward me with, perhaps, the most inspiringly touching event of my life. Draw close so that I might share this memory with you.

I soon walked the lanes and byways of Quetzaltenango, the second municipality of size in Guatemala. This enchanting city lay at the foot of Santa María, an ancient volcano. This very active towering giantess, during her life cycle, has spewed forth a blessing of mineral-rich matter. This material, through time, turns into lush organic soil that nourishes a wide variety of plants and trees. The beautiful emerald foliage that mantles this magnificent mountain, had spread to cover the whole countryside. Its every vista portrays pictorial beauty. Flowers of intense hues set the yards of this city ablaze with color. Flowering trees and shrubs line each street and lane. Here, Flora, the goddess of flowers, has worked overtime, spreading decorative beauty with audacious abandon. She has endowed this land with many facets, all bathed in brilliant, illuminating colors.

As I walked these lovely primitive byways and lanes, I felt I strolled through time instead of a place. I wanted to see as much of this exotic vicinage as possible. I strolled along a zigzag route, completely enjoying myself, when I began to notice scores of dogs. As I approached the heart of the city, their numbers grew to an over abundance. Surely homeless, they lay in the streets, on sidewalks and some in yards. Those that moved about traveled mostly in small packs of three to five. These free-ranging mongrels resulted from inbreeding and crossbreeding. What an underfed, mangy, motley-looking lot. They seemed harmless. They at no time challenged or threatened me.

My amiable walk found me on a bustling avenue, one of the main traffic arteries traversing Quetzaltenango. The flow of this traffic, both trucks and cars, created a dusty, gaseous haze that hung above the pavement and among the tree-lined thoroughfare. The walkways on both sides of this busy artery teemed with people, a majority of them Indians, of Mayan ancestry. The apparel of this ethnic group blazed with bright, dazzling colors. The women's clothing especially, headbands, blouses, and skirts, flamed in the hues and tints of a vivid rainbow. The crowd moved as one profuse mass of color, an ever-changing kaleidoscope, and with the interplay of light on the colors, it had a dizzying effect on the eye.

The morning had grown quite warm and the shady side of the avenue looked inviting. I stepped to the curb to await a break in the incessant traffic. At that very moment, a crescendo of blaring horns, screeching brakes, and squalling tires skidding on pavement broke the morning calm. This pandemonium became the harbinger of one of the most poignantly touching occurrences I have ever witnessed and remains forever etched in my memory.

A roving pack of dogs had ventured into the heavy traffic on the roadway and caused drivers to take evasive actions. One poor critter's string ran out. A large vehicle hit his hindquarters, crushing his spine and rear. As the behemoth continued over him, it threw him about its undercarriage like a rag doll. When the truck finished with this large, dun colored dog he raised himself upon his front paws, unable to move his paralyzed hindquarters. Anchored to the spot, the poor thing's jowls emanated loud, mournful wails of pain. I found myself immersed in morbid abhorrence. An injured, dying dog emits a singularly melancholy wail. His doleful, almost elemental bays rose above the clamor of the street.

A part of the crowd stopped momentarily to take note of the mishap. They moved on shortly, wanting only to get away from this grisly scene. Ensuing drivers veered to avoid the poor devil. The ebb and flow of traffic around him left him an island unto himself in a sea of movement. His isle of refuge could only prove tenuous at best, for surely another vehicle would hit him. His pain-wracked writhing and desperate, mournful howls continued unabated. He could go nowhere. I stood helplessly transfixed by the forlorn, melancholy event unfolding before me. A sense of gloomy sadness pervaded my whole being.

Yet another crescendo of blaring horns, screeching brakes, and squealing tires suddenly broke my reverie. Out of the corner of my eye, I glimpsed a blur of rushing color. To my horror, a diminutive lass with a sleeping baby strapped to her back had bolted from the safety of the curb. She had impulsively raced headlong into harm's way, giving no heed to the rushing traffic that quickly engulfed her. Why? Why? Then I realized that she appeared headed straight for the suffering, ill-fated creature in the street. I shouted in rapid staccato with all my might an unvoiced: *No! No! No.* My throat, dry and pained as if someone grasped it in a vise-like grip, kept any sound from leaving my mouth. Out of dread and anxiety, I could not move. I feared she would die with that poor animal in the middle of the road. By the grace of God and masterful driving, she made it to the mortally mangled animal.

There she extended a hand and placed it on his head. He looked into her face. Her touch calmed the poor thing. His doleful wailing slowly abated and then ceased. His eyes never strayed from her saintly face. With her free hand, she quickly adjusted the baby on her back. The sleeping infant had awakened during its sister's mad dash.

The dog, despite his useless hindquarter, remained propped up on his fore legs. The girl continued her touch to the dog's brow while looking searchingly about her. Then, to my amazed bewilderment, she took a course that petrified me with breathtaking alarm. With both hands, she suddenly grabbed the thick fur on each side of the dog's neck. Then, with great effort, this petite girl began to backpedal, dragging and tugging this sizable animal toward the far side of the road. The dun colored beast helped as best he could with his forelegs. This course of action took them once again into the perilous traffic.

Chaos broke out midst veering vehicles as they took measures to avoid the trio. She continued to heave and pull at a slow cadence through the gauntlet, completely detached from the dangers about her. The dog had not taken his eyes off the face of his savior. The event played out like a bad dream in slow motion. At last, she gained the safety of the far gutter. From the instant I first noted this child's mad dash and her reaching the haven of the gutter, only short moments had elapsed, however, this soul-draining time seemed endless.

Clearly, this creature's strength and vitality faded quickly. The functioning part of his body began to tremble and shudder. The Indian maiden then dropped to her knees and put her palms together in prayer. He licked her clasped hands. The play of radiant shafts of sunlight through the trees dappled the suspended dust that hung over the roadway. This gave the scene a surrealistic aura of ethereal embodiment. A few strollers stopped to give witness to the evolving event at the roadside. The scene captivated me in utter fascination. How wonderful if I could paint a picture of the scene with my words.

The dog's fore legs began to give way causing his paws to slide forward. His head sagged slowly toward his unstable legs. As his head drooped, his constant gaze remained fixed on the girl's angelic face as she prayed before him. His head came to a rest on his extended legs as the last vestiges of life ebbed from his pain-wracked body. He entered that eternal sleep with his last earthly vision that of an Indian girl's tear-streamed face, perhaps the face of an angel. Still on her knees, she then took a crucifix from about her neck, put it to her lips and then touched it to the dog's head. She stood and wiped tears from her eyes. She then slowly backed away from the inert form, not taking her eyes off him until she reached the walkway. Here she paused, then turned to reenter that pageantry of moving color.

I stood muted, with my own eyes bathed in tears and swallowed by emotions. Finally, I jolted out of my reverie. I had to see this child, to look into her face and, in some way, communicate with her. Not waiting, I began to tread my way, discriminately, through the traffic. After discouraging delays, I got to the other side. Not knowing the direction she had taken, arbitrarily I went to the right. In a state of anxiety, I jogged for a short distance with no luck. I then turned and ran back in the opposite direction, but to no avail. I had lost her. I walked aimlessly for a while, mired in a sense of loss and loneliness. I entered a park, found a bench and seated myself. I pondered over this child and her angelic qualities. Who was this young maiden who had been the center of my world for a short while?

She occupied my thoughts and dreams endlessly for the weeks that followed. God gave me this moment in time and I will remember it forever. If there be angels, one must surely walk the hills of Quetzaltenango this day.

Chapter 3

A Letter to Rachel

One of teaching's great rewards consists of the lasting friendships that evolve, to be nurtured by time. My treasured friendships with a young lady named Iris stands as such a reward. We've kept in touch over the years. In time, she married and gave birth to a fine youngster named Ryan.

Around the time Ryan turned three, Iris opted for another child. She prayed for a girl this time around and God answered her prayers. Soon after the baby's conception, she learned from her doctor that she might have a very hard time holding on to this child. He prescribed a whole regimen of medicines and hour upon hour of bed rest. Resolute in her determination to carry this baby girl to birth, Iris followed the doctor's orders.

She spent the long, painful hours in bed each day. To while away the lonely hours, she spent a great deal of time talking to family and friends on the telephone. I became one of those friends.

One sad day, disaster struck. A three-pronged devastating hit befell her: she lost her baby, her husband, and a new home in the last stages of construction. I can't think of a worse scenario, but Iris survived.

I lived in Tucson at the time. Soon after these events, she called to ask, "Coach, may I come down to spend a few days with you?" You know my answer. I met her plane the next day. We spent many hours talking of life with its tribulations and heartbreaks. I endeavored to soothe her aching heart. One night from down the hallway, I heard muted sobs coming from her room. I went to her bedside and we talked until she drifted into a troubled sleep. I then went to my computer and wrote this note to Rachel.

Dear Rachel,

Our Father took you from your mother's womb for reasons we do not know or begin to comprehend. The scriptures tell us that God our Father has reasons for everything he does, but it is hard, at times, for us mortals to understand his actions. Being His children, we do not question his deeds or infinite wisdom, but some day we'll learn why you were given, only to be taken back before you were able to experience the miracle of birth.

Now, as you fly with angels in God's heavenly kingdom, you already know the things that I'm about to say, but I'm going to speak of them, if only to soothe a young mother's broken heart and shattered dreams.

I do not profess to know the conditions of matching an infant to the right mother or the right mother to an infant, but God, in his singular insight, had selected the right woman to bear and mother you. Had you been born in your mother's likeness, you would have had many of her virtues and affections, including a strong belief in God, compassion, devotion to family, a capacity to love and be loved, and innately engendered with an inner beauty of soul of endless qualities.

Rachel, you no doubt would have shared a physical similitude with your mother. Hence you would have been blessed with regal beauty, a radiant smile, and laughing eyes. She is a complete young woman and you, I'm sure, would have been served by these same God-given attributes.

A four-year-old named Ryan anxiously awaited your arrival. He would have been your older brother. In him, you would have found the perfect companion with whom to grow up. Ryan is all boy and it can be seen that he is endowed with many of the same wholesome qualities that your mother possesses, including a gentle, caring disposition. He would have been your protector, playmate, and confidant, a big brother with whom to share a million secrets and memories. You would have loved him, oh, so very much.

Ryan has already matured beyond his four-year-old mind and he understands that Jesus came and took his little sister away. He was saddened by the event. But time, the great healer, will wipe away the ache that he feels at this time. He has been a source of comfort for his mother during this trying period.

I first knew your mother when she was very young. Not yet into her adult years, she spoke at length about birth, children, and motherhood. Even at that early age, she had an innate need for family and children. Rachel, you were a wanted child.

Your mother, being of pure bloodlines, has the qualities of a fighter with grit and a steel-like substance flowing through her veins. Rachel, soon after you were conceived your mother's physician informed her that she was going to have a tough time carrying you through birth. The mental and physical toughness of this young woman took over. She didn't give up, She had no surrender in her. For you, her baby, she battled for six lonely, cruel months of debilitating sickness and mental anguish that only a woman can be subjected to. In this struggle for life itself, she went directly to God. In this confrontation, for hours on end, her delicate, opulent hands were clasped in prayer, beseeching her Father above to let her win this battle.

Yes, indeed, your mother put up a courageous battle. You were the prize. Both your mother and the heavenly Father wanted you dearly. Rachel, your mother is at peace with her God and happy that you now, once again, reside with angels. I saw her just the other day. She thinks of you more often than you might ever dream. At times, a dreamy, far-away look possesses her very being and little tears form to glisten in her eyes. It is at these times that we know that her thoughts have gone to you.

Rachel, in closing, we who love Iris hope that when your Father sees fit, at some point in time, to return you to earth, we pray that He will place you, securely, in the same worthy womb.

A friend

Chapter 4

Jessie

At this time, I think how wonderful if my words could translate my thoughts and feelings as I want you, the reader, to grasp the essence and character of my mother. Though she passed away some twenty years ago, my echoing remembrances go to her often. I see them as moments in time.

Memories of my mother fill the earliest recollections I have of life. They called her Jessie. As a toddler, she stood at the center of my world, a singular catalyst in my life. Through the passing years, a day seldom passes that one of those cherished and delightful memories does not come to mind. Thoughts of her weave through the fabric of my very soul, there to dwell until my passing.

The most pervasive memory I have of this mother of mine reflects the shyness and demure texture of her stoic Indian heritage.

Jessie entered life in Texas during the 1890s.. Her mother, a full blood American Indian, bore the name Molly Hair. Molly had married a white man. This union marked him as a squaw man, and made Jessie what whites called a half-breed. Throughout her life, Jessie maintained Molly's lineage as a member of the Cherokee Tribe, a docile, peaceful people. However, at my mother's death, some of the grandchildren did a genealogical work-up on her family. They found my grandmother born not of Cherokee blood, but, in fact, of Comanche ancestry.

Bewildered by this contradiction, the amateur genealogist went to the County Clerk of Tarrant County, Jessie's birth place. When queried, this official reckoned, "When Molly Hair was born on the Northern Plains of Texas, the Comanche still warred with the US Army and the pioneers of the time. These settlers coveted more farm acreage. They, along with the military, set about to drive the Indians off their tribal lands. A lot of blood spilled on both sides, across the Plains of West Texas during this struggle. The Comanche, a proud people, were among the last Native Americans to surrender. Extremely warlike, they made frequent raids on European settlements over a wide area. They extended their forays as far south as Mexico and kept settlers out of their territory for more than a century. Thus, when Jessie was born, a great deal of animosity remained toward this marauding tribe. Therefore, it was prudent for a Comanche just to say, "Me Cherokee."

I never knew my grandmother, Molly Hair, but a large tintype photograph of her hung in our living room. The picture showed her as a pretty woman with long, braided hair, high cheekbones and black-on-black eyes set in an unsmiling face. Her daring, penetrating eyes dominated the prettiness of her facial features. Those eyes, with an intimation of evil, actually frightened me.

From a vantage spot, high on the wall, Molly's dark, mystifying eyes seemed to follow my every movement in the room. I found this unrelenting gaze unnerving and didn't like being in the room alone. Why, when I had to cross that room I dropped my head and sprinted to the door to get outta there. Yes, this ol' kid dreaded the sight of that elemental gaze. My mother knew of this awe. Those times I misbehaved she threatened me with, "Molly Hair will get you, Sonny." This, along with a good switching with a whip-like mesquite limb, took all attitudes out of this little waif.

To me my mother always seemed old. It surprised me when I saw my birth certificate for the first time found her only twenty-seven at my birth. Now, of course, I realize the clock didn't age her. The worry lines of worriment that characterized her face came from events, hard times and birthing nine youngsters. Also, her dark eyes always had a hint of sadness that bathed her countenance with an aura of gentle melancholia. In retrospect, I figure, I must accept the blame as the principal engraver who etched most of those lines into her face.

I've heard it said that a man learns courage from his father and fear from his mother. In my case, I learned both from my mother. My father and I simply did not communicate well at all. As I pointed out earlier, we never engaged in a warm father-son conversation. He never so much as tossed me a ball, baited a hook or took me to a ball game. Work or other things occupied too much of his life for him to make friends with any of his children. I can say this: to my knowledge, he never physically abused me or any of the other kids. Of course, we got a few spankings. Most of my real disciplining came through Jessie. Man, could this lady of Indian heritage lay the hurt on my rump when I truly needed it. I remember all too well the last whipping she laid on me.

Early in the year of 1942, I cut school to go down to the Marine Corps recruiting office with my cousin, Kenneth Kelly. He had dropped out of college to come home to join up. I picked up the necessary papers to join. Under age for enlistment, I needed a parent to sign these documents before the Corps could accept me. We found my mother in the back yard hanging out clothes to dry. She took in washing to support the family.

I walked up to her and defiantly stated, "I'm joining the Marine Corps and you have to sign these papers." She bestowed a vacant stare on me, took the papers and turned them into confetti. She then walked, wordlessly, to the far clothesline pole that held a coiled remnant of a six-strand clothesline wire. She took it down, turned and strolled slowly toward me. As she walked, she twisted the still-coiled wire into a flexible switch about two feet long. Perceptively I knew that I was about to have some real hurt laid on me. Kenneth faded away. My mom took my left hand in her left hand. She then laid that wire across my skinny butt in staccato fashion. Instinctively I hopped and continued to hop with each lash. At the conclusion of a full pivot, she let go of my hand. I turned to glare at her defiantly. She returned my gaze with eyes drenched in glistening tears. My bravado ebbed. I choked back bitter sobs, not from my physical pain, but rather for the aching heart that lay within my mother's breast.

She dropped the wire. As she stooped to pick up a wet garment, I patted her arm tenderly. With a broken heart, I turned and went into the house, there to shed bitter tears. Several months later, she sent me to the Corps recruiting office.

A prologue to the above event: After my mother's passing in 1982, my sister Helen gave me a bundle of letters that she had found in Mother's possessions. I found among them a letter from the local draft board, dated one month before I joined the Marines. It stated, in part, something like this, "Thiele Fred Harvey, Jr., as the sole supporter of the family, is granted a deferment from serving in the military service of the United States of America." . She had kept it from me because she knew I'd have felt a moral responsibility to accept the deferment it offered. Being very perceptive, she also knew doing so meant a broken heart for me.

I went to Dallas, along with three others, to take the Marine oath of enlistment. We then traveled to the Marine Boot Camp in San Diego. On the trip west our train laid over in Odessa for thirty minutes where they held a prearranged celebration to see us off. Hundreds of folks showed up. Odessa always stood proud, a patriotic West Texas town. The participants included schoolmates, families and part of the OHS band. We had a gala affair. Law! I got kissed by girls that I never in my wildest dreams could have kissed. Teachers shook my hand and slapped me on the back. Mostly, I think, they were glad to see me leaving town. During it all, I kept looking for my mother. When I located her, I saw her pushing her way to me. I moved toward her.

Silently she took my hand and led me into the shadows of the depot. There she commanded, "Sonny, you're a man now. As a man there are four things I expect of you." To emphasize these calls she held up four fingers. "First," she indicated as she turned down one finger with her other hand, "You will come home to us! Second, you don't come home no coward! Third, you don't come home no drunkard! Fourth, you don't come home with no tattoos!" With four fingers in my face she asked, "Do you understand?"

"Yes, ma'am." I did keep all of her commandments.

After a lingering hug that lasted long enough to bring tears to our eyes, she wordlessly gave me a gentle shove toward the waiting train. As I backed away from her, an eerie, sobering thought crossed my mind. Could this be the last time I might see this mother of mine? She, the catalyst of my life and the center of my world.

After a tour of duty overseas with the 1st Paramarines, my unit returned stateside and integrated into the newly formed 5th Division of the Marine Corps. A buddy of mine, Peter Adam, had not served in the Corps long enough to know that you never volunteer for anything. One day while in company formation, a call went out for volunteers for a new concept in Marine rifle units. Peter stepped forward, pulling me with him. He had volunteered us for the assault squad. In this unit, I trained as a demolition expert, ya know, blowing up things. They picked Peter to carry and operate a ninety-pound flame-thrower. He bemoaned this turn of events. With mock sympathy I said, "Go out there and set the world on fire. And," I added, "ya idiot, don't ever volunteer for anything in this man's outfit again!"

Right quick–like, I saw this volunteerism as a big, big mistake for me too. I had to tote a pack of TNT that weighed between 20 and 25 pounds along with two shape charges that weighed in at 15 pounds each. At the time, I myself, tipped the scales at one hundred and twenty pounds. Law, even my shadow had holes in it. In addition to the explosives, I had my backpack, a gas mask, an M-1 rifle and several bandoleers of ammo to lug around. They had told me I'd get a side arm (pistol) to replace the rifle. Unfortunately, though, the Marine Corps didn't have enough pistols to go around. I ain't a-conning you on this. As you know, the Corps makes up an integral part of the Navy. Now this Navy, along with the Army and the Army Air Force, at the time, treated the Marine Corps like a bastard step-child. We got leftovers or, in some instances, hand-me-downs.

With this turn of events, I had to get me a pistol. I had won a little money at poker and Peter let me have enough to cover the rest. I checked every gun store in Southern California for a Colt 45 Automatic, to no avail. Other Marines had beaten me to them. In desperation, this Gyrene wrote Jessie an urgent letter, asking her to check Odessa for a pistol. Just so happens, the big O had a gun shop, owned by a Mr. Armstrong who operated out of a trailer house located next to the train depot. The moment she read the letter, Mother walked the fifteen city blocks to the gunsmith's trailer. Later I heard from her this account of what occurred at the gun shop.

She introduced herself and then told him that she wanted a Colt 45.

"I have only one," he said. "It's brand new, never been fired."

"How much?"

"Two hundred dollars."

"I don't have that much."

"Now, I have some smaller, used pistols that I can let you have at a good price."

"No, I need a Colt 45."

"I'm sorry."

With this, she turned and departed. She had gotten about a block down the street when she felt a tap on her shoulder. It was Mr. Armstrong.

"Mrs. Harvey, a Colt 45 is a big, heavy pistol. Just why do you need a gun that size?"

"It's not for me, it's for my son. He's a Marine and he needs that type of gun."

"How much you got?"

Dejectedly she allowed, "I have only seventy-five dollars."

"Mrs. Harvey, you come on back to the shop. I think we can do some business."

Out of the goodness of his heart, he parted with that pistol for seventy-five dollars. He has my eternal gratitude for that pistol, for it proved instrumental in saving my life.

As those events unfolded in Odessa, my outfit, the 26th Marines received hurry-up orders to board ships in just a matter of a few days. The powers that be tapped us for floating reserves for the Guam invasion in 1944. With this turn of events, I gave up hope of having a pistol in-hand before we shoved off. Due to the secrecy of our mission, I couldn't get word to my mother of our pending departure. There was no way that she could locate, buy, and mail a pistol to me before our ship departed. In fact, I forgot about it. But I had underestimated the Indian tenacity of my mother. Had I known, I'd never asked her for help.

The saga of Jessie and the pistol continues. That very night, after the purchase, my mother boarded a Greyhound bus for San Diego. Her itinerary took her over the torrid, hot deserts of the Southwest USA, in mid-August on a bus without air conditioning.

Add to that the wartime situation and bus travel proved both tenuous and grueling. She got bumped three times, making for long layovers and delays. Thirty-six hours later, she arrived in San Diego. The trip took its toll. She'd followed hell's trek.

We had worked 'round the clock with very little sleep when one late afternoon I pulled sea bag detail. We had to truck these personal bags from Camp Pendleton down to the attack transport awaiting us in the port city of San Diego. On this trip, several of us sprawled atop a stack of bags on an open truck bed. I lay on the stack tired and about half asleep when we pulled up to an exit-gate at Pendleton. A guard called out, "Is there a guy named Harvey up there?"

Cobber, my buddy Lee Dortch, yelled, "Yes!" and shook me awake.

I looked over the edge, and there stood my mother. She looked up at me with just a hint of a smile showing on a tired, drawn face. Shock and amazement permeated my whole being. I slid off the truck. I embraced and hungrily hugged her. The event so took me I couldn't speak. At that moment, Sergeant Joe Fisher stepped out of the truck's cab.

"Harvey, is this your mother?"

"Yes, Mom, this is Sergeant Fisher. He is my platoon leader." She nodded.

"Mrs. Harvey, how did you get here?"

"By bus."

"You came all the way from Texas? You must be very tired. Do you have a place to stay?"

"No," she said wearily.

He then took her arm and led her to the open cab door, saying, "You can ride into town with us."

I put her handbag, in actuality a brown grocery bag, inside with her. He then closed the door and we crawled atop the sea bags with the other guys.

We had traveled down the road a little ways when the sarge

51

said, "Harv, I'm taking you off this detail. Find a hotel room for your mother. You report to the docks early in the morning and wait for us. Now, you are out of uniform so I'll write you a note in case you run into any SPs. I hope that they'll understand your situation."

About 6 o'clock that evening, the truck let us out near the docks downtown where Broadway, San Diego's main street meets the bay. At ten, we hadn't yet found a room. We had walked the whole downtown area, but it seemed no open rooms existed anywhere. Mom was out on her feet, dog-tired and sleepy. We had visited every hotel, flophouse, YMCA and YWCA in town, when out of desperation I asked a policeman if he knew of any hotels that might have a room.

He named a few we had already visited. He then said, "Ya know, my wife might be able to put you up if you don't mind staying at my home."

I jumped at the offer saying, "Sir, we'll take you up on the offer if it will not be an imposition on you or your wife."

The three of us walked down the street to a café where the officer made two phone calls. First he called his wife. From his conversation, I knew that she welcomed us. The second call went to the police station. He asked his supervisor to send a patrol car to pick us up. A nearby unit nearby reached us in two minutes. He sent us on our way after telling us he'd reach home in about an hour. The policeman's wife welcomed us with open arms. Our angelic hostess filled a bathtub with warm water and told my mom to take as much time as she wanted. My refreshed mother emerged from the bedroom about the time that Mr. Hanks arrived home. We all sat down to a great meal. Back in those days patriotism prevailed throughout the country.

As a result, my mother had a place to lay her weary head. Our host family had two sons, both in the Navy. Mom slept in their room and I slept on the sofa. I reported for duty each day and spent the nights in the Hanks' home with Mother. At the onset of the third night, when Fisher dropped me off at the policeman's home, he spoke furtively, "Harv, you had better put your mother on the bus tomorrow morning. I can't tell you more, as we are under secret orders. Also, do not say anything about when we might be leaving. Give her my regards."

During my hitch in the Corps, I felt blessed to have served under two great sergeants, Ott Farris in the Paramarines and Joe Fisher of the 26th Marines.

I had my pistol, thanks to my mom and several very kind, caring people. During those war years, my spirits alternately soared and plummeted. This time they soared.

Jessie had a prevailing aura of mystery about her. This, in my mind, grew out of her descent through her Indian bloodlines. Between her and the images I had of Molly Hair, they could lay some real terror on me. With your indulgence, I will put this in a more understandable context. She could literally scare the pee out of ol' Sonny! Once, she unwittingly had me believing that I was going to be shot to death.

This all took place during the early days of the Great Depression. The Harvey family, dirt poor and destitute, had very little food on the table and a critical shortage of clothing. Nine chronically hungry siblings aggravated this state of affairs. What little food came into the house led to a great competition. Ol' Rip, my dog, had to eat too. Why, when my mom threw ol' Rip a bone, he signaled for a fair catch, like in football.

Of course we didn't have a lock on hard times. You found poor everywhere you looked. Money had gone out of style. All of our friends and neighbors suffered alike. With cash in short supply, no one had radios, or nickels and dimes for the movies. Under these conditions, conversation took center place as a very popular and affordable pastime. Weather permitting, nearly every night some assemblage of folks gathered on our front porch. After a time, parents sent the kids off to bed. In those days, my bed proved highly portable, as it consisted of a quilt only. On these nights, I threw my pallet near an open window so that I could listen to grown-up talk. These conversations usually centered on talk of jobs, welfare, politics, gossip and lawbreakers.

In those days, our family got something known as relief. Relief consisted of a handout of food commodities to the poor by the government. Each needy family had a specific day and time to show up and receive these rations. This foodstuff usually consisted of canned meat products, flour, peanut butter, hog lard, sugar, and an assortment of canned fruits and veggies. With such a large family, it took all the able and available hands to haul these items across town. We didn't have a car so we carried everything on foot. Mother took me along with my three older sisters (Frances, Helen and Gerry) to make this weekly trek. These trips humiliated my sisters, as friends and schoolmates saw them and realized we were on relief. Me, I loved this chore, as it meant that at the end of the day I'd have a full belly. We made the trek for our food commodities on Tuesdays.

Now, Jessie did not talk much during those nightly gatherings but when she did talk everyone listened. One Monday night I had retired to my listening post to eavesdrop beneath an open window. The conversation often took up the plight of all the indigent poor of the country. This night, I heard my mom clear her throat. This emanation shushed the small gathering. Then we heard her say, "Ya know, tomorrow when we go downtown to the welfare department, them people ought to line all us poor folks up in front of a machine gun and shoot us down like a bunch of dogs." With these words, the gathering remained silent until the gravity of her words sunk in. Then I heard murmurs of agreement. To be shot down like dogs. I didn't murmur an assent. Heck, I wet that quilt. Her words of doom ushered in a long, sleepless night.

Some time during that endless night of tossing and turning, Mom's view on the treatment of the poor took on the shape of a real possibility. I resolved that I'd not let anyone shoot me down like a dirty dog. The next morning, when Mom put out the word to assemble, I instead crawled under the house. When I did not show for roll call, she sent out search parties to find this no-show. Folks searched the house, outhouse and all the trees to no avail. I thought that I had beaten the rap but Francis, my oldest sister, knew I had an inclination to head for the dark confines beneath the house. On hands and knees, she looked through the portal of my hideout. Words and threats did not bring me out. With force as their only recourse, Francis and Helen each grabbed a foot and commenced to pull and tug at me. I latched onto a 4x4 floor support and hung on for dear life. I wasn't going to no certain death without a fight. I held forth until Jessie came on the scene and lent her size and strength to the tug-o'-war. I came out screaming, yelling and a-crying that I did not want to die. While I lay on the ground doing a tantrum of some magnitude, one of the girls doused me with a bucket of water. That took the fight outta me.

My bizarre behavior bewildered my sisters and mom. When I calmed down, I expressed my apprehension and terror of the death-wish that Mom had laid on me the night before. Their bewilderment turned to jest. They each took turns trying to assure me they weren't leading me to slaughter. Unconvinced, I reluctantly fell into the trek across town.

At the door of the distribution center, I made one last attempt to avoid the firing squad. In my desperation I did, indeed, put on a show for the other poor folks. My antics in front of all those people thoroughly embarrassed and enraged my sisters. Jessie took over and whopped me across my skinny little butt. You know what? That crowd applauded her action. Now I found myself humiliated but elated to find no machine guns set up to mow me down.

Mother's Native American heritage made itself known in many ways. She saw and felt omens and forebodings in many things. She had a morbid fear of death, not only for herself, but for her loved ones as well. Out of this phobia she saw omens that brought on fears of an impending death. The forlorn wail of a nocturnal coyote, a howling dog, or seeing a falling star brought on visions of a pending visit by the pale horse. During these foreboding events, she gathered her brood about her to protect us from the specter of death. This dread manifested its fear in many ways.

We brought my mother to Colorado to live with us. One evening, at the supper table, my son Chuck and I fell into a conversation about Indians. Well versed in the lore and culture of the tribes of the Great Plains, he remarked, "Ya know, Dad, the Indians in this area took their old and infirm and put them in a cave with a little food, water, and a blanket and left them to die. The elderly knew and accepted this cultural practice." The talk centered on the tribes throughout the meal. Jessie listened but took no part in the conversation.

The next morning, as usual, my mom sat in the dining room, waiting for me to come through on my way to the kitchen to brew her morning coffee. As customary, I gave her a cheery greeting, but she did not respond. Instead, I heard a soft, but audible grunt.

As she sipped her coffee, she did not say a word. Our usual dialogue turned into a one-sided monologue. This worried me, but I did not question her silence. That night I received the same treatment at the supper meal, but to her quietude, she added a blank, cold stare. I found this unnerving. I resolved to get to the bottom of her problem the next morning.

I got that same grunt in response to the usual salutation I'd prepared for her. I planted both feet and with sternness in my voice, I queried, "All right, Mother, what's troubling you, what's your problem?"

"You know," she shrugged.

"I do not know! "

"Yes, you know."

"No, I do not know."

"Now, tell me what's wrong."

"I know what you and Chuck are planning for me."

"I have no idea what you're talking about."

56

"Y'all are going to put me in a cave."

"In a cave, what are you talking about?'

"You're going to put me in a cave with a blanket and a little food and let me die there."

My heart sank as I realized what she meant. An unbearable sadness filled my whole being. What had I done to make her feel such a sense of looming finality? Bitter tears welled into my eyes as I tried vainly to ease her aching heart and terrorizing anticipation. Her nights, fraught with terror, must have seemed endless. I don't know if I fully allayed all of the fears and anxieties that our innocent conversation instilled in her mind. Chuck and I agreed not to discuss Indian culture in her presence ever again. Seemingly, her fears ebbed away, as the peaceful countenance returned to her face in the days that followed.

Several years later, Jessie's perceptive mind began to wane away. It soon got to a point where we needed to place her in a nursing facility. There she assimilated well. Alzheimer's disease slipped in and occupied that part of her brain that held memory. She eventually saw us, all her children, as strangers. What a sad outcome to life.

The lines of despair ebbed from her face, replaced with a peaceful, but vacant look. I prayed that God had filled the void of loneliness with sunrays to take away the shadows and darkness present for so much of her life.

I saw very little of Jessie in her twilight years as I lived in Korea during that period of her life. Each summer I returned to Texas for an extended time. I spent as much time with her as possible. At those times, she looked at me with vacant, unknowing eyes. A complete stranger to her, that look hurt me like a circle, never ending. Somewhere in the recesses of her mind, she retained memories of her children but only those of their early years. On one occasion she asked, "Do you know my son Fred?"

Greatly taken aback by this, I answered, "I see him all the time. He asked me to come by to see you. He loves you very much."

"Is he taking care of himself?"

"Yes, he's fine and hopes to see you soon."

"Ya know, we called him Sonny."

"Yes, I know. We call him Sonny some of the time."

"Sonny and Lee (Dortsch) went away to war. Do you know Fred?"

"Yes, I know him well. Fred and I are best of friends. We look after each other."

"Ya' know, Fred has a brother and seven sisters."

The following summer I returned to Odessa to visit Mother. Once at mid-day I found her asleep. The drawn curtains left the room in a half-light mode. The nurse had told me that she was sleeping and added that she stayed in her bed nearly full time. What I saw saddened me deeply. The hue and texture of her skin showed me just how much her health had declined. I hadn't expected this, so the situation found me unprepared. I pulled up a chair close to her bed. I took her hand into mine and held it for ever so long a time. As I sat looking into her sleeping face, I noted that it had a peaceful countenance about it. A sense of melancholia engulfed me as a myriad of memories wended their way through my thoughts.

What had happened to this woman, this mother of mine. Why had her mind dimmed? Did the brutal labor and utter sadness of her life play a part? I couldn't recall ever hearing her laugh out loud. I saw only, at most, a smile light up her face. She existed as if she were chained by hopelessness. Had she ever known real happiness and joy? I doubted it. I feared that fullness of life had evaded her.

After a while as I looked into her face, I saw her lips form into a smile as they emitted soft-spoken words. She spoke so softly I couldn't understand what she said. Shortly, her eyes opened and the smile held on. Elated by this, I anxiously spoke, "Mom, you must have had a good dream, as you were talking to someone as you slept."

"No, I was not sleeping. My dear departed mother was here and she said that she was coming to take me home." She repeated these words of joy several times. I choked up with emotion as I shared in her elation. I had not seen my mother show this much happiness in a long, long time. I felt certain that she, who had feared and raged against death all her life, had conceded to the inevitable. What a beautiful way to accept her time. Her mother was coming to take her home. Within me, the despair ebbed slowly away.

My mother served as the catalyst in my life. I'll never lose the memories or the thoughts of her. Even now, in moments of nostalgia or in my dreams, the subtle and touching tone of her voice tug at my recall. Jessie entered life, survived it, and died in harmony with the stoic Indian nature of her Comanche heritage.

If I could step back in history to the days of my past....

Chapter 5

Getaway Lairs

As a youngster, I had an innate penchant for trouble. It seems as if my propensity for getting into hot-water exceeded the average for a kid of my demeanor. I can rationalize and lay part of the blame for this quirk in my character to a couple of considerations. For starters, I had seven sisters. Yep, seven of these critters bedeviled me throughout my youth. Why, on any given day at least four, roamed around the house who could whoop up on me individually. Bigger than the other three, I could handle each of them in a one-on-one situation. Heck, then they got smart. They just ganged up on me and beat the tar out of me.

The other quirk in my personality stemmed from the little-guy syndrome that pervaded my total being. As the runt of the litter I always felt I had to prove something, like many little guys. These two factors, lots of sisters and the proverbial chip that I hauled around on my shoulder, kept me on the defensive during my formative years. Of course, I brought most of my problems on myself. I had the tendency to lay aggravation on just about everyone I got around, especially those sisters. Therefore, it seemed prudent that I have an escape plan for times when this hoard set upon me. I had the quick feet, but a couple of my siblings could out-run me. In looking around, I found the perfect hideaway: under the house. This space made the perfect hideaway 'cause none of those gals dared venture into my den of darkness and fear.

Have you ever crawled under a house? Well, when you scurry under a house, you find yourself in another world. Back in the old days, before they built homes on concrete slabs, houses went up with a crawl space beneath them. These areas had about thirty inches in height and held gas, water, and sewage pipes. My lairs, however, had their drawbacks. Crawlspaces, always dank and dark, serve as a haven for all sorts of varmints. Among the vermin you might find troublesome spiders, tumblebugs, rats, stray cats and, at times, dogs or even snakes. On occasions, a skunk showed up, but I knew enough not to contest those demons of odor. Sure, these retreats held their terrors, but nothing like the terror of seven irate sisters. Why, when they came after me, it felt like fighting off a swarm of bees. So, I adopted the bowels of the house as an ideal haven to escape the marauding hoard.

There came a time when the never, never lands beneath the house also served as a hiding place for illegal alcohol products from the law. I think the statutes of limitation will protect the Harveys from prosecution at this late date, so I'll just tell you about it. My dad had started to build a home for us on the outskirts of Abilene, Texas. We moved in when he had completed two rooms and then he just built the rest of the house around us as time and money permitted. When the Great Depression hit in the early 30s, the house remained unfinished. The bathroom sat in that part of the house he'd only roughed-in. It lacked a sub-flooring.

When these hard-times fell upon us, the law of the land still included prohibition. Out of work and dirt-poor, my Dad took to concocting homebrew (beer) for the purpose of distribution. Yep, we became a family of bootleggers. I say family as we all had a hand in this brewing process. My role in this utterly illegal, nickel-a-bottle enterprise involved stashing the finished product under the house. Now, beer needs refrigeration and without such a capacity in the house, my dad elected to store it under the house, as this damp, dark place proved the only cool spot available to him. Of course, the fact the beer sat out of sight in case of a police raid certainly didn't hurt. To stash the longneck bottles, I simply stood on the ground beneath the floorless bathroom while someone handed me a bucket with three bottles of the product in it. I then crawled under, a-dragging it to an ideal cool spot. Of course, this made me the wheel in the distribution of this illicit venture, since only I had a small enough frame to maneuver in the catacombs beneath the house.

When a customer showed up, Dad detailed me to retrieve the number of bottles requested. This gave me a feeling of importance and usually meant a tip of a penny or two. In those days, a penny meant a tidy sum, as my dad received only a nickel for a bottle of his popular homebrew. My mom took charge of this gratuity. This made me feel great, as I usually got a warm hug from her.

On occasions, the law did swoop down on us in raids to uphold the Volstead Act. For you youngsters who slept through most of your history classes, the infamous Volstead Act created the 18th Amendment to the Constitution that outlawed the sale, production, and consumption of alcoholic beverages. Clearly, some of our neighbors did not approve of the Harvey mini-brewery operating in their midst. When one of these raids occurred, seemingly, we received several hours advance warning of the pending incursion. How or why we got this alarm never trickled to my level of the illicit enterprise. A pending police visitation usually ignited a flurry of action in the Harvey house.

These visits by the police proved nothing more than a sham. Heck, hundreds of families during the Great Depression did the same thing, just trying to get by. No one got rich, but such efforts made enough income to exist just above a starvation level. The cops knew very well, without reservations, our plight and never stepped in to curtail any part of our operations. My mom explained this all to me about the time I turned ten years of age. Out of this, I gained a great deal of respect for our policemen. This regard and admiration holds true to this time.

A raid went something like this: a couple of squad cars rolled into the yard and expelled about four lawmen each. They rushed into the house where peace and tranquility reined. They shook hands with Dad and Mom, then the conversation went something akin to this:

"How are things going, Bud?"

"Pretty good, nobody has starved yet."

"How are all the kids doing?"

"Just fine, getting ready to go back to school."

"Bud, you been able to get any work?"

"Yeah, I got a day in last week with the WPA."

"I hear tell that lots of folks are moving to California and finding work. Y'all thought about going west?"

"No, ain't got gas money to get outta town on."

"Jessie, have those tramps from the jungle 'cross the tracks been giving you any problems?"

"No problems. They're good people, only poor like us and hungry. We help 'em when we can."

"Bud, you got any empty bottles we can fill with water?"

"Yeah, I got about twenty bottles filled with water with caps on 'em."

"Good."

Each of the policemen then took two bottles in each hand and went into the front yard, there to make a show of uncapping them and pouring the contents on the ground. They did this act to please the nosy neighbors. They all went back inside and each bought a bottle at five cents apiece. They drank their beer and talked about the hard times with Mom and Dad. When they got ready to go, they each bought one to go. For these, I had to scramble below to bring them up. For my efforts, they each rewarded me with a penny and a pat on the head.

As they left, I asked, "Have y'all caught Bonnie and Clyde yet?"

"Not yet, son, but we will." I always got a big kick out of those raids.

One hot summer day, a crisis developed in our bootlegging business. It seems Dad might have gotten in a hurry to bottle a batch of beer and he capped it while still green. It had not fermented fully. When the heat of the day hit this green beer, it caused it to blow its top, so to speak. Generally, such bottles just blew its cap off. However, some of the caps didn't give and the bottle itself exploded. When this happened, you could hear fragments of glass peppering the floor throughout the house.

My dad called out, "Sonny, take this opener, get down there and pull the caps off those bottles as fast as you can."

Man, I jumped into no-man's-land to save our stash. I gave no thought that danger could come with such a venture. Just as I leaned over to jump into harm's way, Mother grabbed me by the collar and shouted, "Don't you send Sonny down there. He's liable his get his eyes put out!"

Right off, I saw her logic. For a moment, my parents had a tug-o'-war contest with me as the rope. Of course, I threw in with my mom. We won the contest. In the end, when the cool of the evening set in, the bombardment abated. The next morning, I went under to bring out any good bottles. We uncapped them and poured the beer back into the crock to ripen a week or so more. I'd say that batch of brew had some kick to it.

During that early period of my life, I took to hanging out with some older boys from up the road. I couldn't really belong to the gang because of my age, but they let me hang out with them. They constantly moved about in search of adventure and play. Sometimes their ventures did get them into a little trouble. I say older, but in reality, I'd describe most as about nine or ten. One or two might have reached to old age of eleven or so.

One day they gallivanted a far piece from their usual range with me in tow. We came up on an old vacant house. In the back yard we found a couple of old, rusting Model T trucks. They had no engines or wheels, but they had axles attached to frames. We played around these old derelicts for a while. The suspension system of those old relics were comprised of simple leaf springs that attached the axles to the frames. One of the guys proposed that these old springs might make great swords and with them, we could play pirates. Rust covered all the nuts and bolts that held these springs in place, so we needed some tools to break them apart. A couple of the boys took off at a dead run to get wrenches and hammers from home. It took them about an hour to get back, and then another two hours to dismantle the springs.

The swords (springs) went to each according to size. I got one of the smallest units. We then fashioned hilt guards out of pieces of wood and attached them to the blades with baling wire. We then tried them out with a few slashes at imaginary enemies. We saw an immediate problem. The blades bowed the wrong way. We needed to straighten them. So we laid the blades on a concrete sidewalk and tried to straighten them out with the hammers, no good. The hammers only bounced. One of the boys had a bright idea, "Two of you guys hold one of 'em on each end and I will run and jump on it with both feet." Another wrong call. The spring catapulted him high into the air where he lost control and landed with a thud in a classic belly flop. Adding to his woes, he had a bloody chin. The holders, for their trouble, wound up with bruised and cut knuckles. No one else volunteered.

We then threw the swords aside and headed home into a setting sun. We had not walked but a few hundred yards, when one of the older guys stopped short and said, "Hey, if we laid those swords on the railroad track, the train will take the bend out of them for us."

A chorus of yeahs sounded, and we all did an about-face and ran back to retrieve our weapons.

As we walked, one of the sages in the group stated, "It's too late to bend them tonight so let's do it tomorrow morning."

We lived less than a hundred yards from the railroad tracks so we decided to do our thing at a near-by spot where our road intersected the railroad sat both a water tank and a message station.

All of the freight trains on this Texas & Pacific line stopped here to take on water. We agreed to meet about 9:00 to place our swords on the rails. Each of the eight or nine of us in this group had a blade that needed some work done on it.

The next morning the leaders figured we should place the springs, bowed side up, about a hundred yards down the track from the water tank. We put half the springs on one rail and the other half on the other rail. We knew that a fast-moving passenger train, the Sunshine Special, went through later in the afternoon, but we wanted a slow-moving freight to flatten our steel for us. A freight train moved real slow, as it took at least a mile to gain speed after taking on water. Of course, none of us, especially me, had any idea what to expect when the engine passed.

Soon, we had everything set. We had about an hour to wait for the next train. So we positioned ourselves in the drainage ditch that ran parallel to the rail bed. Excitement reined. We watched with glee as a slow-moving engine moved into position to take on water. Mr. Baxter, the telegrapher at the message lodge, came out to pass the time of day with the train crew. I knew him well, as I spent a lot of time hanging around his office and the water tank talking to him and the hobos that got on and off the trains that stopped there.

At long last, a blast from the engine's horn sounded its warning as it made ready to move out. With a great snort and the hissing of escaping steam, the wheels of this behemoth machine began to spin. When the whirling, staggering, steel wheels caught hold of the steel rails, the mass began to move, ever so slowly and noisily forward. It had moved but a little ways down the track when all hell broke loose. The engineer had spotted the obstructions in the path too late. A deafening blare of squealing steel against steel screamed as he applied the steam-driven brakes. Wheels spun in reverse vainly in an attempt to bring the train to a halt. A sickening groan followed as the wheels began to slide, uncontrolled, off the rails. Then all of a sudden, everything came to a stop. The first three pairs of wheels had slipped their bonds. The crashing sounds of boxcars bumping into each other marched the whole length of the train. I looked around. I stood alone. I watched in awe as engineers, brakemen, and hobos came running to make sure the engine stayed upright. Clearly, they feared it might roll down the embankment, but it held.

I figured the time had come for me to fade out on this building scene so I moved back into our yard where my mother and sisters stood watching. They took no note of me. In a very short time, dozens of police cars and trucks and hoards of men merged on the scene. About an hour after the mishap, I noticed a group of policemen, railroad officials, and Mr. Baxter at the front of the engine. Several of the men had picked up the swords to examine them. Not until that very moment did I realize that our slats of steel might have caused the derailment. When Mr. Baxter pointed in our direction and the group moved toward our place, I figured I needed to fade even farther. I backed toward the house, keeping my mom between me and the on-coming lawmen and officials. I went unseen by the others nor did Mother seem to note my retreat. I scrambled beneath the house, my sanctuary.

When this stern, unsmiling group reached my mom, I heard Mr. Baxter ask, "Mrs. Harvey, is Sonny around?"

"No, he was here a while ago, but I guess he is off playing."

"Would he know anything about these things?"

"I don't think so. What are they?"

"They are leaf springs from an old Model T car."

"We don't have any old cars around here."

"Have you seen any older boys around here today?"

"I saw some kids earlier this morning, but Sonny is too young to run with them."

"Do you know where they might live?"

"I don't know, but I think they live up toward town."

"Thank you."

They left, but I remained under the house for a long time.

When I did venture out, I found that my older sisters had set up a lemonade stand in the front yard and did a brisk business with the workers and sightseers. A beehive of activity buzzed around the crippled engine. By this time, efforts aimed at getting the engine back onto the tracks, but with no luck. The heavy boxcars couldn't move. They then got a switch engine to come in from the rear and pull most of the cars back, but they feared that if they moved all of them, the engine might slide down the embankment. I knew all this because I hung right with the work details. No one seemed to pay any heed to me. Heck, I even helped myself to a baloney sandwich set out for the work crews.

Late in the afternoon, several Greyhound buses came out to the scene. They came out to pick up the passengers from the Sunshine Special, the elite passenger train of the T&P Railroad. They took the passengers into Abilene to board a waiting train hastily assembled to carry them on their way. As you can imagine, some of the passengers reacted with real agitation.

The work continued through the night. I stayed at the scene until my mom called me in. Sometime during the night, they moved a flatcar into place real close to the idle engine. This special car carried a heavy-duty crane. By daylight, they appeared all set to try to put the engine back on its tracks. The crane's cables dropped down and the mother of all hooks caught hold of the front of the engine. Workers then connected a sister engine to the crippled one. The crane took a strain and with great effort lifted the cripple about two feet in the air. On signal, the sister engine pulled it backwards and then the crane diligently lowered it to the tracks. Done! A loud cheer went up. Unfortunately, the success ended my sisters' lemonade business.

My hideout beneath the house had served me well. As far as I know, they never apprehended or prosecuted the saboteurs. Hopefully, the statutes of limitations have run out on this bit of mischievousness or I might get myself in a heap of trouble telling this yarn.

It wasn't long after the train wreck, that my mom came down sick. She was in great pain. An ambulance showed up which horrified me, since little or no difference between an emergency vehicle and a hearse existed in those days. I thought for sure my mother was dying. When the attendants opened the back doors to slide the stretcher inside, I tried to scramble inside, too. They pushed me out, closed the doors and proceeded to move slowly away. With that, I picked up rocks and began to pelt the vehicle with some damaging hits. The vehicle stopped abruptly and the attendants took out after me with malice written on their faces. You guessed it. I headed for my hideout and hit the portal with a headlong belly slide. That took the chase out of them. Ain't nobody going to follow me into my own special place. I stayed there sobbing and crying. My older sisters prevailed upon me to come out. When my dad came home, he coaxed me out after assuring me of my mother's good status and her imminent return home the next day. Sure enough, that same ambulance and crew showed up with my mother and a baby sister. Just what I needed, another sister. My parents named her Patty Ruth.

The environs beneath the house served as more than just a place of sanctuary or a hideaway from trouble and harassment. At times, I sought it as a place of solitude in which to mourn or grieve a personal loss. Case in point: I had an old dog. I presume he belonged, as at the dawning of self–remembrance, I found him there. I have no knowledge of when and how I got my dog. To me he had those important good animal qualities: great companionship and fierce loyalty. Just the type of pet that a boy kept with pride, a *sic 'em* type. He never groveled, or stuck his tail between his legs in fear at anything or anybody. When I said, "Sic'em," he went after any danger that threatened me. I named him Rip.

Now, old Rip happened to be an outside dog. At no time did he try to come into the house or even want to come in. Rip, either very perceptive or by instinct, always knew what part of the house I was in at all times. If I came out the back door, he greeted me there or if I came out the front door, he met me there. Although we could not afford to feed ol' Rip anything other than a few table scraps, he seemed surprisingly well fed. The country where we lived had plenty of varmints to his liking. Lots a' times, I rose at the break of day and loped with him down to old Highway 80 in search of road-kill. You need to get there early, as we competed with hoards of buzzards and crows for these morsels of the roadway.

I loved Rip like kinfolk. Sadly, one summer day events took him violently out of my life. On this fateful day, I went out the back door to frolic with him. He didn't meet me. Mildly surprised, I yelled his name, but got no response. I figured he must have gone down in the back part of our acreage, hunting. At a trot, I went in that direction. I soon saw him at a distance among some weeds. I stopped and called out to him. He came at me in a slow, unsteady walk. His walk turned into a stumbling, reeling trot. It had me concerned. As he neared me, I could see foamy saliva about his growling mouth.

Instinctively, concern turned to terror. I turned and exploded with mach speed toward the house. With each stride, I yelled, "Mother, Mother!" She responded to my pleas magnificently. Our back porch had eight steps and Rip gained on me steadily. With my adrenaline flowing, I took those steps in about two desperate bounds. That gave me the edge that put me through the screen door that my mother held open for me. She slammed it shut just as poor ol' Rip hit it. She was prepared, as she had a broom in hand which she pressed against the screen to keep it from giving way. She yelled at me to get ready to close the regular door. With the broom, she gave him a good shove through the crumpling screen. We timed it just right. She stepped back and I slammed the door. This put a wooden barrier between us and the rabid dog. In those days, folks called a rabies-stricken dog a mad dog. They also called rabies *hydrophobia*.

My mother stepped back panting, collected her thoughts and

calmly said, "Sonny, I'll keep ol' Rip busy here. You run up the road and tell Mr. Johnson we have a dog with hydrophobia down here. Please come and help." I tried to say hydrophobia, but couldn't say it.

Impatiently she said, "Just tell him we have a mad dog down here. He will know what to do."

She turned and kicked the wooden door to let ol' Rip know she still meant business.

He responded loudly.

She yelled, "Now go!" With that, I lit a shuck through the house, out the front door, and up the road to Mr. Johnson's house, a quarter mile away. I must have covered that distance in world-class time.

Mr. Johnson worked for the Lone Star Gas Company and did his work mostly from an equipment building out back of his company house. I found him there. I couldn't talk at first due to my gasping, panting and uncontrollable trembling.

He saw me under a lot of stress, so he turned to a cooler and drew me a paper cup of water. "Drink this and relax," he said, as he patted me on the head.

I gulped the water down, took a deep breath and blared out, "Mad dog, mad dog!"

He pointed and said, "Get in the pick-up!" I jumped into the cab and watched as he hurried to a locker and withdrew a double-barrel shotgun and loaded it with a couple of shells. This stunned me. Why did he need a gun? I had no idea as to what treatment lay in store for Rip. I never dreamed that a shotgun held the cure for the malady that plagued him.

When Mr. Johnson settled in the pick-up, I asked him, choking back tears, "What do you think is wrong with him?"

"I think he might have rabies."

"No, my mother said he had hydrophobia."

"Sonny, hydrophobia is rabies."

"Can you help him?"

71

"No, I can't help him. No one can."

"Can we take him to a dog doctor?"

"No, not even a doctor can help your dog. I'm sorry."

"Why are you taking your gun?"

"If he has rabies, I will have to shoot him. If he bites you or your sisters, you might die."

"Please do not kill ol' Rip."

"I have to. There's no other way. I'm sorry."

I pressed my face to my knees and sobbed. He stopped in front of the house and, seeing no action there, he then pulled around to the back. Plenty of action there. Rip still attacked the screen door. He had the metal fabric torn to shreds and the frame hanging from its upper hinge only. Foam and blood mingled about his whole head. I reached for the door handle. Mr. Johnson implored me not to leave the cab. "He is too dangerous," he said, as he tugged lightly at my shirtsleeve. He patted me on the head and said, "I'm sorry, but this has to be done."

With shotgun in hand, he left the vehicle and walked slowly toward the elevated porch. Rip didn't notice him as he moved to get an angle so that the shot would miss the house. He then calmly picked up a rock and tossed it at Rip. This got his attention. With rage, he came off'n that high porch, airborne, directly at Mr. J. With collected calm, he emptied both barrels into poor old Rip who hit the deck without so much as a quiver. I opened the cab door and made a mad dash toward the inert animal. Mr. J. dropped his gun and grabbed me. With me kicking and screaming, he shoved me back into the cab and in my face he railed with sternness, "Now, you stay put and don't you dare come out! That white stuff on him can kill you!"

He then commanded my mother not to walk on the porch. "You better get as much hot water as you can, add lye soap to it and, with a mop, scrub every inch of that porch."

"Yes, I'll do that right now."

"Get the door, too. I'll tear off the screen later. Make sure you do not touch anything."

I watched through stinging tears as Mr. Johnson looped a piece of wire around a hind leg of my Rip, took a shovel from his pick-up, and then dragged ol' Rip to the high weeds. There he buried him. At this point, I ventured from the pick-up, making sure to avoid any spot that the sick dog might have trod, and then crawled under the house, there to grieve for my friend Rip. Later I heard my mother call me to supper. I sat quietly at the table, not touching my food. Gratefully, no one spoke. As my sisters finished eating, each one of them patted my back silently. I appreciated their caring sentiment.

Later, mom put me to bed and stayed at my bedside, talking to me in a way to mend my broken heart. I fell into a troubled sleep as she spoke. As I fell asleep, I remember her saying to me, "Sonny, you should go over and thank Mr. Johnson tomorrow for what he did for us today. He put himself in a lot of danger in helping us." The next day at mid-morning, I traveled up that lonesome road again. Without ol' Rip at my side, I had loneliness as my companion.

As a youngster, I had uncles galore. Both sides of the family produced so many. The family tree had a real glut of them. Now, they've all gone and I have fond memories of them, with the exception of a despicable one. I considered him vermin. I didn't mourn his passing.

The era of the Great Depression forced the family to move into the city of Abilene. Here, we came in contact with one uncle who ended up something like a weekly visitor to our house. He drank a lot, and it seemed whenever he showed up at our house, night or day, he had a snootful. Sometimes, these visits turned into overnighters. Heck, with nine kids, we really had no room for him. As a matter-of-fact, I slept on a one-blanket pallet, since we had neither a room nor a bed for me. I usually threw my bed down each night where the notion struck me. This guy, I'll refer to him as Uncle Nuisance, usually bedded down on the sofa in the living room.

Now old Nuisance, the endless drunk, took to pawing my sisters at times. They tried to avoid him when he came around. We lived in a two-bedroom house where the older girls, six of them, shared two beds in the same room. One of the older girls always prevailed upon me to throw my pallet down in their room when Nuisance showed up. Sure enough, deep into one night, I awakened to muffled sounds of "no, no" followed by whimpering. I jumped up and in the dark, I saw his dim outline on his knees with one of his hands under the covers. At nine years of age and weighing less than a hundred pounds, I knew he outmatched me. But, he had a thick, full head of hair so, in desperation, I grabbed two hands full of that hair and tugged him toward the door. He followed that hair on hands and knees. He had no chance to get up. I ended my tug-o'-war in the living room. I released him and hurried back to the bedroom. There I rolled up in my blanket against the door. Out of the dark came a, "Thanks, Sonny." I spent a long sleepless night, but had no other problems. Before daylight, he had left. From then on, I slept against the door and stayed between my sisters and him anytime he showed up.

Sometime later, we moved to a large two-story house in which my sisters had two bedrooms upstairs. When Nuisance showed up, I couldn't guard both rooms at the same time, so I just threw my pallet at the bottom step. He showed up one evening just before bedtime, drunk of course. My mother gave him a pillow and told him to sleep on the sofa in the living room. On this night, too hot to sleep under cover, I just lay on top of my blanket. From a sound sleep, a hand fondling my anal orifice woke me. Before I could shake off the cobwebs of sleep, he attempted an insertion. This got my full attention. I flipped over and, at the same time, I placed a knee where he *lived* with all the power I could muster. This had to smart. He let out a hideous groan. With everyone else upstairs asleep, no one evidently heard the commotion. Now I moved with the speed of small-town gossip and raced out the front door before he could shake off the hurt that I had laid on him. You guessed it. I went for the safety of my hideout under the house. Old Nuisance came out after me. From under the porch, I heard him stumble across the floor above.

He circled the house several times, calling out in a hiss, "Sonny, you little bastard, where are you? When I find you, I'm going to kill you. Don't you dare tell your dad or I'll come back and get you."

After a while, I saw him waddling up the street. I came out from my den and watched him. When he got under a streetlight, I saw him clutching his crotch. I hated this guy with a passion.

One night several weeks later, some of the neighbors and their kids gathered out front of our house for an evening of play and talk. The folks sat on the porch, discussing the events of the day, while the kids played games in the dusky light. I loved those gatherings which happened quite frequently. As we played a lively game of red-rover, I happened to look up, and there in the street light I saw my nemesis coming. By his gait, I could tell he had drunk his fill at the bar. I drifted to the sideline of the game and watched.

A vacant lot sat next to our house and, out of habit, he cut across this lot to enter the house at the back door. I made a decision to confront him at the back door. Since that hateful night of terror, I thought about his actions, night and day. I determined to resolve the problem for the sake of my sisters and myself. You might ask at this point, why I did not go to my parents with this burden. To me, I didn't see that as an option.

At twelve years of age, I saw it as my problem. And I intended to take care of it. I went through the front door and felt my way through the darkened house. In the kitchen, I took a big butcher knife out of a drawer. I then went to the back porch and took up a position at the top of the several steps that led to the door. I waited and watched as he groped his way up. As he put his foot on the last step, he looked up and evidently saw my image in the twilight of the closing day. He paused. I slashed at him with a wide, swinging motion. He threw up his arm in panic and fell backward down the steps. On the way down, he hit a little red wagon parked mid-way up the steps. This made some noise. The wagon and my uncle lay in a heap on the ground below. I saw no movement from Nuisance's inert form. Horrified, I backed away from the scene and returned the knife to the drawer. I did not know if the blade had hit its mark or not, but reckoned it had, as he did not move after he hit the ground. I returned to the front and sat down on the edge of the porch. My body began to tremble out of control as I realized the dread and horror of my act. Fearing that someone might note my convulsive shaking, I slid off the porch and tried to take part in the games. I couldn't get my heart into it, as the act replayed itself over and over in my mind. It grew worse with each passing moment. In time, by chance, I looked to the street and saw him tottering his way through the aura of a nearby streetlight. I watched as he moved through the glow into the shadows of the night. Tears welled into my eyes. I hadn't killed him after all. I slipped under the porch, there to shed bitter tears of relief.

He did not return to our house for several weeks after that ominous night and its events. When he did return, to my surprise, he came sober. During that day of sobriety, I caught him staring at me with a questioning look in his eyes, as if asking, "Are you the one?" In time, we moved to Odessa, never to see him again.

When we lived in the countryside, we seldom had a problem with traffic as few autos traveled our by-ways. As a result, I had never learned to stop and look both ways before crossing a street. When we moved into an urban area, my old habits moved with me. Heck, I just dashed into harm's way, paying no attention to the dangers automobiles presented. One day my string ran out.

We lived on a busy roadway. In fact, old Highway 80 that ran coast to coast, went right by our house. One hot afternoon, I stood in the front yard when I saw something of interest across the way. I hit the pavement at a dead run and about half-way across a Model

T pick-up hit me. Rather, I hit it. I never saw it until the instant I stepped on it. My foot came down on the rim of the left front wheel in a way that simply tossed me into the air. I might have done a flip, I don't know. In any case, I came down on an arm, side, and leg and skidded on the asphalt pavement. I came up running. In the front door I went, through the house and then out the back door. In a high state of panic, I scrambled under the house. My side burned like a bonfire from the abrasion I took. I suffered in silence. Directly, I heard a knock on our front door. My mother answered. A voice said, "Ma'am, my truck knocked a kid down and he jumped up and ran in your house. Was he hurt badly?"

My mom hysterically blared out, "Oh, my God, I don't know. I didn't hear him come in. I'll check." I could hear her as she walked about the house, calling out my name. I heard her say, "I have a boy, but he is not here now. Are you sure he came in this house?"

"I sure thought he did, but I could be wrong. Are there any other boys around?"

"Yes, but they live down the street."

"I will check around, thank you." My mom, seemly having lost interest, responded, "You're welcome."

After a while, I heard the man crank up his Model T and drive away. I waited a few minutes, then crawled from my hideout. My ol' bod smarted something fierce, so I felt compelled to face the wrath of my mom. She wasn't too upset, as her concern centered on the injuries.

"Where have you been?"

"I was hiding."

"Why?"

"I was afraid that man was going to get me 'cause I might have broke his truck."

She laughed. "You didn't break his truck. He only wanted to help you. What happened?"

"I think I stepped on his wheel and it threw me down. It hurts real bad."

She grabbed my ear and gave it a jerk. "From now on, every time you cross that street, you stop and look both ways for cars. Ya hear?" As she talked, she helped me out of my clothes. She then went to the back porch and brought in a gallon-bottle of kerosene. She called it, like other folks of that era, coal oil. For my mom, her coal oil cured any and all ailments that the human body came up with. It burned like hell, but it sure enough healed my wounds.

We moved to Odessa at the height of the Great Depression. This far-West Texas town seemed on the verge of a real oil boom, so workers had a chance at finding paying jobs. Homes or living quarters, however, proved in short supply. We had to take anything available at the price we could pay. We ended up in a two-room house without doors, windows or sills, or indoor plumbing. We had to tote water from two blocks down the road. I got that assigned task. I carried two buckets at a time. With an eleven-member family, it came close to a never-ending job. This poor facsimile of a house sat on piers of concrete blocks about thirty inches off the ground. The site on which it sat covered a full city block, but it didn't sit there alone. Piles and piles of used bricks, rocks, lumber, rusting tin, worn-out machinery, and even several old cars took up much of the lot. This hull of a house, midst its sea of litter and waste looked a travesty, but we called it home.

The house and its entourage of debris and trash appalled my older sisters, more mature and self-conscious of our poverty than the rest of us kids. To me, all of this land, junk, and waste just meant I had places to explore, play, and build. Also, it gave a home to lizards, horn-toads, cottontail rabbits, ground squirrels, and countless other varmints just begging for capture or chase. And I found plenty of other guys around who enjoyed playing in my yard.

That summer my life consisted of toting water and playing. Actually, I found it a gratifying period in my life. Heck, except for the chronic hunger, hard times didn't bother me that much.

The house, of course, didn't really accommodate a family of eleven. My mother had to figure out a way to place every one. Privacy proved impossible, so it didn't factor in the allotment of space. She put a bed in the kitchen for herself and dad and a cot for my little brother T. W. In the other room, she strung up a rope and draped a blanket over it to separate me from the girls. The girls got about 80% of the room, as they slept on two mattresses simply thrown on the floor. As for me, I didn't need much, because I still got by with a quilted pallet. My pallet, as I called it, did not take up much space a-tall. However, my 20 percent went to nothingness in a very short time.

One hot summer's day, a '34 Chevy coupe pulled into the yard. It brought to us the Chaney brothers and their girlfriends. The state had recently released these young men from prison where they did time for armed robbery. I trembled with excitement, not about the people's visit, but because as ex-cons they had stories to tell. Also, the coupe which had a rumble seat piqued my interest. I really wanted to ride in a rumble seat. I dropped a few hints about riding in that seat in back. They took the bait and promised me a ride.

As it turned out, the brothers, sons of an old family friend, had come to Odessa looking for work. My dad got them on where he worked. Along with the job, they, the four of 'em, moved into my 20 per cent behind the hanging blanket. However, the space enlarged to about 50 per cent.

In the compression of my sisters' room, they not only lost space, but one of their mattresses. Apparently, no one thought about where ol' Sonny should sleep. Heck, I just rolled with the punches and looked around for another spot of my own.

I opted to take up quarters under the house. With the summer weather, I figured I'd find it nice and cool down there. Sitting about three feet off the ground and open on all four sides, the area had good ventilation. Sure enough, it turned out a great spot and, after I bragged on it, a couple of my younger sisters wanted to move their blankets down there, too. Mom, however, wouldn't hear of it.

I guess I had slept under the house for about a week when a scary incident occurred. This thing happened one evening just as the sun dropped below the horizon. Just before it got completely dark, I dropped to my knees to crawl into my bedroom. Luckily, I heard it before I saw it—a big ol' coiled rattlesnake.

Now this ol' belled varmint lay directly in my path, just daring me to come on. Of course, I did not take his dare. I retreated smartly, found me a long stick of wood and went after him. I could not find him under the house, as he had slithered away. I circled the house, to no avail. He had vanished into the confines of the litter that abounded in the yard. To answer the question you might have on your mind at this time, no, I did not sleep under the house. Heck, I made like that belled snake and slithered right into the kitchen and spent an uneasy, but safe night on the floor.

Oh, yes, our houseguests slithered away the next day. Seems as how the law had some questions about the ownership of that rumble-seated coupe. I never got my ride, but I did reclaim my 20 percent behind the hanging blanket.

Ya know, that snake just about cured me of venturing under houses. Yet, I did have an occasion to risk going beneath a house in later years. Back in '43, we Marines invaded Bougainville in the Solomon Islands. After a couple of weeks of fighting, we had achieved our objective, just enough land to establish an airfield. The rest of this big island stayed in the hands of the Japs. Those troops had two choices, attack and die or starve to death. Our forces had them isolated.

Seems some chose to fight. Their first move consisted of putting long-range artillery in the mountains about nine miles from the airfield. When the shelling began, our command decided to send the 1st Paramarine Battalion and elements of the Marine Raiders up in the highlands to wipe out this harassment. The plan involved sending a lightly armed combat unit up the coast in landing craft. We shoved off about 0200 and made our way along a coconut grove beach. As usual, I got seasick and spent this cruise with my head over the side. Now, ya ain't been sick until you've been sick on a pitching and bucking Higgins boat.

At the ten-mile mark, plans called for us to make a 90-degree turn into the beach. Once ashore, we figured to regroup, move out and do our thing up in the hills. Then we planned to return to the same spot for extraction the following night.

I couldn't believe it, we landed in a Jap staging area. I went ashore close to a sizeable thatched structure. This building or house rested on stilts about five feet high. It sat a few feet from one of those big ol' banyan trees. As the rest of the unit came ashore, I took this opportunity to flatten out to settle my stomach. Just as the Eastern sky began to show the dawning of a new day, I felt the need to empty my bowels. What a dilemma, I really, really had to go, but the word to move out might come at any moment. The call-to-arms had to wait as the call to drop my dungarees took priority over all else, war or no war. The war could just wait on me.

With a sense of urgency and panic, I waddled under the elevated house. Picture this. Here I stood in a war, waddling tight-kneed, holding on to my rifle, and at the same time trying to unhitch my belt. I felt I might lose the effort to beat the pending spill. I beat the odds by just a stomach spasm. What a relief! Before I could savor the moment, another problem presented itself. Dang, I had no paper to finish this job. The answer to this problem grew just outside the perimeter of the house. So, still in my squat position, I laid my rifle across my thighs and waddled like a duck to a plant with nice big leaves. A leaf does not have much utility in a situation like this, but it sure beats nothing. You gotta go with something to clean the venting orifice of metabolic waste. Else, in a hot, steamy jungle you're going to have real aggravation in that part of the anatomy where the sun seldom shines.

Just as I finished my job, I heard the order, "Move out on the double!" As I stood between the house and the banyan tree buckling my belt, something in the vague, misty light caught my eye. I stood in rapt amazement as a guy came diligently down the tree. I could see that he had only a piece of cloth around his waist. When he reached the bottom, he bent forward as if to pick up a sandal. I watched in utter wonderment as this scene played out before me. Just a little guy. When he straightened up, I stepped up and brought my rifle stock across the back of his head with a glancing blow. He turned as he crumpled and landed fully on his back. I looked down and to my horror found myself looking at a female instead of a male. Stunned and shaken by my act, I choked on a sob and trembled uncontrollably. What had I done? As I stood there bathed in pity and compassion, all hell broke loose. The shatter and clatter of small arms fire broke the silence. Trying hard to choke back sobs, I raced to join the firefight, glad to leave that pitifully pathetic scene and act.

An outnumbering force pinned us down all day long. Although desperately busy during this time, my thoughts kept going back to the base of that banyan tree. At midday, our ammunition ran low. The sergeant ordered me back to the rear to find more. I veered from a direct path to the beach to pass by that tree of infamy. I found neither her nor her body. I quickly ran around the tree and under the house, to no avail. I ventured up the steps to look inside the house. Inside it looked like an infirmary or aid station, but empty. I hoped that I had only stunned her and she had walked away from the area.

After the incident, I gave a great deal of thought to that lady in the coconut grove. Definitely of Oriental heritage, I wondered her purpose there? I thought of several possibilities. She could have served as a nurse in the service of Japanese military or a resident of the island brought there by the Lever Brothers Soap Company to work in the coconut groves. Also, she might come from Korea, one of the many Korean women kidnapped by the Japs to serve as prostitutes for their military. No matter the reason, I hope and pray that she survived the blow to her head and the war.

In my life's span, I have stored many, many items in my arsenal of memories. The memory of that day, so very long ago, rests among my most vivid. The memorable events on that lonely beach on the far side of planet Earth have not dimmed over time nor distance. It all took place because I crawled beneath a house to…. I think I lost the last vestige of the little boy within me that day.

Chapter 6

Tarzan Broke My Heart

During the Thirties, people throughout the nation faced hard times. The Great Depression held a firm grip on all locales, especially the small towns of the Lone Star State. However, the oppression of the era we felt less keenly in my hometown of Odessa than in most towns in West Texas. During the late twenties folks discovered oil in and around Odessa. Despite the Depression, the demand for Black Gold called for an increase in production. During the mid-30s, Odessa stood as the hub for the production of West Texas crude oil. This oil play brought the town out of its economic slump.

The boom had started. People from all over the South and Southwest began to converge on the small town of Odessa. Drillers' boots began to blend with cowboy boots on the sidewalks of town. Hard hats took their places among the ten-gallon hats of the cowhands on the streets. The smell of crude oil hung like a pall over the area. The pervasive smell of cow droppings permeated the cattle ranges. In time, the noxious smells of crude oil and cattle dung melded into one delicious odor, MONEY. The aroma of money drew folks like flies to the above-mentioned dung.

They came by Model T's and Model A's. Every slow moving freight train that passed through town disgorged those seeking work. Likewise, the bus station served as the final destination of many downtrodden folks. They all came, the hungry poor, the con man, the adventurer, the rich to get richer, the evil, the devout, and those of unknown quality. Among this group of dubious characters one man stood out above all, Jay Brown.

For Odessa, Jay Brown seemed somewhat of an enigma. Due to his very private nature, rumors abounded about him. Some claimed he belonged to the Black Hand, as the Mafia was known in those days. Some of the gossip had him down as a hit man. Some talked of him as an escaped convict on the run. Others surmised since he chain-smoked and had a persistent cough, that he had tuberculosis and had come to let the warm dry climes of West Texas cure him.

Romantics, in the gossip loop, determined he came to forget the heartbreak of a lost love. Yes, the proverbial rumor mill ran rampant about this tall, angular man. Adding to this man's mystique, he exploited the color brown to proclaim his name, Jay Brown. Hey! This guy appeared to be on quite an ego trip, with his brown or tan shoes, socks, trousers, belt, shirt, vest, coat, tie and hat. He always dressed trimly in a well-tailored suit. Of course, all his suits came in tones and shades of brown.

When my bunch talked about this man, Jay Brown, our vocal utterances lowered to virtual whispers as if he might hear. We held this man of mystery in awe, tempered with a degree of fear.

During the mid-thirties, boomtown Odessa had only minimal amusements and entertainments. At the time, we had a couple of picture shows in town. In addition, several honky–tonks with bands that played everything from country to waltzes plied their customers with entertainment. The Ace of Clubs and the Texas Tavern stood among the most popular hot spots of the honky-tonking crowd. Occasionally, a skating rink came to town. These tent-like arenas arrived, remained in town for a couple of weeks and then moved on. As for spectator sports, we had the Odessa High School Broncos, but the football and basketball season, together, lasted only six months. That left six months with no spectator sports at all. Jay Brown saw the need and an opportunity to fill the void. He brought professional wrestling to the Big "O."

During the Depression, the profession of grunt and groan (wrestling) wallowed in its infancy. The wrestling game followed a defined circuit. In a given area, cities and towns had arenas and designated nights with scheduled bouts. The wrestlers got on with it every night except Sunday. They didn't get much pay, but they made a living. To save on traveling expenses, the wrestlers usually traveled in one or two autos and shared hotel rooms. Promoters printed up the posters advertising these bouts a week in advance and distributed them to each town on the circuit. Only the name of the town and dates differed for each city.

Each wrestler had a ring name which he fought under. To recall a few of these names, let's see, we had Man Mountain Dean, Killer Kane, Sailor Watkins, Ali Baba, The Shark, Gorgeous George and Tarzan Krause. Of these, I chose Tarzan as my favorite, my very first hero. Now, Tarzan was a deaf-mute. He heard nothing and said less. He lived in a world of silence. Why, he couldn't even grunt and groan the verbal logo of the pro-wrestler. A small man in comparison to the other brutes of the profession, his size and his handicap gained him the sympathy of the crowd. Our crowd backed him all the way. When the proverbial villain resorted to dirty tricks on ol' Tarzan, that crowd and I went into a frenzied rage to warn our hero. To no avail, the poor guy could not hear a thing. One night things got so critical for our boy that my uncle Garland Kelly, a deputy sheriff, jumped into the ring and, at gunpoint, took a nail file from one of those dastardly cads.

One Tuesday night, the arch-villain of West Texas, Sailor Watkins, did a real number on my hero Tarzan. Sailor whooped up on him after he had rubbed black pepper in his eyes. Dang-it, the poor guy could not hear, talk, or see. He really found himself up stink creek. Old Sailor even beat up the referee and threw him out of the ring. The fans, incensed and out of control, bordered on a riot. Other wrestlers, six of 'em, finally jumped in the ring and subdued the madman. A doctor took care of the impaired Tarzan.

The next day, the sports page of the local newspaper blazed with condemnations of the sorry turn of events at Jay Brown's sports arena. Folks called for and demanded a re-match. The Sailor refused. People called him a yellow dog, but he refused again and again. The State Wrestling Board threatened to revoke his license. Then it happened. The newspaper quoted Jay Brown as saying, "I have used all of my powers of persuasion to induce Sailor to meet Tarzan once again in the ring. The wrestling fans of Odessa are deserving of seeing these gladiators of the ring in a fight to the finish. They have agreed to a winner-take-all in this grudge match. I have labeled it as the fight of the century."

Jay Brown, the master entrepreneur, had set up the inevitable rematch between these two. The lovers of grunt and groan went wild. Ticket sales ballooned and seats sold out quickly. Heavy betting took place and for the week prior to the fight, the upcoming fight held everyone's attention. I didn't see a sell-out as a problem for me. Heck, I hadn't missed a Tuesday night wrestling match since Old Brownie had opened his arena. I'd become a gatecrasher deluxe.

At long last, the big day arrived. I awoke wild with anticipation. I left the house at 2:30 for a 7:30 opening bell. Why so early? I'll lay it all out for you as I go along. To begin with, I lived on the north side of town and the arena sat way over on the south side.

This hot, airless August afternoon, I headed south on Grant Avenue. I set a snappy pace, as my bare feet rebelled at any lingering contact with the searing heat of the sun-drenched asphalt pavement. As a youngster of twelve years of age, I gave no heed to the sun's relentless bombardment on my body. I walked shoeless and shirtless with skin burnt to a leathery brown with not so much as a penny in my shapeless pants. I moved with a mission. In my determination to see and support my hero, Tarzan, I wasn't about to let anything stop me.

I will go into detail, as this turned out a very memorable day in my life. On this day I withdrew from a world filled with boyhood fantasies and dreams and catapulted into some of the realities of the real world. A whole lot of the little boy that lingered within me ended up lost forever. A sad day, indeed.

In most small municipalities, the core and geographical center of the town lay at or near its railroad depot. The train station, the heart and hub of my town, sat on Grant Avenue where it crossed the tracks. When I arrived at this point, a slow-moving Texas & Pacific freight train blocked my way. The delay found me hopping from one foot to the other in a rapid cadence to minimize the incessant heat on the soles of my beleaguered feet. Except for the foot department, I did not mind the delay. Trains had always held a great fascination for me.

The sluggish pace in which the train had to move through town gave me an opportunity to study each boxcar as it moved slowly by. I saw and smelled the cattle cars from which emanated a very noxious odor and ominous bawls of cattle facing an apocalyptic future in some slaughterhouse. Tank cars passed, filled with West Texas crude oil, these too, exuding their own pestilent scent. Most of the cars held heavy loads, leaving me to wonder what exotic goods and wares lay beyond their sealed doors.

Some boxcars offered open doors revealing their human cargo, the vagabonds and drifters of the roads. The Great Depression and the hard times of this period compelled many men and some women to hit the road in search of employment.

These unfortunate souls sat or stood at the open doors, seeking relief from the stifling heat. The leisurely pace of the train offered a chance for me to carry on a semblance of a conversation with some of these weary Knights of the Road.

One hobo called out, "Hey, kid, what town is this?"

"Odessa," I yelled back. With this, two hopped off, one clutching a battered handgrip and the other with a burlap bag slung over his shoulder.

Voices from another open portal asked, "Is there any work here?"

"I think so," I replied, "Lots a' folks work in the oil fields."

With this, several others hopped off with their meager belongings in tow. A couple of them stopped to ask directions and advice as to the best place to find oilfield work. Being a kid of the street, I could help them in this area. With a sense of self-importance, I told them of the Driller's Club and the Turf club, two of the local pool halls. I knew this, as I often worked those places with a shoeshine box.

As the train continued on its westerly course, the caboose finally showed and its passing gave me access to the tracks. As I moved on, I felt good about the sage advice and information that I had just rendered at the crossing. I turned toward the east. The steel rails looked cool. I hopped on one set, spread my arms for balance and did a tightrope act for a few paces only to find them way too hot to handle. I elected to run along side the tracks in the sand. I couldn't escape the heat. Being out at that time of day gave proof that evolution can go in reverse.

Just a block away, at Texas Street, I turned south again. I say street with reservations, as most streets in Odessa at that time consisted of little more than unpaved lanes without curbing or drainage. In those days, road workers simply staked out the path with wooden pegs connected with a heavily twined cord. They laid out two of these lines to run parallel. A grader then lowered its blade and scraped the mesquite brush, weeds, and loose sand to each side of the road. In a couple of months, traffic had these roads well defined, cutting trenches about a foot deep. The arid, prevailing winds of West Texas also helped chisel these sunken roadbeds of the Big O.

Yep, I arrived kinda early for a 7:30 bell time. My game plan for those weekly nights of mayhem dictated that I get to the arena early and before guards came on duty. A typical August day in West Texas, the air hung motionless making the heat torrid. From here on out, stealth took over. I slowed my pace to make sure no one already about the arena saw me. Just as I got within about three blocks, I noted the open double doors for truck passage. Uh, oh. Problems. So I jumped behind a mesquite bush and waited. In time, an ice truck exited, followed shortly by a Coca-Cola truck. None other than Jay Brown himself came to close the gates behind the departing trucks. After a while, everything quieted down again. So, I hopped back on the road and sauntered ahead, but ever so vigilantly. At this point, I could not accept a mistake. I had to get into that arena to see my hero Tarzan. He had to beat up on ol' Sailor, the tattooed type of bully ya loved to hate.

There it stood, like a colossus in the desert, the emporium for gladiatorial wrestling in Odessa. It looked like a castle of olden times, but surrounded by a moat of sand and tumbleweeds instead of a water-filled ditch. The arena harmonized with the scene and the site in which it stood. It carried a harsh, sterile, bleakness about it. With times so hard, Jay Brown had gambled with the investment in such an enterprise. With the potential profit marginal, at best, he'd built it on a shoestring and likely, without benefit of an architect.

Like a frontier stockade, the building surrounded a mat-covered ring. The ring's square perimeter consisted of rough-hewn 4x4s, joined by 2x4s. Used, rusting corrugated tin form the skin of this skeletal configuration. The roofless structure lacked paint of any hue or color. The ring (a misnomer, since the structure formed a square, not a circle) also had so-called ringside seats. These seats existed solely for the more affluent fans. The real fans sat in the bleachers or nickel seats. Within its four walls you found the ticket office, concession stand, restrooms, and, of course, dressing rooms for the combatants. I arrived there on that hot August afternoon to lay siege on that structure. I had to win.

Other than mine, the shimmering heat waves made the only other movement along the road . This phenomenon, produced by a torrid, blistering sun, seemingly gave movement to the whole structure. About one hundred yards from my objective, I went Indian and I could have passed for a young warrior, except for the cotton-white hair. Utilizing the stealth of a hunter, I took an encircling route around the looming bastion. I first checked for any guards who might have come on duty. On my second sweep, I stopped and squatted behind a mesquite bush on the far backside of the arena. After making sure the coast was clear, I made a mad headlong dash to its right corner. At this point, the incessant wind had eroded a hollow beneath the tin wall, just wide and deep enough for me to shimmy through.

I developed the habit of concealing this passageway by stuffing it with tumbleweed. I had this routine down pat, as I had done so every week for months.

When I got to the sink, I paused to catch my breath, jerked out the tumbleweed, dropped to my knees, and like a snake, began to slither. When about halfway through, I felt a hand grab my hair with a yank. The first things I saw, as my line of sight cleared the rim of the hole, were a pair of brown shoes, brown socks, and brown trouser cuffs. Damn! "Gotcha, you little bastard," said the man in brown as he pulled me to my feet. My thoughts quickly centered on jail time, for sure.

Jay Brown took me by the collar and pushed me wordlessly toward the far side of the arena. There he halted before a stack of soda pops and cooling trays. The trays contained the recently delivered blocks of ice. He pointed at these items saying, "You're going to earn your ticket tonight. See those bottles?"

I stammered a "yes, Sir."

"I want you to put all those bottles into those trays. Then I want you to chip that ice over them. Tonight, you will sell pop during the fights. Now, if you don't want to work, then I'm going to kick your skinny butt out that gate."

I viewed his want as my command. I went after those soda pops without even giving him another word. Man! I'd done hit the jackpot, a legal ticket to see my hero Tarzan whoop up on old

Sailor and a paying job to top it off. With the going rate for pop at ten cents, my cut amounted to two cents on the bottle. I planned to give ol' Brownie a day's work for a day's pay. Gee, and the old guy thought of this as punishment.

The dressing room for the wrestlers stood right next to the concession stand. As I started my new job, my thoughts centered on the fight of the century and how Tarzan should beat up on Sailor. I worked at a fevered pitch and sweated like a dog, when, lo and behold, the door of the dressing room swung open. To my amazement, out stepped Tarzan, followed closely by the arch villain, Sailor Watkins. I stared in awe.

They walked in deep conversation toward the ring. My muted hero did his share of the talking. Here my legendary, supposedly deaf, hero seemed to easily hear the spoken word as well. They then climbed into the ring and proceeded to rehearse their pending bout. I stared in disbelief, utterly devastated. My eyes formed a stream of stinging tears that flowed downward to mix with the sweat of my cheeks. I sobbed quietly as I stole peeks at the sham taking place in the ring. Clearly, they had fixed the fight and Tarzan had the win. The elation I had felt just a short time before turned to total gloom. My first hero, no less, faded into myth. A legend came into my life and radiated in my heart and then died. A whole lot of little boy within me died that day. With it, an imagination and dreams as big as all outdoors faded, something I never recaptured.

Chapter 7

The Day I Won my Wings!

The Army called them Paratroopers. The Marines called those who jumped Paramarines. When I dropped out of high school in '42, I planned to join the Army paratroopers, but changed my mind when I learned that the Marines had their own jumpers.

When I finished boot camp, I shipped out to Camp Gillespie, the Marine Corps parachute school located just east of San Diego. After a short and uneventful truck ride out to the camp, the calm broke soon after entering the gate. The troop transport pulled up in front of the headquarters and stopped suddenly.

The driver yelled, "Hey, you guys, they're going to jump. Get out and you can watch them come out!"

We quickly hopped off the canvas-covered truck. A plane flew at about one thousand feet over the landing zone. Just as the plane got even with us, out they came in a mad rush. Each man came out head first in a flat dive. Attached to a static line, their chutes deployed when they dropped fifteen feet, the static line pulling white nylon canapés out of backpacks. The chutes then filled with air to let each man float to the deck below. When the eighth man came barreling out, to our horror, his chute failed to open. He fell like a rock. We could see his arms and hands flailing franticly as he plunged toward eternity.

Heck! He wasn't flapping his arms and hands in a futile attempt to fly. He coolly, but busily pulled nylon out of his reserve chute.

When a trooper jumps, his main chute sits folded in a backpack. As I pointed out, a static line connected to this chute pulls it out of its pack, aided by a very small, spring-loaded pilot chute. This little chute assists in the deployment of the main canopy. When a trooper jumps, he also packs a reserve chute which has no static line or pilot chute. By necessity, the jumper carries this emergency chute on the chest. When needed, he pulls a rip cord to open the pack. However, he has to pull the nylon out by hand. Then you hope it catches enough air before the deck catches you. When all else fails you buy the farm. Then the rake and shovel gang takes over.

This hapless trooper had to pull the ripcord on the reserve chute, and then pull the nylon out by hand. His flailing wasn't lost motion. In pulling textile out of that pack he hoped that he got it out soon enough to catch air. He raced against time and death itself. Fortunately, as we watched he got enough out in time for the wind to open the chute. Within a millisecond after that chute popped open, his feet hit the deck.

At this point, our truck driver queried, "Any of you poor bastards want a ride back to boot camp?"

Like me, the others gave this offer some serious consideration, but we all hung tough. Although we saw the human meteorite as one lucky Marine, luck didn't tell the whole story. His training had taken over in this situation. However, his ordeal hadn't ended.

Before he could get to his feet, we heard a siren sound from

94

our left. A Jeep carrying three guys raced toward the obviously stunned Marine. The driver slammed on the brakes near the poor guy and two men jumped out and jerked the man to his feet. They quickly unbuckled the harness that held the two chutes. They then hustled him into the Jeep and proceeded to slap another chute to him as the Jeep raced toward the taxiing plane which had quickly landed.

The plane stopped as the Jeep pulled up next to the plane's door. They hustled Ol' Lucky to the door, where two other guys hauled him aboard. The plane then revved up and took off in no time at all. The aircraft gained altitude quickly and came back over the jump range. Through the open door, out he came followed by the two jumpmasters. This jump went perfectly. When he landed, his teammates cheered and welcomed him. Why, you wonder, did they hustle him back on that plane and all but force him to jump again? Had he had a chance to think about his flirt with death, he might never have jumped again. Instead, he earned his wings.

I joined a platoon starting a six-week course to be hammered into a jump unit. At our first assemblage, the base commander stood forth and said, "Today, as you stand before me, there are one hundred and twenty of you who want to be paratroopers. In six weeks I will pin wings on but sixty of you. The Paramarines are a select, elite unit, but we have to remain small in numbers because of budget restraints. So, the training will be harsh and demanding. We know of no other way to reduce the numbers. Those of you who have what it takes will certainly earn the wings of the Paramarines."

Ya know, he had it pegged to the number, as just sixty of us graduated six weeks later. At times along the way I had serious doubts about wearing the wings of a jumper. At the onset, I feared they might eliminate me because I suffered acrophobia (fear of heights) and had no idea of my reaction way up yonder. Heck! I had never even ridden in a plane before. Yep, if I got above the ground floor in a building, I felt a shiver go through my whole body. Now, on a bridge over water I really hit the panic switch. But I stood resolute and intent on getting those wings. Also, I wanted the $50.00 bonus given each month in the name of jump pay. My mother needed it to feed and clothe my siblings.

That afternoon after the speech, we went to the quartermaster building to receive our fitting for jump boots. When the sergeant measured my feet, he looked up and blurted, "Hell, mate, we ain't got no boots to fit you. How did you get in this man's outfit?" He did not give me a chance to answer before he called out to Warrant Officer Hersel Blasingame, "Sir, we got a problem here. This kid has only a size 5 ½ foot."

The WO came over and looked me over, saying, "Son, how much do you weigh?"

"One hundred and eighteen pounds, Sir."

"I don't think you're big enough to fit into a parachute harness. They don't make them that small." My heart sank as a tear began to form in my eyes.

The sergeant saw my dejection and said, "Sir, we have some of those old Army/Navy chutes and I think they come in smaller sizes and he might fit into one of them. I'll put in a special order for some size six boots and he can wear a couple of pairs of socks to make them fit better."

"All right, Sergeant, get a requisition in for those boots. Until they get here, he can wear his boondockers. Later get him over to the loft and get the riggers to find a harness for him or cut one down to fit him."

I saluted the WO and shook the sergeant's hand. That made me one happy Marine. The riggers found an adequate chute, but I had to make one jump wearing my boondockers. (The Marines called the high top shoes issued to every Marine boondockers. They had thick rubber soles and tops made of unpolished leather, rough side out. The name comes from the word boondocks, the term for the wild hinterlands where maneuvering took place.)

We spent each morning learning the nomenclature of a

parachute and how to pack it for jumping. After lunch, we spent time in the gym where we learned to control a descending parachute. We accomplished this in harnesses suspended from the ceiling. We learned how to land properly by jumping from platforms onto mats. We worked the last three hours of the workday on the landing strip. We did calisthenics to the point of dog-ass tiredness, then we had to run for a couple of hours through the boondocks. This physical conditioning served to cut the squad. We stayed busy, on the run, pushing every minute of the day. I loved it.

In the packing room, I got to the point where I could pack a parachute in twelve minutes. I puffed out my chest, very proud of my speed at getting it packed so quickly. However, during week five, they gave us the word, "All right, troops, today you will pack your chutes and you will make your first jump tomorrow. Take care." I did. Ya know, it took me all of thirty-five minutes to pack my chute that day.

The next morning we went to the loft, picked up our parachutes, inspected them and quickly strapped them on our backs. After I made all necessary adjustments to my harness, it still hung loosely on my skinny frame. But I felt secure. My anxiety, however, rose to the point of flat-out horror. We then climbed aboard trucks for the trip down to the airstrip. On the trip down, no one talked, but I can guarantee a lot of thinking and soul searching went on in that silence.

By virtue of the fact the Marine Corps grouped all units in alphabetical order, I had a guy named Herman right next to me. When we loaded on the plane, Herman, of course, lined up to follow me out of the craft. He had the jump seat right across the aisle from me. He looked at me as the plane began to taxi and asked, "Harv, are you scared?"

"You bet. I'm really scared!"

"I'm so scared I feel like I might crap in my pants."

"Just make sure you have your pants tucked in your boots! I

don't want you messing up my parachute." I don't know the truth of this statement, but I heard it said the reason that paratroopers wore their pants tucked in their boots to prevent that possibility. Regardless, I glanced down to check his boots.

A jump plane's cabin configuration allows it to carry a maximum number of troops. Speed and safety take top priority. Tactically, it's necessary to get troopers out the door and on the deck as quickly as possible. A man in a descending parachute presents a completely helpless target to any ground fire directed at him. Also, they have to come out in an orderly manner so that all will land in a compact area ready to fight as an organized unit. For these reasons, a white line painted on the deck of the plane's cabin ran the length of the fuselage and made a 90-degree turn to terminate at the cabin's door. Following this line got the troops out quickly in an organized manner. Above this white stripe, near the ceiling ran a steel cable that, too, ran the length of the fuselage. I guess this cable probably hung about seven feet high. When the plane neared the jump zone, the jumpmaster gave the order to stand and hook up. For safety's sake, he then moved quickly down the line to ensure each man's static line securely snapped to the steel cable. He then moved back to the door and, on a signal from the pilot, he gave the order to go.

We followed this procedure the morning of our first jump. The jumpmaster had guided us through the routine many times in a mock up of a plane's fuselage. We stood ready. When he gave the command to jump, we headed down the white line in a dead run. We moved with our arms folded across our reserve chutes to keep them from hitting us in the face at the opening shock. When I arrived at the right angle bend of the white line, I turned, took two running steps and dived headlong into nothingness, shouting "GUNG HO" at the top of my lungs.

In milliseconds, I felt the opening shock that gave me a bone-jarring jolt that felt great. I knew my chute had opened. I found that ride down glorious and exciting. I made a great landing, hitting the deck and rolling as taught. I jumped up, ready to go again.

Ol' Ken Herman ran over to me and slapped me on the back, shouting, "We did it, we did it, Harv, we did it!"

Talk about two happy Marines. I rolled my shroud lines and canopy into a bundle and climbed aboard the truck for the return to the loft building. On the truck, I noticed that I had a burning sensation on the inside of my thighs and below my armpits.

When I finished repacking my chute, I went into the head to inspect my legs and sides. I found abrasions on both my thighs and side made by loose straps. Obviously, I lacked the necessary size for the harness. The chute opening took up the slack very quickly, causing the abrasive action on my hide. But I refused to complain. After giving some thought to the matter, I figured to wear two sets of dungarees. This helped to a degree, but chafing soon became the least of my jumping problems.

The next morning everything went just fine until the moment my chute opened. When it opened, I found myself standing on the canopy of the jumper below me, up to my waist in nylon. I didn't worry until I looked up and saw my canopy fluttering, due to the lack of stabilizing weight on the shroud lines. I quickly scrambled off and continued to the deck.

I still lay on my belly gathering in my chute, when an officer and sergeant hustled over to me with the sarge yelling, "What the hell happened up there?"

"I don't know. I just came down on the parachute below me."

The lieutenant queried, "Did you have any trouble getting out of the door or with your chute opening?"

"I don't think so, Sir." They asked more questions. I had no idea why they seemed to worried.

The sergeant then said, "Lieutenant, this guy has an old Army/Navy parachute and it, being silk, opens a lot faster than the nylon ones."

"How did you come by this chute?"

"They gave it to me because it has a smaller harness, Sergeant." They theorized the silk chute had caused the problem, so no big deal. This supposition took care of any questions I had.

On the truck, Ken and I talked about the jump. When I told him that I had ridden down part way on another guy's canopy, he said, "Hey, that was me!" I gave this some thought. Then I concluded that something appeared very wrong here.

"How did I get above you when I went out of the plane before you?" Neither of us had an answer. I told him what the grading team had figured. Of course, God didn't give either of us great mental powers, so we gave it no more thought. But, as it turned out, the problems of that day only foretold of more troubled jumps.

The next day, our chutes opened at nearly the same time and Ken's arm got entangled in my harness and we came down together. Our canopies tilted against each other. This tilting effect caused air to spill from the sides, thus dropping us too dang fast. We dropped down like a run-away elevator. We hit the deck like burlap bags filled with wet manure. Of course, the graders jumped on us immediately. Guess who got all the attention. Me.

The lieutenant screamed, "What in the hell is going on? It's you again. This is it. You're going to kill yourself and no telling who else. You're out of this program!"

I made every effort to stand at attention but in a state of utter devastation my whole body shook, completely out of control. He looked as sour as clabbered milk, but when he saw my condition, his countenance changed to a look of compassion.

After some thought, he calmly asked, "Son, how much do you weigh?"

In a futile effort to control my tremors, I took a deep breath and answered, "One hundred and eighteen pounds, Sir."

"We're going to drop you from this program because you're just too small for the equipment we have. Sorry, son."

In shock and with a choking voice, I begged, "Please, Sir, give me another chance." I just didn't make pleas like this to an officer, but I found myself in a desperate situation. Thank goodness for a caring sergeant who spoke up, "Sir, it might be that the chute he is using is the cause of the problems he is having. Why don't we try a regular chute on him tomorrow?"

After a thinking pause, the officer said, "Okay, you take him up to the loft and get him fitted up with other equipment. See if the riggers can come up with something." We saluted the lieutenant and piled into the Jeep.

"Thanks, Sergeant, you saved me."

"Don't thank me because, the way you're going so far, you could lose your life, then we'd all be in trouble. I hope this works out for you, Harvey." The sergeant made some suggestions to the riggers and they modified a harness on a nylon chute. It fit a lot better. Me, I could've jumped for joy.

Later in the day, the sergeant's words came back to me. "Lose your life." Was I just barking at a knot at this parachute business? Maybe I should just go in and resign, but my mom's second command echoed, "You don't come home no coward!" (Read chapter entitled *Jessie* to learn the other commandments.) So, quitting didn't seem an option. Anyway, jumping didn't scare me, but when I jumped I did feel a degree of fear. That, however, represented a controlled fear. I guess every jumper feels a certain degree of apprehension, no matter how many times he jumps.

The next day, the lieutenant checked my modified harness and said, "Good luck, son, I'm going to have my field glasses on you when you come out the door."

"Thank you, Sir." I just knew everything would work out fine. Unfortunately, my luck continued running muddy. Jump number four went bad from the get-go. When my chute opened, I found my right foot tangled in the shroud lines and I went down head first under a fully opened canopy. I was in dire trouble. In no longer than the lull between the beats of my heart, I whipped out my issued K-Bar knife and cut the two lines that had snared my boot. (My boots had just arrived the day before.) I flipped upright just in time and landed a little hard, but okay. I figured that I had made my last jump. I pulled my chute into a wad and cradled it in my arms. I then sat on the deck and buried my face in the soft confines of the canopy to wait for the inevitable. The lieutenant and sergeant stood a few yards away from me, involved in some heavy conversation. When they did come over to me, the officer said, "Harvey, do you have any idea what happened up there?"

"No, Sir, all I know is that my boot was caught in the lines when my chute opened. I cut the lines."

"We saw all that. You did well, Marine. Also, we saw something that we did not understand. It looked to us that you did a forward flip as your static line played out. Tomorrow one of us is going up with you to watch from up there." Man, another reprieve and I welcomed it like money. I felt better, but still harbored self-doubts. Maybe serving as a paratrooper didn't fit in my future. Another endless, sleepless night followed.

The next day seemed just another day of pendulous spirits and tumbling confidence, but my hopes buoyed somewhat, when the lieutenant joined the flight. He wore a parachute. He had not given up on me.

While taking a seat next to me, he said, "Harvey, I'm going to jump, too. I want to watch you all the way down. I will be following Private Herman out, so that I can see what both of you are doing. Relax, and do everything that you have been doing. We hope to get some of your problems straightened out this morning." He had given me hope. His care and concern deeply touched me.

As things happen, this day of our fifth jump required us to carry weapons. This, I feared, might cause me problems, adding to my already tenuous situation. To hold on to our weapon during the jump and descent, we buckled it to the belt on our reserve chute. To make it more secure, we cradled it with both arms and held on for dear life. With this added burden, my spirits began to drift into dire straights. When the signal came to stand and hook up, Ken, who out-weighted me by thirty pounds, had trouble maneuvering himself and his weapon into line.

On the go command, I went down that white line holding onto that Reising gun like a long lost girlfriend. At the right angle mark, I turned, took two running steps and dove headfirst through the opening. Just as I started to clear the door, something hit my gun, the butt of which smacked me fully in the face. The weapon, in turn, tore from my grasp and the strap that held it. I realized I was on my back, as my static line and chute played out. When my chute opened with a jarring jerk, I found I'd lost my gun. My face hurt like hell. I figured it felt something like getting kicked in the face by a mule. I swiped my hand across my face and it came away a bloody mess. The gun had broken my nose. As I continued to drift down, I lost it. I had very little command over myself. Convulsive shivers engulfed my whole body. In landing, I made no attempt to do it by the book. I just crumpled to the deck and lay there, wanting to just die.

The sergeant got to me first. When he turned me over, he asked, "Are you all right? Get a Corpsman over here on the double!" A Corpsman got me cleaned up and on my feet. A chauffeured Jeep pulled up next to us. In in sat the lieutenant and a dejected looking Ken.

The officer noticed my face and came out of that Jeep asking, "Are you okay, Harvey?"

"Yes, Sir, I'm fine, but I lost my gun. I guess this means I won't be a Paramarine." I lost all hope of earning my wings.

"Private Harvey, you will make it, as you have earned it. Your buddy here is the cause of all your problems. His actions up in the Blue Goose (the name given affectionately to a jump plane) could have gotten both of you killed. I'm about ready to survey him out of this man's outfit." He then addressed the Corpsman, "Is this man all right?"

"I think he has a broken nose and a loose tooth. Other than that, he's fine."

The lieutenant then motioned me to get in the Jeep, in the

backseat next to Ken. My buddy gave me a sheepish look when I settled in beside him. The lieutenant got in the front seat next to the driver. He turned to us and said, "I'm taking you two guys over to the mock-up to show you what has been taking place on your jumps. Then, Harvey, I'll take you to the sickbay and get you looked at."

When we got into the simulated cabin, he said, "Harvey, see this white line?"

"Yes, Sir."

The lieutenant stood on the line and began to walk atop it. As he moved, he said, "You stayed on this white line until you went through the doorway."

He then returned to the back of the line and motioned me to get in front of him. "Now, Harvey, you move ahead of me just as you would in a real jump. Walk through it, don't run, as I will follow you and show Herman what he is doing wrong." When I got to the 90-degree turn, he stopped me. "Now, when Harvey got to this point, you cut across at a 45-degree angle and you both went through the door at the same time. You hit him while he was in his dive in the doorway. Since you out-weight him, you knocked him around like a badminton shuttlecock. When y'all went out the door today, you knocked him into the side of the door. His Reising gun hit the side of the door and was ripped from his grasp and the strap hit him in the face. He actually went out feet first, and was facing the aircraft when his static line played out. This must have given him a real jolt when his chute opened."

Before we left the mock-up, we did a couple of simulated jumps together. These were done with harnesses hooked to a down-slanting steel cable. The lieutenant, although satisfied with what he saw, warned Ken one more screwup and he'd kick him out of the program.

He then took me to the sickbay. The doctor packed my nose and put a couple of stitches in a small cut on my jaw. As we walked down the hallway, he asked, "Harvey, do you want to finish the program?"

His question took me aback and I said, "I surely want to finish if it is all right with you."

"Private," he said, as he shook my hand, "I'd soldier with you anywhere any time. By the way, why didn't you report to me what was happening in those bad jumps? Your buddy could have gotten you hurt or even worse, killed."

I replied, "Sir, I thought it was my fault that caused the problem. I figured that jumping was like that, and everybody went through the same thing."

"No, son, we rarely see the problems you have had. Tomorrow you will, hopefully, have no problem because we have straightened that guy Herman out." With his words, my thoughts of despair and self-doubt ebbed away. That officer's name was Hersel D. Blasingame, an outstanding Marine in my book.

The next day, as predicted, the jump went off without a hitch. As we floated down, Ken joined me in singing the Marine Corps Hymn. Once again we made two very happy Marines. Ya know, I had never made first string in any sport because of my size. But when they pinned those wings on my chest and shoved a rifle into my hands, I had at last made first string. With that rifle in my hands, size no longer seemed relevant. I had made the team and found a home. The Marine Corps filled all my dreams and needs.

In a matter of a few weeks, I shipped off to New Caledonia, an island in the Southeast Pacific. There I joined the 1st Paramarine Battalion. It rained as I arrived at the tent camp. The only one to join this outfit that day, there I stood in pelting rain with no one in sight. This gray day matched my blue and lonely feelings. You felt this way when transferring from one unit to join another. I spotted a tent across the way with PX stenciled on its front. I shouldered my sea bag that contained all my worldly possessions and headed for it. A Marine walked guard in front of the tent. I figured he could give me some directions. The guard hunkered down under his poncho. As I neared him, a thoroughly soaked, mangy dog rounded the corner of the tent. The critter presented quite a sight, soaking wet with his tail tucked between his hind legs. The guard bent over and commenced to pet the wretch, a big, big mistake!

For out of nowhere came a booming voice, "Corporal of the guard, corporal of the guard!"

I turned to find the source of the escalating shouts. There stood a barrel-chested, heavily muscled man. Short, with a red face highlighted by an even redder, bulbous nose, he had his stubby, bowed legs set in an *I dare you* posture. His demeanor looked menacing, but there stood a MAN, a Marine's Marine, Major Richard Fagan. I learned later the troops referred to him as Lock 'Em Up Fagan.

The major's command for a corporal brought forth an NCO on a dead run. He stopped abruptly in front of the officer and surrendered a smart salute and received one in return. The corporal rendered an "Aye, Sir?"

"Corporal, lock this man up and keep him there 'til he can learn to walk his post in a military manner at all times!"

Now, during my span of years I have come across but two men who induced fear into my reasoning. Joe Coleman, my high school football coach, a tough, profane and driven man, stood as one. Compared to Lock 'Em Up, however, Stumpy Joe seemed like a Sunday school teacher. Night and day, we found ourselves at the mercy of the diabolical Major Fagan.

He, as a young lieutenant, had served as a platoon leader in Nicaragua during the late 1920s. During this period, a rebel leader named Augusto Sandino wreaked havoc throughout the countryside of that Central American country. The Marines received orders to take him out. Fagan and his platoon moved ashore with orders to sic 'em. The unit moved in without any logistical support from the Navy. Without this support, they had to live off the land. The jungles had little to offer. To survive, they had to buy from local farmers and merchants. They resorted to paying with written scrip, basically worthless. Fagan and his platoon earned the infamous title of Fagan and His Forty Thieves.

After the Nicaraguan campaign, Fagan shipped off to the Orient, there to serve with the Marine Corps' China Marines. When World War II broke out, Fagan and contemporaries bore the title *Salts* from the Old Corps. Those of us who came in during the war looked upon these salty Marines, both officers and enlisted men, with awe and respect. During those early days of serving with the 1st Battalion, I lived in a constant state of fear of Major Fagan. He schooled us in the harshest manner possible. His methods bordered on that of cruelty. But in the heat of combat action, when the chips were down, his methods and training paid off.

When I joined Company A of the 1st Battalion, luck supported me. I joined Sergeant Ott Farris' platoon. This NCO taught me the art of soldiering. He always defended the driven harshness of Major Fagan. Ott trained us much in the same way. Though not much older than his men, he treated each in a patient, fatherly vein. His dedication to his troops saved my life one night during the Battle for Bougainville in the Solomon Islands. I respect and love this Marine. Sergeant Farris went on to serve in the Korean and Viet Nam Wars. He rose to the rank of sergeant major in the Marine Corps, the highest enlisted rank attainable in the Corps. I still see my sergeant from time to time and talk to him frequently on the telephone. I'm amazed that he remembers all the names of the men who served with him. I went on to spend 45 years coaching high school football. My coaching methods carried a whole lot of Farris' and Fagan's teaching methods and treatment to the young men who played the game. I could say a great deal more about my heroes Major Richard Fagan and Sergeant Major Ott Farris, but their stories make a whole book in themselves. I will get around to it if ever I finish this one.

Before leaving the era of my life in New Caledonia, I've got to pass this yarn on to you. Remember the guard, the poor old dog, and the tent? If you recall, the tent had big lettering splashed on it indicating it held the PX, the Post Exchange. At the PX the troops could buy the essentials like tooth paste, soap, shaving gear, etc. Y'all know what I mean. Also, they sold things like candy, crackers, and even Van Camp Pork and Beans. The only drawback on Van Camp's stemmed from the fact you had to buy them in case lots. Being a world-renowned chowhound who bordered on gluttony, I bought a whole case each monthly payday. Now, Mr. Van Camp boxed his wonderful fruit in cases that contained 48 cans. Now, others bought beans by the case lot as well. As I remember, all the guys in my tent did the same thing. Every night we, meaning the seven other guys in the tent, each opened a can of beans.

Of course, the atrocious noise and odor that emanated from the anal orifices of eight Marines the whole night through created a real downside to this ritual. War was hell. With that said, remember, lots of you have said, "Say it like it was."

Two times each week the chow hall featured mutton on the menu. On those nights, about half the battalion opted to pass on this meal. Such nights I usually treated myself to two cans of Van Camp's specialty. One of those nights, I started to open that second tin when I looked up and there he stood with a dung-eating grin on his face, my worst nightmare and nemesis. I nearly threw up. Ken Herman had returned to make misery of my life. Without preamble, I said, "Ken, you can just turn and walk your sorry butt out of this tent and out of my life." This threat only served to widen that afore-mentioned grin.

He opened with, "Tex, I knew you'd be glad to see me."

In rebuttal, I came back with, "You SOB, you've been my onus, a real harbinger of disaster. How in the hell did ya get here?"

"I was put in company C of the 1st Battalion just today."

With that, I stood and we embraced like two long lost brothers. The other guys had sat agape at our tit-for-tat sham. I introduced him around and they welcomed him aboard. Of course, we replayed the near debacle at the parachute school to everyone's enjoyment. I loved having ol' Ken around again. We hung out together during some of our leisure time.

One time, Ken went down to Noumea some 40 miles down island from our base. The trip gave real meaning to snafu (situation normal, all fouled up). He didn't return on time because he missed his bus. Predictably, Fagan locked him up with a sentence of five days of piss and punk (to you land lubbers, bread and water). The battalion brig consisted simply of an eight-man tent enclosed in a high barbed-wire fence. At the time, most of us had packed and stood ready to board ship to go into action. When Ken had served two days of his sentence, I went over to the PX and bought myself a box of Babe Ruth candy bars. The sun had dropped below the trees. Dusk, the early part of night, had set in, cutting visibility to a minimum. With a box in one hand and munching on a good ol' candy bar, I decided to venture over to chat with Ken, the jailbird.

As you've already guessed, this proved a big, big mistake! As we talked, he made a desperate plea for one of my candy bars. We did give-and-take for a while, his incessant pleas and my steadfast refusals. In the end, I succumbed to his whining, and with it nearly dark, I dared to toss a couple of bars over to him. Yep, through the glooming came that sickening cry, "Corporal of the guard, over here on the double!" The response came hasty and sure. They met and ambled toward me. My spirits sank so low I could have crawled under a snake's belly.

Fagan opened with, "Throw this idiot in with that one. Five days of piss and punk!"

"But, Sir, there is only one cot in there and the rest have been stowed away."

"How long has that one been in?"

"Two days, Sir."

"Put this one in and release that one."

"Aye, Sir." The corporal opened the door and motioned Ken out and nodded for me to go in. Ken walked by without looking at me. I didn't know what to do with my box of candy, however, Fagan knew the answer. He took it from me after I saluted him.

Inside the gate, I turned to see him walking away. Damned if he wasn't eating one of my candies. The corporal pointed to the two candy bars that I had tossed over the fence and gave me a knowing wink. The next day ol' Ken had the audacity to come by, eating a Babe Ruth. And do you think he'd toss one over to me?

In the brig on bread and water, you get regular meals every third day. After I ate breakfast following the second day, Corporal Myles released me. "What's going on?" I asked.

"Ya better report to Lieutenant Hall. It's a military secret, but we're shipping out tonight. You are one lucky bastard."

"How do you figure that?"

"You didn't have to serve but two days."

"This will go on my record and the Old Man will not forget this. Hell, with a grievance, he's going to save it like money!" Tortured with self–doubts, I trotted over to Lieutenant Hall's tent. Once inside, I gave him a smart salute. He returned in same.

"Harvey," he said with a document in hand, "I was ordered to write you up, but I can't put it in your records as all our records have been stowed away to remain here. I'll have to carry this paper with me, and it will surely get lost in the jungle before we get back to civilization." Again, I got a knowing smile and a pat on the back. "Now get outta here and forget what has happened. Get your gear in order. I think we're taking a boat ride."

I gave him the smartest salute possible and said, "Thank you, Sir. I appreciate what you have done for me." I think I might have skipped to my tent, filled with a deep joy and the deliciousness of being a Marine. I left my troubles behind me and soon got to feel the thrill of combat.

I realized soon after, in the heat of battle, that the harsh, demanding training that Major Richard Fagan, Sergeant Ott Farris and Lieutenant Ralph F. Hall put us through paid off. We performed well under fire. Farris and Fagan received wounds in the battle of Iwo Jima. Lieutenant Hall died in the battle for Iwo Jima. I shed bitter tears when I heard the news of his death.

He was a great Marine. At Iwo, Fagan earned the Navy Cross. As we fought for Bougainville, Sergeant Farris did some amazing things for which he received the coveted Silver Star. Later at the battle for Iwo, he earned the Bronze Star and Purple Heart medals. Then he went on to win his second Silver Star and second Purple Heart during the Korean War. Heck, this guy hung around to fight in Viet Nam during the 1960s. A Marine's Marine, I found serving with him a great honor, one of the high points in my life. Even today, 60+ years later, we get together from time to time. What do we talk about? Of course the war and our buddies of that bygone era. That epochal war stands as the defining event of my life.

Chapter 8

The Cob and I

We called him Cobber, or the Cob, quite different from his real name of Lee Dortsch. I couldn't write a truthful narrative of my life and times without mention of the Cob. Our friendship began back in '44 during World War II. The war that brought us together and its fire and steel nurtured and tempered the bond between us. Through the years, the threads of our lives have intertwined into a lasting, durable fabric.

Lee came by this nickname of Cobber while stationed in Australia. In this country down under the word cobber means buddy or comrade. There he got into the habit of calling everyone he met Cobber. Soon everyone took to calling him Cobber, a handle that has stuck to him through time. However, early in our acquaintance, I found him as rough and tough as a corncob. Hence, I referred to or called him simply "Cob."

This part of my narration deals with the period of time from our wounds in the battle for Iwo Jima 'til our discharge from the Marine Corps. This story line includes how each of us received our wounds and the nature of those injuries. Then it embraces and takes into account the hundreds of great people along the road involved in our recovery. Some of their names and events have dimmed by the passage of time, but what a tale. Hang on! Here goes!

In February of '45, we Marines and Sailors, stormed the volcanic island of Iwo Jima. We fought fiercely for several days when one evening, at sundown, our leaders called a halt to our advance. They told us to dig in for the night. We didn't really have to dig, since thanks to the pre-invasion bombardment by the Navy and Air Force shell holes, ready-made foxholes, appeared everywhere.

I hated the nights, we couldn't get any real rest or sleep since the Japs took the nights to do their thing. We tried to minimize their nocturnal activities by simply taking the night away from them. Our artillery units fired flares into the space above the battlefield which floated slowly down to earth, suspended by small parachutes. These flares gave off an eerie green-hued light. This light, though muted, helped to a marked degree.

On this fateful night of dire consequences, Cob, as a scout and sniper, took up a listening post beyond our front lines. This vantage spot really put him in harm's way. We expected a Jap banzai charge, a reckless, utterly ferocious attack by massed troops. Cob's mission concerned alerting our lines should one of these onslaughts appear imminent. A BAR (Browning Automatic Rifle) man named George (not his real name as I don't wish to bring any hurt to his kinfolk) took the post with Cob. In this situation, one stayed awake and watched while the other slept.

Now, Iwo is a volcanic island with a constant flow of heat up through the volcanic ash that covers a great deal of the terrain. With this prevailing heat, you couldn't lie directly on the ash, as it tended to scald. Yet, the bitterly cold nights presented the opposite problem because we still wore the same cloths that we had worn on the tropical islands further south. We solved both problems by laying our backpacks and blankets on the deck to cushion the heat. We then covered ourselves with a poncho, which captured some of the heat to warm our bodies.

During the deep of the night, George stood watch while Cob slept under his poncho. As I pointed out, we had gone pretty much night and day without much sleep or rest and it figures that George finally succumbed to the call of sleep. Cob related a soft whimper, followed by a guttural sound woke him from a troubled sleep. With the poise and stealth that come only with combat experience, he raised the edge of his poncho just a tad. A Jap crouched within an arm's reach of him, astraddle the dying body of George, his throat slashed.

Cob quickly and silently clutched his K-Bar knife and suddenly threw off the poncho and, in the same instant, jabbed the deadly knife into the back of the assassin. He drove the K-Bar to its hilt. The man died instantly. Cob hadn't seen the other two Japs in the huge shell hole. His actions took them by surprise, as they evidently had not realized that someone laid under the poncho. Cobber tried to scramble to his feet, but had gotten only to his knees when the twosome began to jab him with fixed bayonets which penetrated his chest six times with one of them entering a lung. The rest hit rib and breast bone. Instinctively, he had thrown up his arms for protection. Amazingly, each assailant thrust his bayonet through a forearm and each came out the other side of his arm to penetrate both the bicep and tricep muscles on each. Cob's arms flexed and they couldn't withdraw the bayonets. As the pushing and pulling continued, a shell or hand-grenade landed near the rim of the foxhole. This spooked the attackers as they released their rifles and scrambled up the side of the hole and began to run. Cob stood up and shucked the bayoneted rifles off his arms, picked up George's BAR and opened up on the fleeing Japs, bringing both down.

For his heroics and action, Lee Dortsch received the coveted Silver Star Medal, given for gallantry in action.

From sheer exhaustion and loss of blood, the Cob collapsed just as help arrived. Blood bubbled from the pierced lung with each breath he took. One of the guys took a sock and pushed it into the wound. The Cob thinks this move saved his life. They quickly placed him on a stretcher and proceeded to rush him to the rear for desperately needed medical attention. At this point in the telling of this saga, I digress.

Back at Camp Tarawa on the Island of Hawaii where we trained, they used to line the troops up on each Tuesday and issued each of us two cans of Lucky Lager beer. I had no taste for beer, so secretly I passed my ration over to Cobber. He swore me to secrecy. He drank the two cans he received with the rest of the guys. The two that I passed on to him he stashed away. When we hit Iwo, he had twelve cans of Lucky Lager Beer in his pack. Some troops might have killed for that beer, so no one knew of this except me and I had no intention of revealing his treasured brew. Now, on with the story.

Four guys on the stretcher detail taking him back to the rear had a tough time finding their way. The rough terrain and the dark made it tough.

As they moved along, Cob spit up some blood and cleared his throat to say, "Hey, fellows, there's eight cans of beer in my pack back at ...."

He never finished the sentence as they dropped him like a bag of wet manure and raced back to the Lucky Lager stash. See, I told you that "beer is to-die-for." Each of them got two cans. They downed their prizes on the spot. To heck with old Cobber. After they finished off the beer, they hustled back to continue their mission of mercy.

Hell, they couldn't find him. As they groped around in the dark, he could hear them calling out his name, but he couldn't answer because blood partially clogged his throat. Why, he could hardly breathe. They didn't find him till near dawn, with him nearly dead from the loss of blood.

When the Cob and I get together with others, a group usually forms about him. He and his great story-telling skills draws folks like a magnet.

Inevitably, he will point me out and say, "I'm here to tell you, this guy is responsible for nearly getting me killed in War Two."

Then the Lucky Lager story comes out. He tells it as only the Cobber can tell a story. Seems to me, this tale has gotten better with the passage of time.

On this same ominous night, I, along with Sergeant Garland Macia and PFC Albert Goldstein, held a defensive position for the hours of darkness. We found a large hole probably made by a sixteen-inch shell from a battleship. Dang, if Iwo had been a five-star hotel, we had the luxury suite. We enjoyed our digs. The hole gave us enough room to lie down and stretch out full-length for a relaxing night of sleep. Unfortunately, that didn't happen.

We used our entrenching tools to form a ridge to divide our hole into two sections. One man slept on each side of the ridge while the third person kept watch. We put in the ridge to hopefully prevent a direct hit from wiping us all out. We laid out our bedding in the same way as in Cobber's segment above. We settled in for a night of much needed rest.

Here's the way we handled the nights on the front line. Once darkness set in, everyone went to his foxhole. Orders said no one left that hole for any reason. As I pointed out, we ceded the night to the enemy. From caves and tunnels within our lines and units, these adversaries infiltrated our positions. They sought to come into our holes to kill with knives, bayonets, or guns. Some simply moved in close enough to toss in a hand-grenade if they found the occupants on the alert for them. So, we declared open season on anyone moving about above ground.

To combat this type of warfare, each foxhole comprised, more or less, a mini-fortress within itself. The man on watch, with weapon ready, sat near the top of the hole so he had a panoramic view of his surroundings. This proved vital, as the deadly, nocturnal infiltrators came from all directions.

While on watch, you had to stay mentally alert, clear-headed and responsive to any movement near your position. A moving shadow in the night presented a target to challenge – with gunfire.

I had the first two-hour watch. When tired, sleepy, hungry, scared, lonesome, and homesick, a two-hour watch seems like an eternity. The constant booming of incoming and outgoing cannon blasts filled the night air. Intermingled with these ear-splitting blasts, came the prevailing rattle of machinegun and rifle fire. Interwoven with the blare and the clamor of these machines of war, you heard desperate human utterances filled with all the emotions that life allows. When your watch ends, the night calls on you to sleep. Sheer, debilitating exhaustion will put you to sleep, usually a restless, troubled slumber.

In the deep of the night, after my second round of sentinel duty, a staccato of pistol fire at point-blank range startled me awake. I leaped to my feet at full alert. I could see Macia crouched beyond the dividing ridge. In a hoarse whisper, I asked, "What's up?"

He answered, "We have a visitor!"

"Did you get him?"

"I don't think so."

"Where?"

"On your side."

Then I heard it, the dreaded sound of metal striking the wooden stock of a rifle. A Japanese grenade activates by whacking its firing pin against a solid object. This whack ignites a fuse that burns for seven seconds before detonation. Beyond the rim of my hole, hidden by the darkness, an enemy soldier had the drop on me. I had no options or defense for the inevitable. Then I saw it coming in a looping arc toward me, a harbinger of death. The burning fuse gave off a radiant, sparkling light like a kid's sparkler on the Fourth of July. I had to get it out of the hole before it exploded. With a sense of urgency enhanced by stark terror, I cupped both hands together. I caught it in mid-air and shoveled it over the rim of the hole out of harm's way. Sadly, the rapidly burning fuse did not give me time to scoop the missile back in the direction from whence it came.

Macia had my pistol, else, I could have scrambled to the top of the hole and possibly got some shots off at the adversary. But, I could only crouch and wait. The interval didn't last long, as out of the darkness came a notifying sound telling us they had armed another grenade and sent it on its way. However, this grenadier showed some smarts. He held the grenade for about two seconds before tossing it. This delay gave me only five seconds to do my thing. Out of anxiety, I reacted too quickly and bobbled it. As it hit the deck, I kicked it, at the same time throwing up my arms instinctively to protect my chest and head. The kick and the explosion occurred simultaneously. My feet and legs took most of the shrapnel and volcanic ash hatched by the blast. I fell to my butt to a sitting position on the slanting side of the hole.

I felt very little pain in my lower limbs, but my head throbbed with the mother of all headaches. I had a deafening ringing in my ears, accompanied by excruciating pain. I couldn't feel or move my legs. As I sat there stunned, deaf and trying to collect my notions, another grenade landed within inches beside me. Without thought or reason, I hoisted my hips to come down on the glittering missile. This witless act placed the right cheek of my buttocks on the device. My weight pushed the grenade into the loose volcanic ash which absorbed a great deal of energy generated by the blast. Now this one really laid some hurt on me.

I knew that I had to get some help quick-like or I might never leave that pit alive. Help, I realized, sat about twenty-five yards away. I couldn't stand or even feel my legs, so walking or even crawling exceeded my options. Dragging myself with my elbows and hands appeared my only option. Getting to the top and out of the hole took just about all my strength. Kind of like swimming upstream in the waters of a river at flood stage. At the top of the hole, I lost it. I either fainted or, out of futility, acceded to death. I know not which. Lying there in a state of oblivion, an ethereal entity began to take form in my mind's vision. Out of this ghostly apparition came the face and voice of my mother. She commanded, "Sonny, you wake up and get to those who can help you. Don't you dare give up. We all love you and need you to return to us." Aroused by these commands, I began to fight again those ever-shifting, fluid-like sands of ash.

I lost all concept of time. It had no meaning. I alternately floated in and out of my senses. I struggled in that sea of sand until utterly exhausted. I sank into oblivion. Once again, I saw a ghostly image, this time in the form of my girlfriend, Jeanette. I think I might have asked, "How did you get here?"

This dreamy visualization put her before me in a kneeling position, her hands clasped as in prayer. Her moving lips beseeched her God to look after me.

She then rose and said, "Our future is to be shared. Take my hand and follow me." She extended a hand for me to take which I reached into a nothingness to accept. Then as she backed slowly away her image began to fade, absorbed by the darkness of the night. I tried to follow.

Follow I did, with renewed effort, but exhaustion and weariness soon captured me again. I sank once more into a deep languor with no will to carry on. I felt a deep sense of finality. Still, through delirious dreams, another visitor came to me on that fitful night. Like the others, this visitant came in the ghostly guise. My former football coach, Joe Coleman appeared. This man, was something of a paradox to my teammates and me. We both feared and respected him. The long, grueling hours spent on the practice field made a great substitute for war, and at the time seemed like combat on a battlefield. He demanded discipline, effort, and total dedication to the game of football. He pushed us each day to our limits of physical and mental endurance. Yes, his schooling followed the harshest vein conceivable. The lessons and the steel he engrained into each, mentally and physically, proved a life saver for those of us who fought on the seas, lands and air of War Two. To this day, I deeply regret I never told coach that I loved him. He passed away all too soon. To you, reader, tell that special person in your heart, whether mother, father, sister, brother, your children, teacher, coach, friend, or all of them, that you love them. You might not have that opportunity tomorrow.

Coach Coleman, on the practice field, at times resorted to the profane to get a point across. That night, so long ago, he came to me quite clearly as I lay there basking in self-pity awaiting death's release. I lay there plumb out of it. Then there he stood, as big as life, in his trademark beat-up ball cap. His right cheek swelled with his perennial chaw of tobacco. Because of his short bowed legs, we called him Stumpy, but not to his face, for sure. I see him now standing over me, spittin' and cussin'. His maledictions went something like this, "Harvey, you sorry little shit, get off'n your dead ass and move out. There's hell to pay and you gotta pay it. I ain't a-having none of your quitting. Now hustle, else I'm kicking your skinny little butt." When the old Coach spoke, it came out as demanding commands. You listened and you reacted. Ya know, I reached deep inside myself and found the strength and power to drag my failing body the last few yards to help and safety. *Thanks, Stumpy Joe.*

At the brink of the hole, I came to a halt to alert those inside of my presence. Before exposing myself to possible friendly fire I called out, "Sam, (Samuel Bourgeois, the medical Corpsman attached to our platoon) this is Harvey and I'm hurt bad. I'm coming in, now don't shoot." The ringing in my ears had abated

120

enough that so that I could hear them mumbling about the situation. Unfortunately for me, the Japs had people who could speak English better than some of us. They had used this capability to trick Marines into deadly, compromising positions in previous battles throughout the Pacific. Those in the hole took no chances. Desperately I called out again, "I don't have on a helmet. I'm going to wave a hand, and then I'm coming in. Now, don't shoot!"

Anxious hands grabbed my hand and pulled me into the hole. Just before I passed into oblivion, Sam declared, "Hell, his ass is like hamburger meat!" I don't know what Sam did, but he saved my life, according to Naval doctors who cared for me later.

I don't know how much time passed, but I came to find myself lying face down on a stretcher in a deep open trench. Hundreds of other stretcher cases shared that long protective trench. I could feel my right arm tethered to a bag of blood plasma hanging on a standing M-1 rifle.

My first thought and concern went to my boots. I wore those hard earned paratrooper boots, night and day, ever since I left parachute school. I wore them out and had them resoled about six times over the years. I asked a tending Corpsman if I still had my boots on my feet.

He lifted the poncho and said, "Yes, one of them is okay, but the left one has only the top remaining with a heel hanging to it." The damaged boot had taken the brunt of the blast from that bobbled grenade.

"Would you please take them off and give them to me?" He complied and set them near my shoulder. I hugged them to my neck in a gesture of love. I then drifted back into blissful sleep. I slept in the arms of Morpheus, the Greek god of dreams and sleep, with my brain marinated in morphine. *Thanks, Morpheus.*

My next wakeful moment found me on the deck of a Higgins boat in the rough and stormy coastal waters off Iwo. Still face down, I found myself on a wire and steel stretcher they used to hoist me aboard an LST. The stormy sea made the transfer very difficult and dangerous. Since I had woken up, my Corpsman figured I needed another shot of morphine. A soaking rain chilled me. The shot took me out of my misery. In this state, time still had no meaning. I next awoke on the upper deck of a much larger ship, the USS Ozark, a heavy equipment cargo ship. I learned later that the regular Naval hospital ships had exceeded capacity, so the Navy converted this craft into a floating hospital. Just how they got me from the LST to the Ozark, I'll never know, but there I lay, still clutching my boots with a Corpsman standing over me, holding a bag of blood plasma.

You will note that I have consistently capitalized the term Corpsman. I do this out of the respect that I have for those men. If not for this group, along with the many Naval nurses and doctors who cared for me along the way I could not have survived the long journey to recovery. God bless them all.

A doctor soon came by and lifted the poncho that covered me and said, "Take this man now." I remember the doctor's name, Anderson. They took me to the operating room, where they placed me on an operating table, still clutching my boots. Doctor Anderson came in and barked some orders. Things began to happen. Someone tried to take my boots.

I cried out, "No, no don't take my boots!" There followed a tug-o'-war for the boots.

Doctor Anderson interceded, "Let this Marine keep his boots." An anesthesiologist captured the moment with a shot to my arm. I drifted off into a nothingness, still happily hugging my jump boots.

I came to and found myself on my back for the first time since the explosion. I lay on the top tier of a low double bunk bed, clearly the quarters of the ship's crew. A body-cast encased me from the soles of my feet to my armpits.

My first thoughts went to my boots. "Gotta find my boots," I said in panic. Then I did a strange thing. I knew what I did, but had no control over my actions. I saw an open hatchway beyond my feet. I then reached up and took hold of a pipe that ran parallel to the bunk bed. I then swung clear of the bunk and began to swing myself, hand over hand, toward the lighted hatchway. I wanted to find my boots, come hell or high water. I felt like a spectator instead of the player in this scenario. I had to find my boots!

Others in the ward saw my alarming behavior and sent up a howl for someone to stop me. Paying them no heed, I continued to work my way along the pipe. The plaster of Paris cast must have weighted at least 15-20 lbs. Where the strength to perform this trapeze act came from, I'll never know. The pipe that supported me went through the bulkhead above the hatchway. This should have brought my mindless, bizarre odyssey to a halt. However, at the hatchway I made a seemingly impossible move. I swung myself low and through the opening and caught the pipe on the other side. I then found myself in a large room that housed several large ventilating fans that carried fresh air throughout the lower decks of the ship. I did not go far, as I collapsed and fell to the deck in a dead faint.

When I came to, I found myself on a cot in a vast room in the hold of the ship. My cot, sat among forty to fifty other cots, all occupied by Marines with their heads and ears swaddled in bandages. An eerie silence prevailed throughout the makeshift ward. "Strange," I thought. Raising my head as much as possible, I looked around for someone in charge, but saw no one about. Thirsty and wracked with pain, I called out loudly, "Corpsman!"

The sound of my voice caused a sudden uproar of yelling and screaming among those about me. I found this both unnerving and incomprehensible. Silence returned in a short time, but no one responded to the loud uproar. Looking about, I saw that the guy next to me had his eyes open and he stared intently at the ceiling.

Softly I spoke, "Hey, Mack, where are the Corpsmen?"

No response. I figured the bandages that covered his ears muffled his hearing. I could reach his cot so I gave it a nudge, at the same time calling out to him. Apparently, he didn't respond to either sound and movement. What was going on?

The heavy cast that adorned my body immobilized all but head and arm movement. What could I do? Pain and thirst wracked my body and I felt a bowel movement coming on. Now, just how could I handle this situation with full-body coverage? Had anyone given thought to this dire probability? Heck, I didn't have any idea what provisions they'd made down there to take care of the thing that happens. I know that I had peed uncontrollably and it had to go somewhere. I found out later that a tube had drained my urine into a bag.

I lay there for a long while until real urgency and anxiety set in. Out of desperation, I called out loudly for help. Again, clamor and pandemonium erupted from the poor souls about me. My call for assistance brought no one. I gave up hope. As I lay wallowing in self-pity and doubt, I heard a hatch open and then slam shut. I raised my head to see Doctor Anderson. As he walked briskly through the barn-like ward, I propped myself up on one elbow and waved my other arm desperately. I watched hopelessly as he made his way through the room. As he walked, he glanced here and there and shook his head from side to side indicating a great sadness. I never caught his eye. He made his way through the ward and out the hatch at the far end. A deep sense of finality set in. With no control over myself, I sobbed bitter tears.

I watched that hatch, hoping that he might return. Sure enough, he did come through that same portal a little later. I had decided to call out his name if he came back. I waited until he got abreast of me, and then waved my arms, and as loudly as I could, I yelled, "Doctor And…." The uproar drowned me out before I said anything more, but he heard my call and did a 180-degree turn and saw my waving arm. He hurriedly got over to me saying, "What in the world are you doing here?"

"I don't know. I just woke up a couple of hours ago."

"I've been looking for you for a day and a half and could not find you or your chart." He laughed and said, "I figured you had bought the farm. I never thought to look for you here. How do you feel, son?"

"I'm feeling something terrible, Sir. Can I have some water?"

"Sure, you can. Has anyone been down here to look after you? We've got to get you outta here first. Hang on, I'll be back."

"I ain't going no place, Sir. Where are my boots, Sir?"

He smiled, thumped my cast, and left.

While I awaited his return, two doctors and a group of corpsmen came in. They moved among the silent ones. I watched as one of the doctors bent over and applied his stethoscope to an individual's chest. After listening for a while, he shook his head and stood erect. Then the other doc took a listen and then motioned to the Corpsmen. Two of them placed a stretcher by the cot and then put the body on it. The reality hit me like a sledgehammer. Damn, they had come to cull the dead from among my room mates! To say the least, I found this unnerving as hell and I don't resort to the profane very often. I propped myself up on my elbows. I wanted to make sure they didn't take me. When they got to me, they seemed genuinely taken aback by my presence. They looked at me, then at each other. I anxiously declared, "Doctor Anderson is a-coming back for me!"

"How did you get down here?"

"I don't know, Sir. I've been asleep for a long time!"

"Relax, young man. You'll be taken care of." They moved to the cot next to me, applied a stethoscope to the man's chest and then closed his eyes. No wonder I did not get a response from him. Now I really, really felt bad.

In a short time, good ol' Doctor Anderson returned with three Corpsmen. Man, what a relief and joy to see them. The three Corpsmen stood abreast of my cot and lifted me. The doc pulled the cot away and replaced it with a stretcher. Then they lowered me into it. One of them promptly pinned an IV to my arm.

When the liquid began to flow into my veins, Doctor Anderson said, "Harvey, this bag contains both food and drink for you. We can't give you solid food, as your anal orifice is messed up and we can't allow you to have a bowel movement at this time."

"What do you mean?"

One of the Corpsmen laughed and said, "Hey, mate, it means your a-hole's been shot up and you can't s_ _ _ through it."

"But, I've got to do it now, real bad-like!"

The doc said, "You're only feeling the need. There's nothing there to come out. I'll give you something to relieve the symptom when we get upstairs."

Up topside, they put me in a bed and Doctor Anderson administered a shot to my arm. He told me that the ship lay at anchor in the waters off Guam and they were to take me ashore very soon. Before the shot took effect, I said to him, "Doctor, there is something bothering me. While I was down in that big room with all those guys, all of them had bandages on their heads. Seemingly, not much was being done for them. What's wrong with them?"

After a pause, he said in a halting voice, "We've done all that we can possibly do for those poor souls. For them, there's no hope. Those Marines are now in God's loving hands. God bless them all." With that, he touched my head, too choked to say more. He then turned and walked out of my life, but not out of my memories.

Today my thoughts go to that makeshift ward and its row on row of Marines who were in God's hands, waiting silently to be accepted in his heavens above. For a time, I shared that waiting room with the silent ones. By chance or circumstance, God's Hands had held me safe.

I never found my boots.

The shot that Doctor Anderson laid on me and the subsequent ones administered to me kept me in a constant state of total inertness. When next I wakened from a dreamless sleep, I found that I had chewed incessantly on the sheet that covered me. Even out of this stupor, I felt as if I drifted through a void of nothingness. Time and life had no meaning. I found I now lay abed in a Naval hospital on Guam. Joe Malone, a great sergeant from my outfit, occupied the bed across the aisle from me. He had lost a leg on Iwo. Joe tried to cheer me up, but I could not respond. I did not talk to anyone or answer any questions put to me. I didn't feel much pain, as they kept me steeped in pain-reducing narcotics. The heavy cast that embodied me, however, presented a big problem. The thing prevented comfort and caused me to itch like hell all over.

Guam is a tropical island, so folks wore whites and khaki as the uniform of the day for comfort's sake. The heat kept the moisture in the air at near the boiling point. Along with the Corpsmen, we had female nurses there. They wore loose-fitting cotton seersucker uniforms. One morning a young, pretty nurse bathed the exposed parts of my body. Looking down I could see an opening in the cast about the urinary area. I could also see a scab-encrusted penis with a tube in its orifice for the elimination of urine. She leaned over busily cleaning this organ when her blouse fell partially open to expose her braless boobs.

Fearing that the combination of touch and sight might rattle my manhood, I softly said, "Miss, you better button your blouse or I might embarrass us both." She looked at me with a quiver in her lips and a moistness forming in her eyes.

She mumbled, "Oh no, you...." Before she finished her say, she quickly left the ward.

I thought, "Man, I'm in trouble, now," as I had insulted a lady Naval officer.

Directly another, more mature, nurse came out to finish cleaning me. She spoke as she went about her work, "Miss Kirby wants to apologize for losing her poise. Do you realize why she broke down?"

"No, but I guess I made her mad about her uniform or something."

"Mr. Harvey, do you know the nature of your wounds?"

"Yes, my backside and legs are bad off, but I'll be okay."

"You have some serious internal problems also. The doctor

should be around a little later and he will probably tell you more."

"When do you think I'll able to go back to my outfit?"

"Not for a long time, I'm afraid. The doctor will let you know."

In a while, Miss Kirby came back and clasped my hand and said, "Mr. Harvey, I'm sorry that I upset you. Will you ever forgive me?"

Abashed by her candor I stammered, "I wasn't upset. I figured I had made you angry."

"Then we're friends again." She then patted me on the head and went about her work. I returned to my depressed state and sheet-chewing, concerned about what the doctor might reveal.

Two very young doctors showed up about mid-morning. They introduced themselves. I forgot their names, I'm sorry to say. They spent several moments mulling over my medical charts, then one of them said, "Harvey, you have multiple injuries. We think everything will turn out well. Do you have any questions?"

"Yes, do I have any broken bones?"

"No, your chart doesn't indicate any broken bones."

"Then, why do I have this big old cast on my body?"

"You have this cast for several reasons. Your left leg has a great deal of blood vein damage with clots forming in them. The cast immobilizes your leg, hopefully, to keep a clot from breaking loose and going to your heart."

"Why is it on my right leg, too?"

"To hold your foot in an upright position to prevent drop-foot."

"What's that?"

"A condition where you can't lift your toes when you walk, so you drag that foot when walking."

"Why does it come up to here?" I asked pointing to my chest.

"You have internal injuries. One of your testicles was blown away completely."

"Testicle, what's that?"

"Testicles are your balls, ya know, you had two of 'em. The other was damaged and the cast immobilizes it, hopefully to save it."

"If I lose it, then that will make me a queer or something, won't it?"

"No, not hardly. It will mean that you can't have sex."

Being very naïve at the time, I had never heard that term used, except to tell apart men and women. "Sex, what do you mean by that?"

"Sex, you know, what you do with a girl. Son, hasn't anyone told you about the facts of life, the birds and the bees?"

Hearing all this got to me. They talked on, but I didn't hear a thing. The whole situation took me aback and I really worried about the celibate future that lay before me. I lost all hope. A persistent feeling of hopelessness and dejection pervaded my whole being. I wanted to die.

The next morning, a doctor of psychiatry visited me. He began to talk to me about leading a productive life and all that kind of stuff. Hysterically, I told him I didn't want to hear what he had to say. He persisted.

Joe, from across the aisle said with authority, "Doctor, I think it best that you leave him alone. I doubt that he needs your counseling at this time. He's a Marine and will work this out himself." The doc patted me on the head and left. Joe added, "Hang in there, Harv."

Later in the day, a chaplain made his way to my bedside. Now, at this point in my life I believed myself an out-and-out atheist, as I've already pointed out. Before he could get started, I said, "Sir, I don't want to hear what you have to say."

"But son, you need God's comforting salvation at this time."

"No, I don't need to hear your bilge about God's help!"

"It is through Jesus and God ...."

"Get out! Get out! I don't wanna hear none of your hogwash and crap about God. Get out!"

Sergeant Malone again came to my aid. "Sir, just leave the little guy alone. You're making matters worse for him at this time. Please leave him be."

"I'll pray for you," the chaplain said as he backed away, visibly shaken.

From across the aisle, I heard, "Ease up, Harvey. Calm down!"

Soon they came with a stretcher to carry Joe Malone away. He had fought his war and his wounds earned him a ticket home. As they laid him on the stretcher, he asked to be taken to my bedside.

He shook my hand and added, "Harvey, take care and good luck to you. It was a pleasure soldiering with you. Hang tough."

"Thanks, Joe," I said, too choked up to say more. The same for him. They toted him out of the ward to begin his long journey home. A part of me went with him. A photograph of C Company, 26th Marines hangs above my bed. Each night I look at that picture and say a prayer for them. What a privilege to have served with such a great company of Marines. That photo has faded over the years and the names of most of them have dimmed with time, but I remember their faces and each one as vividly as the day we took that photo. At times, I single out Sergeant Malone and say, "Thanks, Joe, God be with you." (Joe lived in Ohio and I have gone to my computer several times in vain attempts to locate him. There are over 100 Joe Malones in that great state.)

The next day, a stretcher came for me. This leg of my long road home took me to Aiea Naval Hospital at Pearl Harbor where I remained for several months. While there they performed countless operations on this old battered body of mine. Upon arriving at Aiea, I still stewed in a very sad mental state of mind. I felt like I sat in a void; that nothing had any meaning for me. Of course, most of this grew out of the fact that I wallowed in a sea of self-pity at the time. They still had me tethered to a perennial bag of life-sustaining fluids. My suit of plaster of Paris still personified a jail cell. Adding to its misery, it had developed some rather rank odor from oozing wounds and tropically enhanced sweat. In short, I smelled like a pigsty. Pain was my constant companion and I longed for the day that I could return to my rifle company.

They put me in small room that faced the plastic surgery ward of the hospital. The cubical held two beds, with one already occupied. The room had all the sounds of a morgue: none. I had no inclination to talk and my roommate couldn't. Only the eyes remained of his original face. The void where most of his face should have been looked like someone had poked a finger into a half-air-filled toy balloon. He took nourishment through one tube and breathed through another. I felt less sorry for myself. If you look around when adversity strikes, you will always find someone worse off than yourself. My roommate's name has faded from memory. *Life Magazine* ran a lengthy article with photographs of him twenty to thirty years later. At that time, he continued to undergo reconstructive surgery in a VA hospital somewhere in Illinois. I held onto that edition of Life for many years, but it faded away along with that courageous Marine's name. I think of him often and wonder how he's getting along.

They didn't do much for me other than IVs that induced fluids into my arms for nourishment. They did frequently sprayed me down with oil of wintergreen to cover the nauseating odor that emanated from my cast. Every four hours I received shots of antibiotics and painkillers. This routine went on night and day. Sleep became a catch-as-catch-can thing. The days seemed long and the nights endless. I hated the nights. Having very little command over myself, time found me chewing incessantly on my sheet. Life seemingly had lost its meaning. I existed chained by hopelessness.

Several days after I arrived at Aiea Naval Hospital someone yelled, "Harvey!"

The authoritative sound marched the length of the long ward like a clap of thunder. Then like an echo, it reverberated again, "Harvey, where in the hell are you?"

That voice could have deafened a rock. I knew that voice. The Cob! I raised my head as far as I could to peer out the window that separated our room from the main ward. The pandemonium he created brought nurses, Corpsmen, and a couple of doctors who scurried to shush and stop him. He had none of it. The head nurse stood in front of him, blocking his progress. She put a finger to her lips and pointed to our room. She then turned and led the way to me. Cobber hadn't come alone. He pushed a wheel chair with Bill Cross, a long time friend and buddy of ours, as the passenger. He had lost a leg on Iwo. Cobber had his arms crossed and bandaged to his chest. When they got to my bedside, I broke into uncontrollable sobbing. Cob took a long look at me and then directed his eyes to my roommate. He sniffed the air and exclaimed in a rage, "What the hell is this place? It reeks of pestilence and death."

"This is a plastic surgery ward," I answered.

"I know that, what's this room?"

"I guess I'm in this room 'cause I smell so bad."

"What are they doing for you?"

"I don't know. They give me shots all the time."

Cob then moved to the other guy's bed and asked, "Can you hear me?"

He nodded a yes.

"What are they doing for you, Henry?"

Henry took up a pad and pencil and scribbled a note, "Look at me. Nothing can be done for me."

"Why do they have you in here?"

Another note stated, "I like it here. I don't like people to look at me."

"Henry, you can't hide out. Get out of this room. People will get used to it. Can you walk?"

There came another yes nod.

Cobber then abruptly left the room and went into the office of the ward's head nurse. Cobber had gone into her office in irate

132

mode looking for a fight. He found it. She, a petite, pretty lady, hailed from Austin, Texas and she lit into him. Cob stood up to her, him a lowly PFC and she an officer. She never asked his rank and she didn't know but what he might have outranked her. This didn't seem an issue with her. I don't know what they said in her office, but Cobber indicated it got heated. Later he revealed that he came out second in the spat.

"I like that lady," he said. "She's tough enough to be a Marine gunny sergeant."

They returned to the room where Cobber opened the conversation. "Henry is in this room by choice, but he should be out with the rest of the guys moving about."

"I know, but he wants to be in isolation."

"How about that, Henry? You want to move out of this room to be with other Marines?"

Henry rolled his eyes indicating thought. He nodded yes.

"Now, why is Harvey in here? Evidently they're doing very little for him. Why does he have that body cast on?"

The petite nurse referred to my chart, which she had brought along. She started at my toes and worked her way up, explaining each of the wounds that lay within the cast. Cobber and Bill listened intently as she talked. She finished by saying that the major problem involved the critical blood clots forming in my left leg.

With a plea in his voice, Bill calmly said, "Nurse, if there's anything that can be done for our Buddy, will you help us to get it done?"

"There's a new doctor here and he'll be making his rounds later today. He's so busy and there are so many of you, but I'll try to get something done for him. You Marines certainly look out for each other. You know, I could run you up for the ruckus you caused here today, but I won't because you've all had enough hell thrown at you already."

Those of us who could salute, gave her a snappy one and

verbalized a heartfelt, "Thanks."

She left.

We three and our newfound friend, Henry, got into some heavy Marine talk. Each of us brought the others up on what had brought us to Aiea Hospital. I hadn't heard anything on either of them before this time. Cobber had heard some of the details of my misfortune and that I had bought the farm. I hadn't felt this good mentally, since the grenade got me. These visits with Cobber and Cross helped more than any other medicine that I could possibly have received. They spent long hours at my bedside every day. With Cobber and Cross nearby, my despair ebbed away.

The next day they moved Henry and me into the ward and put us next to the nurse's desk where we got lots of attention. I finally got solid food of sorts, something akin to baby food. It turned out far less rewarding than I had figured. I had little or no appetite. With the return of solid food in my diet came the need of bedpans. Boy, now this really brought on big problems.

Picture this: three reluctant Corpsmen assisting in the arcane chore of defecating. (Defecate, now I had to go my dictionary with the vulgar four letter "S" word to come up with this one.) I have used the proper name for what I needed to do, but the three of them resorted to the taboo four-letter term meaning the same thing. What an odious ordeal for all involved in the messy affair.

During one of Cobber and Cross' daily visits the head nurse came to us with a scamper in her steps and a smile on her pretty face. "Fellows, I've got some news for you."

Cobber chortled. "That smile on your face says it's got to be good news for a change."

"Yes, it's great news for a change. Doctor Sorenson is coming to see you in a little while. He's one of the best plastic surgeons in the world. These two guys are lucky."

I asked, "What's a plastic surgeon?"

"Quiet simply, he builds new body parts. Don't give this man any of your cheap sass 'cause he can mash all you guys at one time. He was an All American tackle at the University of Minnesota."

That revelation got our attention and we anxiously awaited the arrival of this All American.

After lunch that day, several guys from about the ward hung around Henry and me. The combination of Cross and Dortsch always drew a crowd wherever they settled down. The two of 'em brought some fun to life. Into this gathering came the lady from Austin with a massive man in tow.

"All right you Marines, break it up. This isn't a slop-shoot. No beer served here. Move out!"

Everyone immediately obeyed her command by moving back only enough to widen the circle about our beds. Into this void, Miss Austin ushered in the big doctor and his small entourage of assistants. He acknowledged the circling rubbernecks with a semblance of a salute. These guys all wore bandages and since they occupied this ward to receive the healing treatment of this miracle worker all had a keen interested in Doctor Sorenson. He went first to Henry who sat on the edge of his bed waiting.

"Son, we have a great deal of work to do on you. It's going to take a long time and it's going to be tough, but I believe you're tough and can take it. I want to talk to you in the nurse's office when I finish here." He then stepped over to me. "How do you feel, son?"

"I feel pretty goo...."

Cross interrupted, "Sir, he's kidding you. He feels lousy."

He pointed a finger at Cross's stump, saying, "I'll take your word for that. I can see you're an authority on pain. Thanks, son."

He thumbed through my charts quickly and said, "Nurse, have someone cut the top half of this cast off, but let him remain in the bottom half. I'll see him the first thing in the morning."

Miss Austin scribbled on her note pad.

The doctor shook my hand, saying, "Hang tough, Harvey, we're going to fix you up." He moved out to inspect the other injured. The circle dissolved to hustle back to their beds to await their visit with Doctor Sorenson. From that moment on, things began to happen, thanks to the head nurse, Cross, and Cobber. These two, though not assigned to my ward, spent most of the daylight hours there. With their charm and humor, both ward personnel and patients welcomed their visits.

Later that same day, a bone specialist came in to visit Henry. I heard him say to Henry, "Son, I'll be working with Doctor Sorenson in an effort to rebuild your face. We'll have to move bone up from your hips and graft it so that we'll have a foundation to work from. It's going to take a long, long time and many operations to rebuild your face, but we'll get it done."

He then turned to a nurse who accompanied him. She handed him a booklet. He opened it and pointed to a page that had six facial features sketched on it, all handsome. Henry's eyes indicated that he smiled on the inside.

He looked them over and scribbled a note that read, "Any one of these would be a great improvement over what I had before." Henry showed that he had a sense of humor. He needed it for the many months and years of suffering and loneliness that lay ahead.

The doctor said, "I'll leave that book with you. You decide. There's no hurry."

When Cobber looked the sketches over, he quickly said, "Man, Id trade this mug of mine for any of these right now. Which one you like, Henry?" He threw up his hands in bewilderment.

"Which one you like, Harv?"

I studied them for a moment and allowed, "I think I'd pick number three."

Cross picked a different one, adding to the good-natured befuddlement of all. "We'll just put this to a vote of the whole ward. Come on, Henry, bring that book with you," the Cob commanded. All three went the length of the long ward with Cobber doing the asking and Henry recording the votes with a pencil. The whole ward got involved, including the nurses.

The following morning Cobber came to my bedside and reported that Cross had a meeting with his doctor back at his ward. I, meanwhile, waited for someone to come and take me to the room to have the top of my cast removed. I should have felt happy at this prospect. I had just endured a long, sleepless night filled with agonizing concern.

Cobber sensed the mood that prevailed. "Okay, Harv, what's wrong? You having lots of pain this morning?"

"No, Cob, it's not the pain."

"Don't tell me you're feeling sorry for yourself."

"Yes, I guess you might say that I am. I can handle pain, but that's not what's bothering me now."

"You got no worries. The old Cob is here to take care of you."

"I know, Cobber, but they told me at Guam that I had lost one of my balls and that the other one was badly damaged with little hope that it would mend."

"No s_ _ _, Harv? You poor bastard. Are you sure?"

I told him about the little nurse who cried, the doctor who explained it all to me, the psychiatrist who told me that I could lead a normal life, and the chaplain who wanted to pray for me.

"Hell, Cob, no one has given me any hope. I just want to die."

"Like hell you do. You're going to get through this, no matter what they say."

"I don't want to live to be a queer."

"Hell, losing your gonads don't make you queer. That's something else. I'm going to talk to your nurse."

In a little while, he returned with the head nurse in tow. While shaking a finger at me, she lit in to me, saying, "Now, what's this about wanting to die? Here we are, doing all we can to get you well and you want to call it quits. We're going to take this cast off you this morning. The doctor will be able to see your condition down there. As far as we know, that testicle might be doing just fine. When you get the top half of that cast off, we'll be able to clean you up. The doctor says you can have some semi-solid food today also."

I took the food and prospects of a bath of sorts as good news, but the worried mind hung on.

With the top of my cast off, what I saw depressed me even more. Sores covered my body where the case had been. My swollen left leg looked a sorry sight and grotesquely slopped over the sides of the cast. The right leg looked like a bone with dried skin stretched around it. And the putrid and noxious smell assaulted everyone's nostrils.

After they cleaned me as best they could, Dr. Sorenson came in and ordered Corpsmen to turn me on my stomach so that he could take a look at my backside. I figured he wasn't too happy with what he saw.

He gave the nurse some instructions and I heard him say, "We can't do a thing with this man until the clots dissolve in that leg."

They took me back to the ward where I lay for many days just waiting and hoping for the clots to go away. I received exemplary care during this trying period. Cobber and Cross stood at my bedside a great deal of the time. Without them, I think I might have gone completely off my rocker.

One day the lady from Austin came to me with news of a civilian specialist flying in from New Orleans. A Doctor Faust intended to treat me and some other guys with the same problem. The nurse informed me that this doctor had developed a revolutionary procedure to dissolve life-threatening clots in the bloodstream. When introduced to him, I found him a genial man, about sixty years of age, I'd say. I heard that he had tried to enter the military service at the onset of the war, but they found him a tad too old to serve. He happily offered his service when the Navy asked him to come to Hawaii. Had he not come nearly half-way around the world to treat us, I doubt that some of us would have survived.

Doctor Faust promptly set to work. His treatments hurt like the devil, but they worked, and the swelling began to abate. When my

138

blood circulation improved to the point where they could safely operate, Doctor Sorenson took over. He performed numerous skin grafts on my buttocks. During this period, other surgeons did work on other parts of my body. Doctor Faust stayed about six weeks, doing his thing on my leg from time to time. When he left, he informed me that he had requested they send me to the New Orleans Naval Hospital so that he could look after me further. That idea made me happy.

Cobber and Cross came to my bedside one morning to inform me that they had received orders for transfer to stateside hospitals. They had to leave the following day. I took this news with mixed emotions. I had figured that we'd all go back together. Their departure left me with a deep sense of loss, but at the same time it made me happy to see them move closer to home.

At that time, Cobber and I figured on eventually returning to active duty. Cross, with his loss of a leg, knew that he headed for a discharge.

Just as he left, Cobber said, "Fred, let's keep in close touch so that we can serve together when we return to duty." I assured him that I certainly intended to make every effort to do so. For both of us it was a wistful goodbye.

After six months and many trips to the operating room, they told me I, too, had gotten orders to ship stateside. I wrote Cobber at the Naval hospital located near San Leandro, California of my pending departure. I couldn't give him the exact date or even the place where I'd end up. I left Hawaii before I received a reply from him.

Still married to a stretcher, they put me aboard a Constellation aircraft for the flight to the states. Several others loaded up, still abed in stretchers, but many of the passengers boarded under their own power. Most of this group wore an assortment of casts and bandages. Happiness and glee abounded as we prepared for going home. Alas, this festive mood soon turned to concern. Several hundred miles out, just before we got to the point-of-no-return, the craft developed severe trouble on two of its engines. Closer to Hawaii and bucking a strong headwind, the crew felt it prudent to turn back. Our flight nurse (I wish I could remember her name) reassured us and calmly prepared us for evacuation in the event that we had to ditch at sea. Talk about ironic, to survive Iwo and drown at sea. Fortunately, the pilot and crew skillfully nursed the four-engine Constellation back to Honolulu where they welcomed us as newcomers to the island. Young ladies of Polynesian heritage greeted us warmly and decorated each with leis woven from the beautiful Hawaiian flowers. I saw for the first time a live performance of the seductive hula dance. Alas, the festive occasion proved short lived as a new crew and plane awaited us.

About mid-morning, the Constellation alighted at the Naval air station near Alameda, California. Those of us on stretchers ended up on the tarmac to await placement in ambulances for a ride to the Oak Knoll Naval Hospital. The bright sunlight compelled me to close my eyes. With closed eyes, I felt someone kick my stretcher, and then followed the question, "Where in the hell you been, you little fart?"

With my eyes still closed, I quipped, "You've got to be my worst nightmare. Dortsch, what are you doing here?" Ya know, this guy had met every hospital plane that came in from Hawaii. He had gone to the Naval hospital at San Leandro, California for further treatment on the nerve damage dispensed to his arms by Jap bayonets at Iwo. As a result, he had hitchhiked some sixty miles to the Alameda Naval Air Station to meet those planes. What a guy!

I stayed at the Oak Knoll Naval Hospital for only six days, but the Cob continued to thumb his way there to spend each day with me. On the day that I left for New Orleans, he told me he was transferring to receive more treatment on the East Coast. Again, we had a sad parting of ways.

World War II ended on September 2, 1945. The war's hostilities ceased on that date, but the battles continued in military hospitals for months. Many remained for years.

The further adventures of the Cob and me take up again in the chapter "Down on the Farm." So don't put this manuscript down 'til you read it! Ya hear?

Chapter 9

Down on the Farm

Across the Mississippi River, from New Orleans proper, lay an area called Algiers. Within this suburban community lies a US Naval base. I do not know the mission of this base at the present time, but during WW II, it served as a Naval ammunition depot. Now, an ammo dump needs a great deal of real estate, due to the volatile and bulky nature of munitions. To accommodate its ongoing needs, during that world conflict, the Navy leased a farm adjacent to the base. This package rimmed a portion of the mighty Mississippi. With docks and piers, the tract proved an ideal site for barges to load and unload the munitions of warfare.

Those of us stationed there found that, under the terms of the lease agreement, the Navy agreed to leave the farm intact when and where possible. The plan called for the family home and livestock along with barns, pens, fields, etc. to remain operational. In so doing, the family could move back at war's end without the interruption of farm activities. Obviously, future events superseded the lease agreement as the base remains active to this day.

To stow this fickle, erratic stockpile of destruction, the navy constructed concrete bunkers partially below ground for safety's sake. They, then covered these bunkers with soil. In a short time, the natural flora of the area took root and grew in profusion. Literally hundreds of these mounds, arrayed about thirty yards apart and aligned in neat rows covered the area. The resident dairy cattle grazed peacefully on and around these mounds. This gave the vicinity an aura of pastoral serenity and beauty.

A Marine Corps sergeant put in charge of this farm facility had to care for all this acreage, its structures and the animals left on the farm. The animal population included milk cows, chickens, pigs and several horses. He also had tractors, plows and other units of farm equipment essential to this type of business under his care. The sergeant, an old farm boy, knew his way around this agricultural enterprise. He could do it all.

To help him operate this venture, the Naval hospital in New Orleans permitted a few convalescing patients, on a voluntary basis, to go over to live on the farm and help run the place. The assigned chores fell within the limits of a man's physical abilities. Six ambulant patients at a time went over to this farm and stayed until sound enough for discharge from service or return to active duty.

For eight months, I had stayed in Naval hospitals all the way from Guam to New Orleans. I remember 'em all like a toothache. Now, don't get me wrong. I appreciate the care and treatment that the Naval hospital system afforded me after my injuries on Iwo. But, by now I had tired of the hospital existence. When I could get around on crutches, I began to bug the doctors to let me go to the farm. "Out of the question," they always told me. This did not deter me. I kept after them. After a week of persistent begging and whining, my primary doctor honored my request, but based on these conditions: (1) if I could get by on a cane, and (2) if the farm had chores I could do compatible with my impairments. I leaped at the chance like a hungry wolf. "Mastering the use of a cane will take about five minutes," I declared, raring to go.

"Whoa!" the doc said. "It's going to take a little time to get this done."

A couple of days later the doctor summoned me to his office. He asked, "Harv, what do you know about chickens?"

I answered, "Well, I know that they lay eggs and they are

pretty good eating when fried or their eggs are scrambled."

"You might be over-qualified but, if you'll agree to take charge of the chickens, I'll farm you out," he said.

"Ya know, doc, I'd take care of those snakes and chickens along with all the 'gators over in that swamp just to get out of this ward living for a while."

He came back with, "You might be doing just that. I understand there are lots of those varmints over in that area. As for transportation, a Jeep will pick you up 0800 tomorrow. Just one other thing. You'll catch the base/hospital shuttle every Friday morning and see me, here, in my office for a weekly checkup. Now, do you still want to go?" he asked.

I replied, "Sure do, Doctor, and Sir. I want to express my appreciation and gratitude for all that you and your staff have done for me. I realize that I'm here today because of you and others like you who have looked after me these many months."

I shifted my cane to my left hand, came to attention and gave this man a smart hand salute. He stood and returned the salute. With moistened eyes, I hobbled out of his office. I have a deep-seated respect for Naval doctors, nurses and Corpsmen. A great many Marines would not have survived the war had they not been there for us all the way from the foxholes of the Pacific to the hospitals stateside.

The next morning, bright and early, a Jeep driver assigned to the hospital motor pool ambled in and picked up my sea bag which I had eagerly packed hours before. He shouldered it and preceded me out of the ward. As I walked through the ward, I shook hands with those men still confined to their beds. I looked around for the duty nurses and Corpsmen. Unfortunately, I had to leave without saying goodbye and thanking them for caring for me. Then, at the Jeep, to my surprise a small group of nurses, Corpsmen and fellow patients waited to see me off. Again, the dilemma of good-byes befell me. These people, the center of my world for several months, had become family. With a heavy heart, I hugged each of them and then climbed into the waiting Jeep. Loneliness joined me. It felt like leaving home.

My driver, a big redheaded seaman from 'Bama, informed me that he and his Jeep belonged to me for the day. "Would you like to take a little tour of New Orleans before you check in at the base?" he asked. An assertive aye sent us on an unforgettable tour of that scenic city of my boyhood dreams. Red proved an excellent excursion guide.

After an extended tour of the city, we motored down Canal Street, took the ferry across the Mississippi, continued to the Naval base, and checked in at the office of the Marine detachment. There they ordered me to report to Sergeant Wall at the base farm. I returned to the Jeep to motor the remaining mile or so to the farm. The farmhouse, my billeting quarters for the next few months, proved typical of the many farmhouses throughout the South during that period. The well kept, neat, homey and quite large house impressed me. In fact, as I remember, it embraced thirteen rooms. We found the house devoid of personnel.

Out back in a huge barn, we found a Marine in a squat position, working on a vintage John Deere tractor. I approached him saying, "I'm looking for a Sergeant Wall."

Looking up, he replied, "You've found him. What can I do for you?"

"I'm PFC Harvey, reporting for duty."

"Yes, I've been expecting you." He stood erect and offered me a hand that he quickly recalled because of the black, grimy axle grease covering it. Espying the cane and looking me over, he said, "Hell, man, you're in no condition to work on a farm. This is tough duty. You'll be right back in sick bay in two days."

I countered, "Sarge, I've worked hard all my life and I'll gain weight and strength, you'll see. I can toss grain to those chickens and gather their eggs as well as anybody."

"Okay," he replied, "but you take it easy for a while and don't overdo it. Go up to the house and take any room you like that has a

145

rolled pad on its cot. With that cane you better find one down stairs." As we left the barn he added, "A truck will be here to take us to the base chow hall in about one hour. If that redhead is not in a hurry, he's welcome to chow down with us." As we turned to continue once again, he yelled, "Hey, Harv, welcome aboard."

I liked this NCO.

Big Red grabbed my sea bag from the Jeep and into the house we went. We ambled down the hall until we found a vacant room. Having Red along really made me glad as he pitched in and helped me make up my cot and stow my gear in a beat-up footlocker. When finished, we found a head (bathroom) and washed up. With nothing to do for the next half-hour, we found a room equipped with a ping-pong table, card table, an assortment of books, and a radio. Within a few minutes, five Marines had joined us in the game room. They had come in from their chores to await mess call. After introductions, one of them asked, "Were you, by chance, assigned to the hogs?"

I replied, "No, I've been assigned to the chickens." The look on his face told me he'd hoped for a different response. The other four all snickered. He, in seeming disillusionment, said, "All new guys get the sty. How did you get the chickens?"

"Doctors orders," I answered, at the same time tapping my cane to the deck to bring it to his attention. He pouted. The others teased him.

One said, "Bob, those pigs love you. They'd be heartbroken if you left them, especially them there sows." This brought loud guffaws from the assemblage, including Bob himself.

"Ya want to trade?" he asked.

"Can't, doctor's orders," I rejoined.

He came back with, "Let's flip for it."

"Give it up, Bob, you're married to them sows for the duration," someone added.

I took it that the pigsty was not an enviable mission to have on this farm. Thankfully, the doctor's orders had delivered me from that nauseous job. When a cleaned-up Sergeant Wall came in, Bob went right to him with his "case." Bob, I came to find, when given a grievance, saved it like money. The sarge, after listening to Bob's narrative of mistreatment, amusingly said to everyone's glee, "Bob, when I make commandant of this man's Corps I'll take you out of the hog-wallow. 'Til then, you hang tough." Later, however, he informed Bob that he had simply followed orders to put this new guy on a light duty detail until he gained strength. I figured I'd made an enemy, but on the next liberty call, Bob invited me to join the group for a bash on Bourbon Street. However, he did amusingly needle me about swapping jobs.

Within a few days, I fell into the routine of farm life, which I relished with delight. Military discipline eased up, to a degree, on the farm. Reveille call came at 0500 each dawning, but if you wanted to forego breakfast, you could remain in the sack until police call. The clean up call went out a while after the Sarge and the chow hounds got back from breakfast. Most mornings only the Sarge and I answered mess call. After we policed up the area, Sarge assembled his troops in the front yard and assigned each to any special details that came up beyond their regular duties. We did not have to stand inspections or parades except on rare occasions. For me, duty couldn't have been better.

The next morning, at the end of that first duty call, Sergeant Wall called me aside and said, "Follow me. I'm going to introduce you to our fine feathered friends." As we walked, he continued, "We have about 400 layers and just enough roosters to keep them happy. When an old hen gets in a brooding mode, we segregate her into a special area and give her about twenty-four eggs to sit. At the hatching, the mother hen and her brood remain in that area until the chicks are mature enough to join the main body. Any questions?"

I asked about fryers and he told me that the farm did not try to furnish fryers to the galley. "However," he said, "we do relegate excess old hens and roosters to the boiling pot where they are

147

introduced to raw dough." Being an old Texas boy, I know about this union: chicken and dumplings! A concoction so tasteful folks celebrate it in story and song. To put this subject in proper prospective, I know of no other songs that celebrate the likes of quiche Lorraine, pot roast, or liver and onions. In Texas, chicken and dumplings has always held a special place.

He continued, "You will gather eggs each day and we will take them to the mess hall when we go in for supper." The facilities that the farmer had provided for egg and poultry production impressed me. The Sarge also told me that my duties included feeding, watering , cleaning the coop, and maintaining the hen population at about 400. This number about matched the capacity this facility could house and roost. The Sarge told me that the base mess officer, a hard-nosed demanding type, needed about 250 eggs or more a day to take care of the needs of the mess hall. With the small crew complement on base, the flock met the needs with some to spare each day. This made the budget-minded mess officer happy, according to Wall, as he did not have to go out on the open market to purchase eggs which resulted in big savings.

Life on the farm agreed with me as my weight shot up from 100 lbs. to one-ten in about two weeks. I enjoyed the guys that billeted with me, especially Sergeant Wall. He, in part, helped a great deal in my weight gain. He introduced me to raw oysters. A little fish joint sat just outside the gate and he and I went there two or three times a week and loaded up on these lubricious morsels of the deep. That he had the hots for the owner's daughter might have lured him to this rustic spot. As they mooned over each other, I downed, without effort, a couple of dozen oysters served on the half-shell at each visit. The Sarge and I became good friends.

As I did my thing down on the farm, my foxhole buddy Lee "Cobber" Dortsch went through the discharge process on the East Coast. Cobber found out from my mom that I had gone to a farm located on a Naval base in New Orleans. Hearing this, he thought of an adventure in the land of Cajun culture, never having visited this part of the world before. Cob didn't let much of life go by him without trying to take advantage of it.

When I went to Louisiana, he went to the East Coast. The day the Marine Corps discharged Cobber in North Carolina, he went into town and tried to buy a motorcycle. Unable to find one due to the war, he threw his sea bag over his shoulder and thumbed his way to New Orleans. After eleven rides, three days, and three nights on the road with only catnaps as he rode, he arrived in Cajun Country. He later related his story to me as it had played out.

His New Orleans odyssey went down thus: Noon of the fourth day found him sitting astride his sea bag on Canal Street, the teeming heart of New Orleans, dog-ass tired, sleepy and in a uniform raunchy from prolonged wear. Being an old salt, proud of his uniform, his immediate concern related to his appearance. He took a side street and soon found a cleaning establishment. At the service counter, he explained his plight to the man in charge. "No problem," he said, "Step into that room and hand out your uniform to me. Also, if you have a clean shirt in that bag hand that out too." Cobber complied. Within a few minutes, the good man returned the uniform, brushed and pressed to perfection.

When he opened his wallet to pay, the man flatly refused to accept payment saying, "I have a son in the Army and I'd hope that someone is looking after him in much the same way."

Cobber and I found this sort of treatment from most all the citizens of New Orleans. There will always be a warm spot in my heart for the people of New Orleans, Louisiana. Cobber thanked the man profoundly, shouldered his sea bag and returned to Canal Street.

His next order of business involved finding the Naval base. He asked and found the base lay a far piece from his current location. Taxi fares exceeded his funding, so he opted to use street trolleys when available. As he stood on a corner waiting for a trolley, he noted a Red Cross office across the street. A bright idea came to him when he noted a sign in the window that welcomed service men. He opened his bag and took out a manila envelope containing his official discharge papers. With bag in one hand and the envelope in the other, he strolled across the street.

Looking through the glass door, he saw a lone, matronly lady sitting at a desk. He collected himself, took a deep breath and stepped briskly inside. At this point, I shall tell the story as the Cob related it to me. It's a classic.

"I moved promptly to the desk and placed my bag on the deck. I held the envelope in a protective manner, but where she could not help but see it. She looked up with a start, as all this had taken place so abruptly. In a snap, she regained her composure. The look of surprise turned to a smile and she said, "May I help you, young man?"

"I replied, "I certainly hope you can. Ma'am, I'm on an assignment of important urgency." I then commenced to take papers out of the envelope. When I had them about half way out, I stopped and shoved them back inside. I then looked furtively over each shoulder. These moves really got her attention. In a near whisper I said, "Maybe it's best you don't learn the full contents of this document."

"Her eyes widened with excitement as she haltingly said, "I understand." She looked beyond Cobber at the door. Being a part-time volunteer, the poor dear, really warmed up to this bogus conspiracy. With my bluff in, I really turned up my performance frequency. I looked once again at the door and then leaned across her desk.

"Now, nearly in her face, I whispered, "Ma'am, I've got to get these orders to a Marine at the Naval base with utmost urgency and secrecy. I'm unfamiliar with the area and don't even know where the base is located. Can you help?" Her eyes glazed over and her breathing turned into short gasps. I'd really caught her up completely in the charade."

At this point, as an excited co-conspirator she took over in an enterprising fashion. She picked up the telephone, ran her finger over a list of numbers pasted to her desk and dialed. The base motor pool answered. She requested a vehicle to meet the next ferry at the Algiers side of the Mississippi. She acknowledged his compliance and added, "The driver will meet a young Marine at the off ramp and take him without delay to base headquarters." She then took auto keys out of her desk and, in a half-run, headed to the exit with Cobber in hot pursuit. At the door, she reversed an "open/closed" sign and held the door open for Cob. He stepped through and she locked the door behind them.

His story continued. At the curb, sat an olive drab sedan with a large Red Cross painted on each of its front doors. At her command, Cobber threw his sea bag in the back seat. At quick time, they hopped into the auto. The nice lady then moved into the traffic and drove at an unnerving pace down Canal Street. At the ferry dock, Cobber gave the nice lady a short speech of appreciation that included something to the effect that she had helped in the war effort. He totally disregarded the fact the war had ended several weeks before. He then gave her a warm hug and a kiss on the cheek that left her glowing. Shouldering his sea bag, he walked aboard the waiting craft. As the boat pulled away from the dock, he waved to his waiting benefactor. She waved back, lingered a while, returned to the auto and put it in gear and slowly returned to the traffic of Canal Street. Only the Cob could have pulled off a pretentious act like this and get completely away with it.

As the ferry slipped into its mooring, Cobber saw an auto of a battleship gray hue in the parking lot. He had surmised correctly, as the driver moved the vehicle toward him as he entered the parking area with his sea bag riding on his shoulder. The seaman stopped the car, got out and opened the back door through which Cobber tossed his bag.

As they pulled out of the parking lot, the driver opened a dialog with, "Man, I was expecting high ranking brass, not a single striper. Are you going to be stationed here?"

"No," Cobber answered, "just here on a mission that I can't talk about." With this, the seaman drove in silence as Cobber dozed until they reached the base.

At base headquarters, he alighted, retrieved his bag, thanked the young driver and then headed up to the building. On the porch he dropped his bag and entered the door, hoping that no one questioned his reasons for being there. To his relief, he saw no one in the hallway. He found a head (restroom to you landlubbers). As he washed up, a petty officer came in. Cobber asked him the directions to the base farm. The petty officer told him the farm lay about a mile down the road that ran in front of the headquarters building. To avoid any questions, Cob thanked the man and walked quickly out. He once again shouldered his sea bag and headed down the road.

He had walked only a short distance, when he heard the familiar sound of a Marine truck approaching. He turned and threw out a thumb and the vehicle braked and came to a stop alongside him. The truck reeked with a smell that nearly made him throw up. He'd stopped the slop truck making its daily run from the mess hall to the farm's pigsty. The guy riding shotgun hung his head out the window and asked, "Where ya headed, Mack?"

"To the farm."

"Hop aboard. That's where we're headed," the shotgun allowed. The stench emanated from the cargo aboard. Cobber looked up and saw several lidless barrels of swill on the truck bed. He decided right quick-like that neither he nor his sea bag were going to share that space with the swarm of flies that had already staked a claim.

He opened the door of the cab and tossed the sea bag up to shotgun, at the same time declaring, "Hold my bag. I'll ride the running board."

The driver slipped the truck into gear and off they went. The jostling vehicle and the liquidity of the swill combined to produce a fine mist. To escape this malady, Cobber simply hopped upon the hood and seated himself on the cab.

Of course, I had heard the blaring horn, whooping, and yelling that preceded the truck from a quarter mile down the road. In the coop at the time, gathering eggs, I asked the chickens, "What the hell is going on?" I stepped outside to see.

I saw some idiot jumping up and down on the hood of a truck shouting as it turned in the drive. Then, I heard, "Harvey, you bastard, where in the hell are you?"

In shock and amazement I recognized the idiot as my beloved Marine buddy Cobber Dortsch. I stood agape with awe for seconds until it soaked in what the moment held for me. The idiot jumped off that truck and came running. I dropped my cane and egg basket and waddled over to meet him. We embraced, stepped back and looked at each other. He had tears in his eyes, too. This stands as one of the greatest and most memorable moments of my life.

All the brouhaha and clamor that went with this splendid event including backslapping, laughing, and loud bantering brought about an assemblage of all the other farm hands. After introductions all around, I singled out Sergeant Wall and ushered him to the side. "Sarge," I asked, "can we put my buddy up for a while?"

He answered, "No problem In fact, he can stay as long as he likes or until he is found out."

"Hey, Sarge, I don't want to get you into any kind of trouble."

"Hell, man," he rejoined. "Ain't you heard, once a Marine, always a Marine. We just called him back on active duty."

"Thanks, Sarge."

The three of us got together to set up the spurious game plan. Wall laid it out for us. "Cobber, here is an old ID card of a guy who was discharged about a month ago. While you are here, you are Pvt. William Mann. You will work with Harv in the chicken pens. Just keep your nose clean and keep a low profile around here. Okay?"

With a laugh, Cobber came back with, "You mean this sorry-ass Texan is going to out-rank me and, by the way, when is payday?"

I pulled rank. "Yo, private, grab that bucket of chicken feed and follow me. Payday, in this man's outfit, is every day. You get to slosh down all the raw eggs you like. Shape up or ship out."

"It's great to see you, ya little bastard." Our friendship, how unique and priceless it was for me. This arrival meant a lot for my future.

The tyranny of fate had left me something less than virile since receiving wounds at Iwo Jima. The nature of my injuries had separated me from one of my testicles. Doctors held little hope its partner could ever function as a reproductive organ. Damn! I felt condemned to lead a sexless, celibate life. My morale and spirits marinated in despondency with great regularity. I had succumbed to the pressures of despair. The very idea of living a life of loneliness abhorred me.

I saw my only option to this inevitable fate life had dealt me as self-destruction. I approached this prospect with cool logic and lucidity. Cobber, endowed with a perceptive mind, had sensed this mortal possibility while in the hospital at Pearl Harbor. His concern for my mental state had brought him to New Orleans, I later learned. This friend had come to stand by my side during this most trying and difficult time.

I had relegated these boundaries of fate I had drawn for myself to a back burner. The Cob had arrived! His very presence left me little or no time to wallow in self-pity. For many months, I had not found much to laugh about nor enjoy in life itself, for that matter. Now, his incessant banter garnished with an innate joviality kept me in a state of glee. Happiness and joy gave chase to the dejection and blues that had pervaded my mind.

Within days, we had settled into a routine of daily chores down at the chicken coops. Caring for the chicken took not real effort. We finished our tasks in short order each day, and found time to throw in and help the other guys with their assignments.

They were a great bunch of fellows to farm with.

The hard work and long hours provided just what most of us needed, as our bodies had atrophied from wounds and the subsequent long confinement in hospitals. At the time of my discharge from the hospital, I weighed in at one hundred and five pounds. Cobber, just a little more. To augment the mess hall bill of fare, we took to gulping six to eight raw eggs a day. An arduous, gagging way of ingesting eggs, but seemingly, it helped, as we did increase our body mass somewhat. And, of course, I'd had those oysters.

We took pride in our egg production and continually sought to increase their numbers. As a kid, I had always heard of the term culling in relation to chickens and improved egg yield. So out of our desire to improve the numbers and not knowing how to go about culling, we called a veterinary doctor. Over the phone, he explained that culling meant the craft of ridding your flock of the older non-laying hens and replacing them with young, vigorous hens. He then proceeded to tell us just how to accomplish this. This involved placing two fingers in a prescribed area. Of course, as novices in the art of culling, we got it all wrong. Out of this misunderstanding, we lopped off the heads of a number of the egg-laying population. Egg production took a huge drop in numbers. Of course, this drop came to the attention of the base mess officer. According to Sergeant Wall, on hearing of this misadventure, the mess officer went into an all-out rage. I could tell he was one highly upset Marine. He ordered Wall to bring that dumb-shit in.

As I entered the captain's office, my keen sense of perception told me that behind that desk sat an unhappy camper. My notion soon proved correct. I came to a ramrod-like attention and saluted. I started the usual discourse, "PFC Harvey re...." whereupon he clobbered his desk with both fists.

He snapped, "How in the world did you manage to cut egg production by 75%?" From this, he went into a tirade of ranting and raving, centering on the problems I had created for the mess hall staff. He pointed out several times that with wartime rationing still on, a commodity such as eggs proved hard to get. After a while, he began to lose steam. With a semblance of calm, he implored me to tell him what had happened.

I laid it out for him, leaving out nothing except for the part played by Cobber. As I explained the why and what-for of the events that led to the egg and chicken debacle, I could see his irate fury returning. He suddenly jumped from his chair and in my face, shouting maledictions and dire threats. His threats included a hanging from a yardarm, permanent mess duty, court-martial and sending me back to the sickbay. Man! He scared me so bad I nearly peed in my pants. When he finally ran out of castigations and punishments that he wanted to put me through, he returned to his chair, shaking his head, saying only, "Hell, Marine I don't know what to do with you." If not for my combat veteran status, I think he'd probably had me shot at dawn, no kidding.

At this time Wall, who had stood at-ease behind me, stepped to my side and at attention said, "Sir, with your permission, let me keep him and put him on the worst detail on the farm."

"What job do you have in mind?"

"The hog pens, Sir."

"Damn," I thought. "I'd rather swing from the yardarm."

The captain leered, "Fine idea, sergeant. Work his butt off. Dismissed."

We saluted smartly and got out of there on the double.

Once in the Jeep, I queried, "Really, Sarge, am I going down to the wallows?"

"You bet. I don't intend to go before that man again. Sorry."

"Thanks, Sarge, for getting me off."

My stowaway buddy Dortsch, had missed this disciplining session by the virtue and fact of his non-Marine status. Wall had advised him to get lost while I met my fate on the carpet. He did. We motored around in the Jeep, until we found him down on the muddy bank of the Mississippi, staring forlornly at the far shore.

He looked surprised to see me as he presumed that I'd end up with brig time. When I told him that we had received a sentence to the pigsty, he backed off, saying, "I think I just heard my mom calling me. I'm out of here. Hell, man, why didn't you just take brig time? Really, I'm out of here, as there's nothing worse than a stinking pig sty."

"Like hell you're outta here," I countered. "You're going to serve hard time down yonder in those wallows with me. What ever happened to esprit de corps?"

"What t'a hell, Buddy, I'm with you, but I ain't gonna like it."

Of course, this turn of events made Ol' Bob, the guy in charge of the sty, one happy Marine. Why, he actually jumped with joy. The Cob wanted to fight him.

The work in the sty not only proved dirty, but came with an insufferable stench. And I really hated seeing that afore-mentioned slop truck arrive from the mess hall each afternoon. Dumping those barrels of swill from the truck bed into the feeding troughs brought on real problems. The slimy residue on the deck of the truck bed made it nearly impossible to manhandle the barrels. Slipping and sliding in this muck, combined with the abominable, reeking odor, gave me call to throw up on a regular basis. It didn't seem likely we'd ever get use to it. And the flies! Man, I'm here to tell you, when they settled, they covered the deck like rug. When disturbed, they abounded in such numbers that it looked as if a black cloud hovered over the sty. But after a time, we began to cope with the smell, flies, slime and the hogs themselves. Maybe not used to it, but we coped.

At the end of each day, we hosed each other down, outside with our work clothes on. Water and soap did get some of the offal and stench out of the duds. We then left them hanging on tree limbs to dry, ready for use the next day. After rinsing off, we strolled into the house with towels about our hips. Of course, the other guys always met our entry with jeers and jibes. We refused to let this daily harassment get to us.

In time, we began to take pride in our work. We repaired the fences and drained feeding areas so we could clean around the troughs more efficiently. We fashioned the sheds to give relief to the animals during the heat of the day and sprayed DDT to eradicate at least some of the flies. Once we completed the afore-mentioned repairs, we began to have a little spare time on our hands. By count, we tended to one hundred and twenty of those eating, grunting, lard-producing systems.

One day as we lulled in the shade of an oak tree watching our burdens scouring for acorns, Cobber, to my dismay, said, "Harv, we got enough space and feed here. Why don't we go for increasing the numbers?"

Remembering the butt chewing that I had laid on me over the chickens, I snapped, "Not no, but hell, no. Don't even think about it."

He persisted and then prevailed.

"What the hell! Let's do it," I said. "But first we get Sarge's consent." We did.

We took count. We had a large number of sows, a few piglets and an old boar that was about as big as a damn polo pony. Our experience in the breeding of swine stood about equal to our knowledge in the handling of chickens. Cobber wondered why we didn't have more little pigs around, what with the over-abundance of sows and a boar that looked like he could service females in unlimited numbers.

We watched this big old boar closely for a couple of days. Out of something less than scientific observation, we came to the conclusion that while the sows had a need and Ol' Big 'Un seemed hot and ready, the problem lay in the boar's size. He just weighed too dang much for the smaller sows to support during the act of copulation. We agreed we'd solve this dilemma on the morrow. Heck! We had no interest in Ol' Big 'Un's recreational sex! We needed to support the propagation of the species.

The next morning, Sergeant Wall informed the troops of the

admiral's inspection of the base, which included the farm. The Sarge continued, "Harv, you and Cobber get lost during this inspection, and the rest of you men, turn-to and get ready for the admiral's visit." We heard the usual inspection grumbling, but Cob and I ignored it. In a state of high elation at this reprieve, we lit a shuck to the hog wallows. What a perfect hideout! No way a ranking officer saw the need to venture down to this zone of pestilence.

We donned our work clothes and set about the task of propagating the species. Here again, we had no idea what to do. But, since we didn't plan to eradicate any of these animals, we could see no harm in what we planned to try. The grunts of contentment in the sty quickly turned into a bedlam of panic-stricken, squealing, shrieking, running porkers. All those animals joined into this madhouse of pandemonium except, of course, the big old, endowed one. He just stood watching and grunting.

We cornered one likely female and dragged her by her hind legs to the boar. Each of us grabbed an ear, slid a 2x4 under her belly and lifted. This took away her fore legs. The old boar, seemingly bored by it all, merely stood there. Just as we started to lose it, the big one got the idea. All of a sudden, he reared up and came down on that board-propped sow with all his weight, knocking us down. Bad idea. We got up muddied, but laughing.

Then, we heard chuckles from beyond the fence joining our glee. To our dismay and consternation, there they stood, the top brass and his staff. My heart sank. Talk about big, big trouble. Cobber muttered, "This will get us the firing squad."

The admiral beckoned, "You people get over here on the double." We complied at a dead run through the mud and glop. At the fence, we came to ramrod-like attention. In unison we threw smart salutes, which he returned. Expecting the worst, we heard the Old Salt, a red–faced, burly man of medium build, ask, "Just what in the hell are you two Gyrines trying to do?"

To cover Cobber, I quickly stammered, "We're trying to mate

one of the sows to that big boar, Sir."

"Have you ever done this before?"

"No, Sir."

"Was that sow in heat?"

I replied, "I don't think so, Sir. She had been lying in the cool mud."

This answer led to full-blown laughter from the entourage, which brought on a glowing embarrassment. With a great big grin, the admiral astounded us all by vaulting to a sitting position atop the flat board that crowned the fence. He then proceeded to take his shoes and socks off and tossed them to an aide. He then hopped off the fence, took off his khaki shirt, laid it on the top rail and then rolled up his trousers to his calves. By this time, everyone gaped in utter amazement. He declared, "I'm an old Iowa farm boy and I'm gonna to show you Marines a thing or two about hog farming. Let's go."

As we walked toward the pigs, he put his arm around my shoulder and quietly asked, "What's your name, son?"

"PFC Harvey, Sir."

"Well, Harvey, I didn't intend to embarrass you back there but, in the animal kingdom, in heat means that a female is ready, like being horny. Ya understand?"

In a blush, I answered, "Aye, Sir, I think I understand." He chuckled and gave me a good-natured slap on the back.

We slopped through the muck, three abreast, toward the far corner of the sty where most of the pigs had retreated. When we arrived at the spot where the old boar stood watching over the 2x4, the commodore drew to a stop. He looked at the beast, saying, "Man, oh man, that is one big mammoo. Why, there stands enough pork to feed the crew of a battleship for a week." He then pointed to the piece of wood. "Now, what were you two knuckle heads doing with that board?"

I deferred to Cobber. He said something to the effect that, "We thought the little pig was too small to hold the weight of that big hog long enough for him to do his thing. So we figured that we could help out by holding her up while he was doing it."

The admiral laughed heartily and explained, "Boys, these animals have been reproducing for thousands of years and without any help from a couple of Marines armed with a 2x4. You better stick to storming beaches. However, there are a few things we might do to help in this matter. Come on. I'll show you some things the Corps didn't teach you."

He sure did just that. First, he showed us how to spot a sow in heat. Just so happens, a rather simple task. Then, he gave us the task of bringing the ripe sows and Ol' Big 'Un over to the admiral. Now, this ol' boar had only to get a scent of a ready sow. He got on with it right quick-like. The Old Salt saw the problem and commanded me to run over to his waiting aide to get his white gloves. As he put on his gloves, he told us, "The problem is, these sows give out before this guy can hit the "target." So I'm going to help him."

Help him, he did. When the big boar climbed aboard that sow, his reproductive organ shot out two times like bolts of lighting, missing both times. On the third time, the Salt caught it. "Look here," he said, "his tool is shaped like a corkscrew and he has trouble hitting the mark because of it." With that, he preceded to place the corkscrew into the anxious orifice. Like a bank customer, he made a quick deposit and backed away.

Cobber made a classic observation, "I'll be damned."

By the time Ol' Big 'Un had recharged his batteries, we had another sow ready to go. He serviced two more and retired to a cooling bed of mud to savor whatever hogs relish. We picked out a sub for him about the time one of the admiral's aides came on to the playing field. He alerted his CO with, "Sir, I want to remind you that you have a luncheon scheduled at 13:30."

"Oh, yes, Lieutenant. I'll never be able to make it. You and the others attend and I will catch up with you at the O' Club later. And have someone bring me a fresh uniform. I'll be at the farmhouse." With that, the junior officer left.

We did a couple more sows, and then headed for the hosing-down area. The admiral laughed and talked as I hosed him down. What a great guy. Unfortunately, I can't remember his name. After the hosing, we all walked up to the house and took a real shower. After that we sat around talking, telling war stories, if you can believe that.

Sergeant Wall produced a bottle of Scotch. The old guy had some stories to tell which we really enjoyed. When his uniform arrived, he dressed and stayed on until we'd consumed all the booze. At leaving, he shook our hands and we gave him a crisp Marine salute.

His departing words went something like, "Thanks. I don't know when I've had this much fun with my clothes on." He went to his waiting Jeep and as the vehicle moved away from us, he turned and waved to us until he left our sight. What a memorable day. Cobber and I have told this story many times over the years.

The following week, the breeding project continued. We have no idea how many we bred, but we did a bunch for sure. We got a kick out of doing it.

Several weeks later, as we admired the sows heavy with the seeds of the inspection day orgy, Cobber opined, "Remember, the admiral said these sows would throw their litters in about 112 days. Ya know, in about four months we're going to have more little pigs than we can handle. We better make suggestions to someone to make plans to get rid of some of them real soon."

For the better part of the day, we pondered the thought.

Later, Cobber got a notion, "Hey, Harv, the Marine Corps' birthday comes up in about two weeks. Reckon they would let us sell some of these critters and throw a party, here on the farm?"

"Good idea, Cob, but I doubt the mess officer would go for it. I'm sure, without a doubt, he hasn't forgotten our chicken foul-up. There's no way he's going to listen to us but, maybe we can get the Sarge to talk to him."

That evening while trucking down to the chow hall, we put the thought to Wall. At first, he just laughed at the idea but the others, who had heard the proposition, backed us. "Let me think about it for a couple of days," he said without much enthusiasm. Later, on the truck ride back to the farm, Wall said, "Hey, you guys, I've given the party idea some thought and I'll see what will come of it, but don't get your hopes up. I expect the brass will pack me off to a section 8 ward when I put this to them, but I'll try."

The next day, true to his word, Sarge went before the CO and damned if he didn't sell him on the idea. He came blaring down to the sty in his Jeep with the horn broadcasting his coming. He slid to a stop and hopped out of the Jeep with whoops proclaiming glee. We dropped our shovels and ran to meet him. With a big grin, he showed us the document giving us the permission to sell some of the pigs and to plan a party.

The document further stated that the guest list included the entire Marine detachment, twenty-some-odd men and their spouses or girlfriends. These numbers took the party off the farm. We had only a couple of weeks 'til November 10, the Marine Corps' birthday. We needed to work quickly. We headed, sudden-like, to the farmhouse.

We lined up three slaughterhouses, called them, took the best offer and told them we'd bring in thirty-five pigs the following day. At mid-morning the next day, a junior officer showed up with two dump trucks. The old farm already had a loading ramp so we had a plan for getting them aboard. Unfortunately, the hogs wanted no part of it. It took us, the Cob and me, all of two hours to load the critters. Like the hogs, no one else wanted any part of this loading effort. They all retired to a near-by shade tree and watched in amusement. We thought, "To hell with this," but we kept at it.

The hogs refused all efforts to drive them aboard. So each of us grabbed an ear and hauled it up the ramp and into the trucks. The porkers fought, squealed and shrieked with every step. At the point of complete exhaustion, we got the last one aboard. Tired, sweaty, grimy, we smelled awful.

We figured we had done our part of the deal. We reckoned wrong, as another problem presented itself. The sideboards on the trucks proved too low, as evidenced when one young boar reared up and scrambled over the side.

The young officer solved the problem right quick-like saying, "You men are already dirty so you will have to ride in the truck bed and keep them from jumping out."

At that very moment, I came close to disobeying a direct order for the first time in my military career. Cobber hopped aboard one of the trucks. I had no recourse but to follow suit, mainly to cover for him.

Sarge, bless him, stepped over and said, "Ride in the cab, Harvey, and I'll get up there."

I refused his offer as I reeked. Yep, by this time, I smelled pretty ripe.

Here we went, a convoy led by a Jeep followed by two trucks filled to their brims with squealing, shrieking, stinking hogs and two dog-tired Marines. From the onset, we worked our butts off keeping them aboard. The convoy moved at a rapid pace, tossing me and my pigs about the truck bed like pinballs making my efforts a hell of a lot harder.

We arrived at the river and the folks at the ferry met us with disdain as we boarded to cross. At first they refused to let us board, due to the obvious. The ferry's captain said no. Our young lieutenant pulled rank and we boarded. Of course, his rank meant nothing aboard a civilian craft, but I think the captain's heart went soft when he looked at Cobber and me. The other passengers left their autos in nauseated disgust and made their way to the bow of the boat for the river crossing.

We reached the far shore just at high noon where our convoy of pestilence had to negotiate the stop-and-go traffic of Canal Street. (Reader, if you're weak of stomach, you might want to skip the next several lines. Consider yourselves warned.) In addition to the hot breath-stealing humidity, the hogs developed some serious motion sickness. They began to throw up literally buckets of slimy vomit, adding to their already incessant voiding from the other end. An intolerable stench surrounded the vehicles. If you have never smelled the metabolic waste of a hog, I'm here to tell you, you ain't never smelled nothing yet. Moving on the steel deck of that truck awash with that slimy muck posed a serious danger. Caught up in the moment, I crawled on all fours to the sideboards of that truck, hung my head over the side and threw up. Man, I'm here to tell you, this ol' Marine gave the streets of New Orleans everything I had. I was one sick hog wrangler.

The convoy moved slowly with the flow of stop-and-go traffic. Of course, our escorting, cloud-like army of flies increased in numbers by the moment. As we moved, hub-to-hub with throngs of other vehicles, their drivers and passengers grew incensed with rage. They let their passions out slapping the sides of their cars, shaking their fists, and shouting maledictions. I didn't give a hoot. I no longer cared how those gentle folks of New Orleans felt about me and my swine.

At long last, the scourge of Canal Street arrived at the slaughterhouse. The dump trucks with Cobber and me aboard weighed in and received directions to an unloading pen. By this time, you realize, the crews of those trucks had reached their limits with this whole squalid detail. Yes, and I'm here to tell you, they had had it. In the unloading pen, the drivers took their scorn and spite out on Cobber and me. Without stopping, but at a slow speed, in unison they simply pulled the dumping levers on their trucks. Down I came, slipping, sliding and tumbling the length of the slimy truck bed. You should have heard the bestial squealing and squalling from gross terror those porkers gave up. Surprised, battered and bruised, I hit the deck like a burlap bag full of wet manure.

A little stunned, but with maniacal rage, I came scrambling off'n that pile of future lard and pork chops. Hobbling with all the speed and power I could generate, I zeroed in on the dumb bastard, just as he alighted from the cab. My aim fell true, as I hit him with a headlong butt to that part of his anatomy where he lives. He folded like a greasy taco. I wound up straddling his chest, pounding his surprised face with both fists. Before I could finish my intended assault, Sergeant Wall pulled me off him. He then jerked the son of a bitch to his feet and slammed him into the side of the truck. The enraged NCO pressed him against the truck and drew back to throw a right hook. Before he could launch his wadded fist, he suddenly regained his poise. Still holding him erect and in the poor bastard's face, he gave him a tongue-lashing like I'd never heard before. Sarge finally let him go, but not before informing the poor bastard that he planned to put him on report. Punishment received, thirty days on mess duty. I had watched all this from all fours, for I had sunk to my knees from utter exhaustion. On the other side, Cobber had reacted much in the same way. He got in more damage to his driver before the lieutenant could intervene.

We had to sit on our respective trucks when we weighed out. Cobber moved into my truck once we'd weighed. We sat waiting in the truck bed, feeling and looking like two thoroughly beaten mongrels. The truck driver, through a fat lip, had the audacity to declare, "You guys are going to clean up these trucks when we get back."

In unison, we hollored "Get screwed!"

When finished with the paperwork, the lieutenant climbed into the Jeep saying, "You two guys, hop in. You're going back with us." As we pulled away, we turned and gave the trucks the infamous frigging finger.

The next day the four of us went into town. There the lieutenant reserved the main ballroom at the posh Jung Hotel, planned a prime rib dinner and lined up a seven-piece band. He made all the arrangements right there in the hotel office in about an hour. The Cob and I just went along for the ride but enjoyed it all.

We genuinely earned that holiday for riding herd on those hogs, according to the lieutenant.

The Sarge then trimmed the cake with icing. The son-of-a-gun drove the four of us across town and parked the Jeep in front of an office building. We waited. Promptly at 1200 hours, the lunch bell sounded and the structure belched forth a bevy of young ladies. Like a covey of startled quail, they bolted out of the doors and set out in three directions. At quick time pace, they moved out to do the things that young ladies do during their lunch break. Many of them gave brake to their step to lend observance to the four Marines in the Jeep, only then to hasten on. Mercy, I'd never seen so many pretty women on one range in all my born days. Sarge registered a marked interest in two of 'em. This motivated him to hop out and corner them. They each gave him a knowing, warm hug. He spoke to them briefly. They looked in our direction, smiled, and he beckoned us over.

After introductions, he paired us off. I liked my draw. Babe, a raven-haired beauty with dark flashing eyes and a beautiful face hailed from Biloxi, Mississippi. She was a real beauty. Cobber, too, seemed very pleased with his pairing.

"Hey, Sarge," Cobber said, "We can't wait a whole week to date these beautiful young ladies. Why don't we all go out and get acquainted tonight?" The Sarge seemed receptive, the girls jubilant but I had my apprehensions. Since I had not dated following my injuries, I had no idea how I might respond to the touch of a young lady. At the time, I had turned the corner and had given up all hope of having a normal sex life. I feared she might think me queer or something akin to this, should I show a lack of responsive excitement to her sexuality. And believe me, she came loaded with that commodity. Reluctance and doubt tormented me till the appointed time of our meeting.

That evening, we met the girls at their place. They shared rooms on the third floor of a large rooming house. This large hostel sat on a quiet, tree-lined street near the center of downtown New

Orleans. I feel I should tell you of this sizable dwelling and its placid neighborhood, seeing what happened there later in the evening.

We all piled into a waiting taxi and headed to a place on Rampart Street where Wall and his girlfriend waited. We met at an elegant, baroque restaurant in the French Quarter. we had a gala, fun evening. Naturally, Cobber, served as the life of the party. He charmed us all with his wit and infinite rapid-fire banter. Splendid food and excellent wine really fit the bill. We didn't have anything like this in Odessa. Of course, the free-flowing fruit of the vine enhanced my state of utter bliss.

By the midway point of the festive evening, the beauty and blithe spirit imbued in Babe had completely captivated me . She both pleased the eye and satisfied the mind, filling me with a deep joy. However, I suffered no illusions. I could never possess this jewel or any other for that matter. No young lady wanted to link up with a shell of a man. I feared I'd always have a void in my life.

At midnight, the lights dimmed, signaling the closing time for this memorable restaurant. The gala evening had ebbed to an ending much too soon. Reluctantly, we proceeded to the entrance where taxis waited at curbside. Sarge and his friend bade us goodnight and hopped in the first cab to go on their merry way. The rest of us all piled into the backseat of the remaining cab. Cobber promptly embraced Marie and they got on with some heavy necking and wooing. I reluctantly put an arm around Babe's neck. She snuggled up to me and tilted her head to be kissed. I complied. Damn, her full, ruby-red lips sent a thrill through me. Soon, we both warmed to the occasion. The ride to the apartment ended all too soon.

At the curb, we alighted. As I paid the cabby, Cobber sidled next to me and whispered, "Harv, I think Marie is hot for my body. Do you mind taking Babe for a walk?"

I okayed the request.

"Babe, the night is so beautiful, what say we go for a little walk before we go up?"

She accepted the proposal. At a slow, lingering pace, we headed into a balmy moonlit night, a time for romance. As we walked those empty streets, hand in hand, intermittently she turned to face me, silently soliciting a kiss. At every pause, I hungrily embraced her and sought her proffered lips. With each stop, we grew more impassioned. In time, we found a park bench where we sat and talked for a while. Thank goodness, Babe knew how to carry on a conversation.

A very shy person by nature, I happily let her carry the dialogue. She mostly told of her home and family back in Mississippi. I saw an aura of loveliness interwoven among the threads of her character. Her laughter, her smile, and her zest symbolized all the forces of happiness with life. Infatuation set in. I had never met anyone such as her. I liked this Southern belle. She had filled the void of despairing loneliness that had pervaded my life for the last year.

After a while, the November night grew a little bit too cool for her. I offered her my uniform blouse, which she readily accepted. We made our way back to her place.

As we quietly ascended the stairs to the third floor, she stopped once to whisper, "Will I see you before the Marine Ball?" That she wanted to see me again made me feel great.

I whispered back, "How about every night?"

At the door, we went into a lingering mode, neither one wanting the exciting, romantic evening to close. She took my hands and pulled me to her. I looked into her glistening, ebony eyes which transformed me into a near hypnotic state. I yanked free of her kneading hands and embraced her almost savagely. She hungrily responded in kind. There we stood, like one, from knees to lips, going at each other with elemental fire and desire.

Having very little command over myself, I pressed her fiercely against the wall. Her flitting tongue reached out. My lips parted to accept the sensuality of its touch.. We worked in tandem, our responses mutual. I felt a pulsating tremor engross her whole body. An awakening in my groin gave me a mental jolt. And then it happened, the mother of all orgasms.

A long-time absent reaction had unconsciously occurred and like a pulsating jackhammer, my desire let loose. Babe felt the shudder that rippled through me and momentarily pulled back. We looked at each other in gaping amazement. She clung to me as a shiver passed through her body, leaving her limp.

Pressing to me, she huskily whispered, "What happened?"

In a very clumsy way, I tried to explain to her what had happened and said, "I guess you just have that effect on me, Babe."

She coyly allowed, "I felt you tremble and I think the same thing happened to me."

Quite possibly, she'd never experienced this sensuous phenomenon before. I know I hadn't for a very long time. She seemed somewhat puzzled, but not distressed nor embarrassed by the event.

In all innocence she whispered, "Did we do wrong, Fred?"

"No, Babe, we didn't do wrong. This was just one of the natural, wonderful things that happen between two people. Don't be alarmed. Anyhow, what's so bad about feeling good? I'll see you tomorrow at seven or if possible, I'll pick you up at your office at five." I gave her a fervent, loving kiss and whispered, "I'll explain to you tomorrow why this is the happiest moment of my life. I love you!"

This girl had filled the void of loneliness with her sunshine and taken away the shadows of my nights.

With this, I banged heedlessly on the door and shouted, "Cobber!"

I didn't have long to wait. Shortly the door opened with a rush and there he stood with his shoes in the right hand with his blouse draped over his arm. His left hand held up his unbuckled pants. His face proclaimed a look of absolute dismay, bordering on panic. I led the way down the stairs with intoxicating glee. I strode down those steps, four at a time, and didn't stop until I reached a streetlight across the street from the apartment house. Cobber pulled up right behind me.

"What in the hell is going on, you blooming idiot?"

Lifting my pant leg, I shouted, "Fire in the hole. Cob, I done cranked off a load that would float a battleship!"

"What 'a you mean?'"

"I mean my manhood has returned. Look at this."

Then it sank in. When he realized the significance of the moment, he let out rebel yells that woke up those boarders not already awakened by our headlong scramble down the stairs. The girls opened their window and made a futile effort to hush our clangorous merriment. The Cob rewarded their efforts with more revelry and a jig. This brought giggles from the girls and shouted maledictions from several other windows.

I said, "Cobber, we better light a shuck and get outta here before the Shore Patrol shows up."

He dressed quickly and we headed down the street. At the end of the block, I turned and looked back. I could see Babe still silhouetted in the window. The silhouette hid its countenance, but I felt she wore a sensuous smile. A gentle melancholia tugged at my heart–strings. I had mixed emotions at parting with her this most memorable night. I waved. The silhouette waved back. The thoughts of her and that night still echo in my memories. Through her, the dark shadows of despair finally, truly began to disappear. She had rekindled a meaning to life. No wonder warm memories of her have always remained in the recesses of my heart.

November 10, the night of the Marine Corps' birthday and the gala party finally arrived. Cobber and I picked up our dates. What loveliness and sheer beauty. Their gowns highlighted the deliciousness of their physical merits. They appeared filled with deep joy, with no contradiction between the smiles on their faces and their innate beauty. The Cob and I stood in gaping amazement at the hands we had been dealt.

When I moved to this living, vivid person, to pin a corsage of red roses on her shoulder, I felt reverberations of the heart. When I touched her, I sensed a quiver passing through her body signaling mutual responses between us. I whispered in her ear, "This is not just a party that we are attending but rather it will be more like a celebration, a celebration of love. You are pleasing both to the eye and the mind. Gee! Babe, I've never known anyone quite as lovely and pretty as you."

She rewarded me with a most ebullient kiss. She then grasped my hand and led me back inside where she whipped out a lipstick and redefined her ruby-red lips. I noted little or no contrast between the red, red of her lips and the scarlet hues of the roses that I had pinned to her evening gown. Then we joined the others and headed down the stairs to enter a waiting cab. We headed to the Jung Hotel to join the Marines. Once again, I set off to one of the most enjoyable events of my life.

Everything happened just right, we had excellent food, a top-notch band and abundantly available booze. The lieutenant, acting as emcee, introduced the Cob and me as the prime movers in making the Corps' birthday party a reality. We proudly accepted a standing ovation. Why, even those damned truck drivers came over and apologized for behaving like turds. We accepted their apologies and shook hands. Heck, I couldn't be mad at anyone this night.

On the dance floor, Babe moved with unbelievable grace and vitality. She stood out as one of the prettiest women there. I swelled with pride that she came with me. And I certainly fell under the influence of her charm. At one point during a visit to the head, I dropped this on my buddy, "Cob, I think I have fallen in love with this girl."

"I'm not at all surprised. She's a charmer, but don't fall too deeply in love. We don't have much to offer a woman right now. Just don't make any promises at this time."

"I realize this, but she's a keeper."

Within a week of the ball, I received a medical discharge from the Marine Corps. I had no recourse. I faced one of the saddest days of my life. Adding to my dejection and sense of loss at leaving the Corps, came having to say goodbye to Babe. I had never done well saying farewells and this one proved especially hard for me.

Her tears brought tears to my eyes at departing time.

Baring my soul, I told her, "Babe, you've been very special to me and there will always be a warm spot in my heart for you. Some day I'll return to you, hopefully. I'll write. I want to thank you for sharing a part of your life with me."

With that I climbed into the Jeep where Wall and Cob waited. As we drove away, I looked back at a sad, forlorn Babe. I knew all too well just how she felt as I felt the same. My sense of loss felt worse than an open wound.

Wall drove to the far west side of New Orleans. At the side of the highway, Cobber and Wall drank a beer. I found myself still too heavyhearted to join them. Having to say adios to the good Sarge proved particularly hard for both Cob and me. We stepped out of the Jeep and, out of respect for this Marine, we gave him a smart salute. He touched his forehead and muttered, "Damn."

He drove away. We threw up our thumbs and caught a ride with the first car that came by. We headed west and home. We got into Orange, Texas just across the Texas-Louisiana border on the side of Highway 80 when I had a relapse. I fainted dead away. Cobber ran to a nearby house to call an ambulance. The little lady insisted that he bring me into the house when she saw him in uniform. Between them, they carried and dragged me into a bedroom. I felt so weak I couldn't have broken a smoke ring with a crowbar. She called her doctor and he arrived in just a short while. He examined me and quickly told me not to leave the bed for any reason. While there, I saw a continuous flow of the good citizens of Orange. They brought flowers, food and best wishes. Cobber handled the situation like normal, entertaining all who passed through the house. We stayed there five days. When the doctor released me, the folks of the town tried to buy us bus tickets. We preferred to thumb our way. Cobber and I have passed through Orange many times since 1945, and we always remember the people and the warm welcome we received there 60 years ago. The names of the wonderful lady and doctor have long since faded from memory, but their acts of kindness still echo in my thoughts and heart.

We had broken with a past that had shaped our uncertain futures. Those memories still hang around. I have never had regrets, only fond memories of the time. My WW II experiences changed me. I had left home a boy and somewhere along the way, I transcended that youthful era. I returned home a man. What did the future hold for me? Now, 60 years later, I have most of the answers. Hell! I'd do it again!

Chapter 10

The Silent War

This I call the silent war, as it never made headlines or radio, nor did GIs mention it in their letters to loved ones. You have no doubt come across veterans, fathers, uncles, brothers, or friends, who refuse to share memories of WWII. Their experiences were just too dreadful and vile to talk about. Some have nightmares and flashback recalls of this aspect of their war. I have never suffered the memories of battle, so I take it upon myself to talk for the silent ones. Y'all have a right to know.

Some of you might find this segment of my memoir a little bit too rank and explicit for your inclinations. However, I'll try to smooth out rougher spots to make it a bit easier for you. With this warning and subsequent compromise, I will get on with it.

This chapter takes into account certain psychological aspects of war. I will undress that part of combat which runs the complete gamut of human emotions. Fear, dismay, horror, panic, awe, and reverence all have a part. Since I plan to lay it all on you, I can't ignore the area dealing with the production and disposal of metabolic waste in the human body. Yep, this menial side of life went to war too. Talk about adversity!

This facet of the war deals with the toilet thing. You know, all the things you usually see and do in a toilet. Somewhere back in time, a fellow came up with a word that covered the main thing that happens in a toilet. I'll call it the four-letter S word. This great, all-inclusive word seems to cover it all. Dang, you can use this word or a derivation of it as a noun, adjective, verb and all that. Too bad society has made the word taboo. Now, I won't be so crass to use the S word, so I'm going to do like TV and radio folks did before cable. I'll simply use bleep to replace the S word throughout this text. However, if you want to go the profane route, feel free. Hell, even I've slipped occasionally in this text, but I'm taking care not to overdo it. To help some of you through this awkward phase, I will ease the shock by telling a humorous, but empirical yarn on myself.

My mom substituted mess for the S word and I grew up believing mess a universally accepted word with no taboos about it. When I went into the Corps, and they issued me an oval shaped pan-like metal object, in wonder I asked, "What's this thing?"

"That's your mess kit."

"Gee, the Marine Corps thinks of everything; a little portable bedpan."

"Nah, you dumb bleep (See, you've done well with bleep. Keep it up.), that's what you eat out of in the field and, by the way, the mess hall is where you eat on base."

Man! Less than a day in the Marines and I'd already learned lots, like calling the bathroom the head, a gun a rifle, and the floor a deck.

Before leaving boot camp, I found that bleeping could turn into an ordeal. One night the mess hall served some tainted ham. When you have a thousand or so Marines with the bleeps and only one head with 100 commodes, you have one hell of a problem. I found out right quick-like that an entrenching tool (a small spade) had other uses than to dig foxholes. I dug me a slit trench and squatted over it with a blanket thrown over my body 'til dawn. At that time, I went in the head to shower, as I did not have the luxury of toilet paper. Unfortunately, others shared the same boat, if you know what I mean.

When my unit received overseas orders, I went aboard a ship

for the first time, the Bloom Fontaine. With this my first experience on a ship, I spent my first hours exploring every inch of her while she sat still secured to the dock in the port of San Diego. The Bloom Fontaine, a Dutch ship, used to haul cattle from Australia to the Dutch East Indies. When the war broke out, the Bloom Fontaine and its crew high-tailed it for San Francisco. In Francisco, the Navy commandeered the ship and hurriedly converted into a troopship. Below decks, where they had corralled the cattle, some of the dung which defied scraping, they simply left and spray painted over it. Workers welded in bunks, six high, where beef on the hoof had once roamed. A Naval gun crew joined the crew to man a small 5-inch gun. That made up its armament.

To finish the conversion, they built a long wooden structure on the foredeck. In it, seawater streamed along the length of a long wooden trough and flushed back into the sea. On each side of the gutter, a long pipe ran above the running water. This set-up could accommodate two rows, cheek-to-cheek. (Maybe butt-to-butt draws a better word picture of the scene.) With any term, it still meant bodily functions done up close and personal. With a head of questionable utility, the Old Bloom made ready to go to war.

We learned that once converted the Army brass came aboard the Bloom, smelled, inspected and rejected it, quick-like. Unfortunately, the Marines came aboard, sniffed, looked and accepted it. The Marine Corps, though an integral part of the Navy, sat at the end of the food chain. We felt lucky to get hand-me-downs. In fact, all branches of the military treated the Corps like a stepchild. Only the Naval Seabees (CBs, construction battalions) stood as an exception. We Marines had high regards for the Seabees and they, in turn, respected us.

After being on board the docked ship for a couple of hours, I began to feel a bit queasy. Before long, I hung over the rail losing lunch in waters of the San Diego harbor.

A member of the Naval gun crew saw me and yelled, "Lookie here, we got a tough, seasick Marine and we ain't even gone to sea!"

I should have recognized it as a bad omen and deserted right then and there. I spent about 40 percent of my military time aboard ships, and, yes, I pitched my cookies every time I boarded a ship or landing craft.

We sailed during the night and I did manage to get some sleep, however, I went topside before reveille, as I wanted to see the Naval warships escorting the Bloom Fontaine. I looked in four directions. I saw nothing but empty seas and far-off horizons. Man, Uncle Sam had taken the stepchild thing way too far.

About four or five days out, the pump that flushed the latrines in the head broke down. When nature calls, you gotta answer. Most of the guys squatted near the rail at the stern. They dropped their load between their boots. Then they tossed a bucket tethered to a long rope overboard and pulled up seawater to flush the deck. I did not resort to this method of bleeping as puking kept my bowels empty. The Dutch sea captain ordered his crew to come up with something better. They did, to a degree.

They went to the front part of the vessel (the bow) and built wooden contraptions that hung over each side of the rails. To say the least, they built some ingenious facilities. They looked like great saddlebags hanging on a saddled horse. A guy had to climb over the rail, stand on a narrow platform, hold on to the rail with one hand and unbuckle and drop his pants with the other. Holding on for dear life, he then sat on a 2x4 timber and proceeded to feed the fish. (I hope by now you realize I can't resist puns.) This method of toileting had its ups and downs, as the bow bobbed like a hobbyhorse in the ever-moving waters. The fact each saddlebag accommodated six men at a time proved a big drawback. The smart way to do your thing meant getting on the windward (facing the wind) side, so that stuff didn't come back onto your legs, especially if you had loose bowels. (Are you girls still with me on this? It gets worse before it gets better.) During rough seas, things really got sporting. The bow went up and down like an Otis elevator. One moment your butt surfed water and then you came up like a rocket. When you came down, ya hit bottom with a jarring jolt. Only the brave or really urgent took the elevator in anxious seas.

Seems we always had a line awaiting their turn at the saddlebags. To pass the time, the line did a little betting as to which user could lay out the longest rope. Boys are like that. Did I mention we had females aboard hell's ship? Yep, 13 Naval nurses headed for Australia. They spent their time soaking up rays and fighting off horny junior officers. They did their tanning and leisure thing on the forecastle deck that loomed over the bow of the vessel. They had a clear view of the saddlebags and the guys riding the elevators. I doubt the girls spent much, if any, time watching the troops below. When I finally kept food down and could take a normal bleep, I couldn't let it all hang out because of the nurses. I tried to hold on 'til dark. After a day or two of this, I boldly took a place at the end of the line.

We floated on that tub for thirty-two long days. We spent most of our waking hours waiting in a bleep line or chow line. They only served two meals a day. Basically, you finished a meal and got back in line to wait for the next one. I had mess duty for a couple a' days, where I guarded the potato bin. The bin lay deep in the hold of the ship with air both hot and humid. I threw up a couple a' times, sick as a dog. I sat on one sack of potatoes and laid my head on another. As I lay there, a couple of guys slipped in and pinned my head and shoulders to the bag. Others grabbed a bag of potatoes and took off. Feeling as sick as I did, I didn't give a damn. Later, when relieved to go topside to get fresh air, someone offered me a raw potato. I refused, too sick to eat.

The bathing facilities on the infamous Bloom left much to be desired. Not many took a bath in the provided shower. As for myself, I used a rope and bucket. Soap didn't lather in the saltwater, so I didn't get very clean. I got pretty rank and gamey after a couple of weeks. We washed our clothes by tying them on a long rope and letting them drag astern for about 30 minutes. When we got near the equator, it began to rain nearly every day. I took to lying on deck in bathing trunks with a bar of soap in hand. One and all really welcomed those rains.

The ship of infamy continued to have the worst of luck. We sailed perilously, amid the vastness of the wide Pacific, when one day, all of a sudden, all engines choked to dead silence. I'm here to tell you, somewhere close to two thousand miles west of South America, the old power plant of the Bloom called it quits. You talk about some worried minds. We had over two thousand souls on board. The crew told us to wear our life jackets at all times. They also suggested that everyone keep a look out for submarines. Speculation and rumors ran wild amongst the passengers. We figured we might eventually drift into South America, say in about 40 days. We felt like sitting ducks. I spent my time looking toward the circling horizon for a rescuing flotilla. For two days and two nights, we bobbed on a restless sea. The Dutch crew finally nursed the old engines back to life and the tired old cattle ship continued on its westward journey. We did, however, have one joyful interlude on the trip which developed, by virtue of a crisis.

A report came that a Jap submarine might be operating in the area. The "Bloom" headed for the nearest landfall. At mid-afternoon, we pulled into a lagoon at the island of Tongatapu. As we dropped anchor, we looked to the shore to see a flotilla of canoes coming to greet us. The locals brought with them coconuts, papayas, and many other exotic foods that I had never seen or heard of. For an old boy from Odessa, I could not believe that such beauty and wonder existed. Smitten by wanderlust, I resolved to some day travel the world over, seeking the exotic. That night, the islanders came aboard to sing and dance. The beauty and culture of the Polynesian people astounded me. I delighted in their approach to life. I have never heard "You Are My Sunshine" sung so beautifully. I think of Tongatapu, its beauty, people and culture often. The next day our departure delayed for six hours while a detail went ashore to bring back 13 Marines who had jumped ship over night. Perhaps, had I thought about it, I'd have joined the exodus.

After 32 days aboard the Bloom Fontaine, we finally went ashore at Noumea, New Caledonia. New Caledonia is a tropical French island located east of Australia. Now, I thought we had big mosquitoes in Texas, but they didn't come close to matching those of the tropical South Pacific in both size and numbers. They told us malarial fever didn't exist on New Caledonia, but where we were headed, the fever proved rampant. While at New Caledonia, I met Atabrine, an anti-malarial drug. Malaria took a real toll on folks in most of the lands in this part of the world. They didn't have a cure for it, but Atabrine controlled its symptoms if taken every day. So they started priming us with Atabrine early. When we went through the breakfast line each morning, a Naval Corpsman stood there to toss a pill into your mouth. You had to swallow it or you didn't eat. As a world-class chowhound, I slipped through the serving line at least three times each morning. Of course, I had to take an Atabrine tablet each time. I never suffered an over-dose. However, one morning I walked by and saluted the battalion doctor. He got 'bout halfway through his return salute when he said, "Hold on there, trooper, I want to look at your eyes." He looked intently into each eye and asked, "Son, do you feel all right?"

"Yes, Sir, I feel fine."

He then scribbled a note and handed it to me. "I want you to report to sick call this morning. Show this to your sergeant."

I reported and got a complete physical exam. The doc took a blood sample and dismissed me to return to my platoon. The next day, I returned to the sickbay as ordered. "Your blood sample turned up negative," the doctor stated. "Are you sure you feel okay?"

"Yes, Sir, I feel fine." With this line of questioning, I started getting a little concerned.

"Do you wake up at night, sweating a lot?"

"No, Sir."

"Do you have backaches?"

"No, Sir."

"Son, the whites of your eyes are a browny, amber color and your skin is a dirty yellow and you should feel terrible."

He sat real quiet for a spell, in deep thought. "Son, you have all the symptoms of what we call yellow jaundice, but your blood does not show it."

"Yellow jaundice, what is that?"

"Jaundice is a disease of the liver. Maybe the Atabrine is making your eyes and skin show a yellow tint." He then went into another thinking mode. He asked, "How many Atabrine tablets are you taking a day?"

Dang, I figure here comes big time trouble, as we weren't supposed to go through the breakfast chow line but one time. I could not lie. "Sir, I have been taking two and sometimes three pills every day."

"What are you saying? Why are you taking so many?"

"Because each time I go through the line, they make me take a pill."

"Harvey, you mean to say you go through the line two times? Do you eat all the food dished out to you?"

"Yes, Sir. They wouldn't let me go through the line if I didn't take a pill."

He took out his pad and scribbled a note. "Harvey, you show this note to those people and it will get you through the line two times, but you will take a pill only the first time through. Don't you go through but two times, ya hear? I want to see you in two weeks."

"Thank you, Sir!" With a salute I got outta there one happy Marine. I checked my eyeballs. Sure' nuff, they looked back at me a putrid yellow. My skin had the same tint as the enemy. Sure happy I had round eyes.

When the Marines invaded an island, we called the day, D-day, and we called the hour, H-hour. On D-day we usually woke at 0100 and ate a better-than-average breakfast, sometimes we got steak and real eggs. We then went below to check and recheck our gear. We went over the side of our attack transport in the pitch dark. Some of those transports loomed about three stories above water level. Getting down the net into a pitching and bucking Higgins boat proved a tough, dangerous ordeal. When the boat reached capacity, we moved a short distance from the transport, there to go round and round until all other boats joined us. You know the steak and eggs I told you about? Turned out I had them just on loan. The fish of the deep ended up the final recipients of that good ol' meal.

Somewhat unfortunately, I have always answered nature's call pretty regular in the mornings. So, right about 0700 my bowels called upon me to do my thing, ya know, bleep. Unless you have tried to bleep off the back of a bucking Higgins boat, you have never had a real problem. You really need a couple of great buddies who will lend a hand. With every inch of the landing craft wet and slippery, each buddy has to hold an arm as you teeter on the very lip of the boat. You do what you have to do as quickly as possible. You save the paper work until you're safely on the lower deck of the boat. The poor ol' coxswain (naval boat driver) usually takes offense at Marines taking dumps off the aft deck of his craft. He stands right next to the act, in harms way, especially if a guy had the trots (diarrhea). Speaking of the trots, in the tropics I suffered this malady about 30% of the time. Now that's a real aggravation.

After two or three hours on a Higgins boat, you're wet, grumpy, cold, seasick, and ready to go ashore under any conditions. By the time H-hour rolls around, you'd attack hell itself. My first combat action took place in the Solomon Islands. These islands lie just a few degrees south of the Equator. We encountered heat and humidity so dense it seemed like trying to breathe under water. We had to use machetes to hack a path through the thick jungle flora, absolutely crammed with vines, bushes and trees. Due to the heat and humidity, a slasher lasted only five minutes before someone else had to take over. Of course, bugs and insects abounded. The ants could really lay some hurt on you. But, of all the parasites the jungles had to offer, I hated the blood-sucking leeches worst of all.

Then, we found this vine with sharp thorns configured like barbs on a fishhook. When one of these babies latched on to you, best stop real quick. If you pulled or jerked, those little barbs dug in deeper, bringing forth blood from a painful gash. Those guys who had shed their dungaree tops wisely put them back on. We took to calling them wait-a-minute vines. When one of them grabbed you, you automatically said wait-a-minute, as you didn't want the next guy to bump into you, causing further damage.

The Japs took pride in their presumed status as the best jungle fighters in the world. Hell! The Naval Seabees and Marines just tore up the jungle and they didn't have an arena to fight in. We admired those tough and fearless Seabees. One day, with their bulldozers, graders, and trucks, they got ahead of us. When they began to take sniper fire, we hopped aboard their equipment and rode shotgun. We had fun that day and rushed for lots of yardage.

Once we arrived on the Solomon Islands the toilet problem really manifested itself. For starters, we never had enough toilet paper around. If you did get lucky enough to come by a roll to keep in your backpack, the rain and humidity soon turned it into a big, useless spit-wad. If you had to bleep sans paper, you had limited choices, none of them good. Of course, we always had plant leaves about, but most proved too slick to really grab. Also, the tropics had lots of toxic plants that could lay some real grievances about the anal orifice. The wrappings off packages from home made great wipes. Newspaper clippings served also. I used love letters in dire emergencies.

Jeanette Bowden, my high school sweetheart, was a lass of

innate beauty and wit. She wrote to me avidly while I served overseas on my first tour of duty. When I joined the Marines, she went away to college.

When I returned on my first leave, we found that our love had begun to wane. I had found a home in the Marine Corps and her interests lay in other areas. However, we continued to write and remain friends.

The relationship finally ebbed into nothingness because some of the wounds I sustained left me temporarily impotent. It was a hopeless situation.

On one occasion, she proudly displayed a bundle of letters I had written to her. She had bound them with a golden ribbon. When she asked what had happened to her letters of love, I prudently deviated from the truth.

The toilet thing wasn't too big a problem during the daylight hours. I encountered real troubles during the night. We took the daylight hours to go on the offense. The Japs picked the dark hours of night to do their thing. We hoped to rest at night, but that didn't happen. Those folks got real offensive in the dark. In fact, you could say they got downright obnoxious. They didn't let us sleep very much. This situation threw my usual morning constitutional completely off kilter. Some nights, I had as many as two bowel movements. I could say the daily consumption of C- and K- rations caused the problem, but in reality, the Japs scared the bleep outta me.

At each day's end, we received orders to dig in for the night. Enough said. We whipped out those entrenching tools and got on with the digging. We wanted nice, deep holes of abode when the devils came calling. The buddy system came into play. At least two men worked the same hole for mutual protection. One stayed awake to watch for movement. We had strict orders not to leave our holes for any reason. This included bleeping. Already you're wondering, how? Well, it wasn't easy. I usually tried to take an empty ammunition box to bed with me. The first time I did this, I tossed the box outta the hole and it took two shots from a trigger happy PFC. See what I mean about staying in your hole? Since you couldn't always find an ammo box, you had to find other ways to keep your real estate neat and sanitary. I talked the problem over with a salty sergeant and he gave me some sage advice. "Harvey, when you get your foxhole deep enough for safety, just dig a little slit trench in the bottom. After you have finished bleeping, cover it up." Marines have, out of necessity, always coped with the worst situations quickly and smartly. This time, too. The word quickly spread and everyone went to this method of waste disposal. Rumor has it that a Marine brought this idea of waste disposal to the States and gave birth to present-day landfill technology. Just about every city in the US uses this method of garbage disposal. Don't know if it's true, but if so someone should build a monument to the guy.

In the jungles of the South Pacific, you also had limitless rains to contend with. As a result, you didn't dig very deep before you found subsurface water. You'd dig a nice foxhole and by morning, you'd find yourself sitting in a water well. More than just a few fellows woke up to find their landfills had failed and floaters drifted on the morning tide. When you heard a loud outburst of real bitching, you knew a floater had gotten cozy with an enraged Marine. When I heard of this phenomenon, I took to tamping my landfills securely. Luckily, I never had a floating visitor.

Whenever we went on a combat foray, we received an issue of a substance which we applied to our faces. This served to blend us into the foliage in which we worked. That's right, we had camouflage and everyone took camouflaging seriously. When on the march, we got a 10-minute rest break out of each hour. Each guy usually spent this recess period in a beneficial way. Some slept. Others smoked, ate a K-ration, played cards, wrote, or used the time to take a good ol' country bleep. When a guy had to do a job, he could not venture too far from the group, else he might get lost in the thick jungle vegetation. Because of this, a guy usually did his thing amid a dissenting audience. One day I made a keen observation, "Look, Sarge, at that big shiny butt on ol' Ruff. What a target he makes. I think that you should make it a requirement that everyone should camouflage his butt along with his face."

His reply, "Harvey, that's a great idea! I want you to write it up and present it to Major Fagan."

"No, Sarge, I think you ought to write it up."

"Harv, you got me down for dumber than I really am." Ya know, using my keen insight and wit, I never got around to writing such a request. I could just see Fagan kicking my skinny butt, with or without camouflage.

As a Marine, you learned the art of scrounging. Sometimes this scrounging turned into outright looting. At Vella Lavella, the Army moved in to take over the duty of guarding the airstrip. They did this so that we could prepare for another assault in the island-hopping campaign employed in the Solomon Islands. Before the main body of army troops moved in, much of their equipment and supplies arrived.

At that time, New Zealand governed much of the Solomon Islands. For some reason, New Zealand troops took control of all supplies.

We noted a bit of laxness in the way the NZ people guarded the supply dump. They had surrounded it with a two-strand barbed wire fence. One night a bunch of us borrowed (I think they call it grand larceny) a small army truck and used our military training to loot the place. With the truck parked fifty yards behind the dump, we cut the fence and slipped in. Then, we picked up about 15 cases of assorted canned food. One of the guys discovered a big pile of brand new jungle hammocks. We shucked some of the food to make room for about 30 of these babies. We had never seen or heard of jungle hammocks. That happens to stepchildren, ya know. We got outta there with no problems. The next day we heard reports that Japs had raided the supply dump.

I availed myself of one those jungle hammocks and strung it up between two trees. These things had a rubberized roof, with built-in mosquito netting, and a false bottom that prevented snakebites. When I crawled into it, I found it just what the situation called for. Heck, compared to a waterlogged hole in the ground, that hammock seemed like moving into a 5-star hotel. Talk about one happy jarhead. Unfortunately, I hadn't counted on piss-call Pete or washing-machine Charley.

These two Jap planes came over nightly to bomb and strafe our positions. They didn't do much damage or hurt, when we dug in, but they laid down some aggravation on us. Sure 'nuff, the first night in my luxury accommodations, the gruesome twosome came calling. For once I slept well and I didn't hear the air raid alarm. But I sure heard the blast of bombs as they drew near. Getting through the double-zippered netting proved too slow. Outta sheer panic, I whipped out my K-Bar knife and slashed my way out. Heart-broken over the damage to my new digs, but alive I sewed up the slits, but got real smart. I dug a trench deep enough to lower my hammock into it, so I slept suspended below ground level. Others followed suit.

The jungle's heat, humidity, mosquitoes, malaria, puke, dysentery, scorpions, snakes, wait-a-minute vines, Charley, Pete, fungi, loneliness, endless nights, death and injuries all stood as the squalid realities of tropical combat. These factors made up your silent war.

Of the many maladies listed above that befell the troops in the tropical climes of the vast Pacific Ocean, of course, I found death the most gut wrenching. I won't lie to you and claim I had no personal fear of death. But dealing with the conditions of the death of a comrade really troubled for me. Yes, death topped the dread list. However, loneliness, I found, ran a close second.

When we made contact with the enemy, most of the time we had air support overhead. This close support constituted a unique and legendary venture between the Marine Air Wings and ground troops. The combination worked like a well-oiled machine because both units took pride in training and working together. The air wing embedded their own personnel with the ground troops. Those air wing ground guys stayed in constant communication with the pilots above. We put highly visible cloth panels in front of our positions and gave the air wing open season on anything that moved beyond. Let me tell you, it felt great to see and to know we had help. In the beginning, we saw the planes as inanimate objects in the skies above with the names Wildcat, Hellcat, Dauntless, and Corsair. But in close air support, another dimension appeared. In their nearness, we could clearly see a pilot's face. This aspect gave the machines of war a finite quality about them. Those were Marines up there.

When feasible, the pilots worked with and above us from sunup to sundown. With daring, they flew in harm's way as they took ground fire on every run they made. Some died. The Japs shot more than a few from the sky, only to bail out to land behind our lines. Out of this working relationship, things grew close up and personal. When the pilots finished a sortie, they flew low and parallel to our lines. As they passed, we stood to wave and cheer. They acknowledged us with a thumb-up gesture and a waggle of their wings. From time to time, they fashioned little parachutes out of pieces of bed sheets, bandanas, and old parachutes to drop poggy-bait (candy), cigars, gum and canned food down to us. Why, one evening, two of them came over to drop some cooked pork chops.

When these guys soared above, doing their thing, we didn't feel so alone. Through them, we stayed in touch with the outside world, an orgy of spirit. When the long shadows of evening began to show, the carriers called the birds of war to come home to roost. On their final mission of the waning day, some pilots soared low and slow over our lines. With canopies open, they pressed their palms together in prayer. We saluted.

As the sounds of the radial engines faded into the dusky evening, the sounds of yet another jungle night mounted the stagnant air. During these moments my spirits began to run kinda muddy. The unseen tyranny of loneliness took hold of my heart and held it the night through.

I hated the nights with a passion. Even now, some sixty years later, the thoughts of jungle nights still echo in my memories. I shared a hole with others, yet I sat alone. Loneliness seemed my one constant companion. The nocturnal hours carried a thousand alien sounds, many of which I figured came from infiltrating enemies. Seclusion and despair take hold of your heart and make it sting as if touched with a red, hot poker.

The Paramarines, Raiders and other combat vets returned stateside to form the core of the Marine Corps' new 5th Division. First we trained at Camp Pendleton, our first training base, then we moved to Camp Tarawa, Hawaii. Shortly after we arrived there, I developed stomach cramps.

As the days went by, the cramps worsened. One day while on a field exercise, the pain got so bad that I passed out briefly. Arthur Light, one of the Naval Corpsmen assigned to my company, called for an ambulance that transported me back to the sickbay. They kept me overnight, gave me some medication and released me back to the unit the next day. A couple of nights later, the cramps hit me again. Peter Adam and Euel Renfroe got me over to the sickbay where they gave me something for pain. A doctor, who suspected appendicitis, checked me over, but the test showed negative. The next time it hit me, the docs sent me to a nearby Army hospital where I underwent x-rays and all kinds of other tests. They, too, failed to find anything wrong with me.

I lay there about five days. Peter Adam and a couple of others came to visit me.

When they left, Peter returned to say, "Fred, the scuttlebutt around the company is that you're too yellow to go back into combat again."

This stunned me to tears.

He continued, "I know you're not, and I've challenged those who have said this."

I found myself too choked to speak. He soon left, sensing that I needed some time alone.

Cobber and Cross came over later. They indicated that they had heard nothing of what was being said about me. They, however, served in another platoon and lived in another tent.

Cobber said, "Harv, I'm going to find out about this s---. Cross and I will whip anybody's butt that says anything bad about you."

"Y'all talk to Pete. He says it's coming from some of the guys in the assault squad." They left in a storm, looking for a fight.

Late that afternoon, a psychiatrist came to escort me to his office.

He told me to have a seat and then mulled over my records. "Harvey, I see that you've been having chronic stomach pain. You have been tested for everything which could be a source of the problem. Nothing seems to be physically wrong with you. Were you drafted into the service?"

"No, Sir, I quit school nearly three years ago to join the Marine Corps."

"Three years? Have you been overseas before?"

"Yes, Sir, I was in the 1st Paramarines in the Solomon Islands."

"Were you scared when you were in combat?"

"Yes, Sir."

"When the shooting started, did you feel like running away? Are you afraid of dying?"

"No, I never thought about running away and I do not want to die."

This line of questioning went on for a couple of hours. He spent a great deal of time on questions on my home life and my mother and her situation. In time he said, "Harvey, I think that you worry too much about your mother and sisters and brother. Worry may be causing your stomach problems along with reluctance in going back into action. I'm going to recommend that you be discharged from the Marine Corps."

His words shocked me. I begged, "Please, Sir, don't do that! This is my home now! I love the Marines! I won't cause any more problems!"

"Son, there's no other way. Even your medical doctors are saying this. I'll call you in again tomorrow."

I had on PJs, house slippers and a robe. I went out the side door of the hospital and walked the side roads back to Camp Tarawa. I reported to the clinic on base in the hopes that they could get me out of the clutches of the Army. Also, I hoped someone could get my boots and dungarees from the hospital, since I didn't want to go there again for any reason.

In the clinic, I found Corpsman Light on duty with a doctor I hadn't met before. Light introduced him to me and I proceeded to tell him of my problems. This young physician, serving his internship in the military, ended up playing a definitive part in my life.

I told them everything that had happened to me since I had my first symptoms, right up to my walking out of the Army hospital. He then had me lie on an examining table and punched around my stomach, the same as five doctors had done before. When he finished with the examination, he asked, "Harvey, have you been overseas before?"

"Yes, Sir."

"How long were you over there?"

"About fifteen months, Sir."

"Can you name all the islands you were on during that time?"

"Yes, Sir. I was on New Caledonia, Guadalcanal, Vella Lavella and Bougainville. I was on Guadalcanal only two weeks, and did not see any action."

"Did you say Bougainville?"

"Yes, Sir."

"Did you go barefooted a lot while on Bougainville?"

"Yes, Sir. After we set up a perimeter, my position was in a

192

coconut grove near the beach. I went without shoes when I was not on guard duty."

"Harvey, I think I might know what's wrong with you."

"Are you kidding me, Doctor? I've had many to examine me and they could not find anything wrong."

"I wouldn't kid you on something so important to you and your health. I was reading a medical journal on the ship coming over, and it indicated that many South Pacific islands are infested with hookworm, especially Bougainville."

"Hookworm, what's that?"

"Hookworm is a parasite that gets in your intestines through the soles of your feet. Going barefoot gives them that opportunity. There are other ways they get into your body, but most likely, you picked them up on Bougainville. We have hookworm in the States. In the Southern states lots of kids get them through the soles of their feet."

"Can you get rid of them?"

"Yes, if you have them, we will get rid of them tomorrow. Light and I are going to take you back to the hospital right now, before we all get in trouble."

They called for a Jeep and got me back into my ward. Some hospital, they hadn't missed me. The young doctor promised to return early the next morning before they could cashier me out of the Marines. He indicated that he intended to stay with me until I safely returned to my unit. He told me not to eat anything until he saw me the next day. My spirits went to an all-time high.

I waited for them on the front porch the next morning, arriving there before dawn. I didn't want that shrink to find me before my people got there.

When the young doctor and Light found me, they took me to an examining room. There they took a stool specimen that I had surrendered to a bedpan. They left the room for about 30 minutes and returned with three red pills that looked like miniature footballs. "Swallow these and wash them down with this glass of mineral oil," the doc said. Man, I nearly threw up when he said mineral oil. I hated mineral and castor oil with a passion. I did manage to get the pills and oil down, but only with great effort. Even today, when I think of that six-ounce glass of mineral oil, I gag.

After my retching stopped, they placed me on a portable commode. In about thirty minutes, I gave that pot the mother of all bowl movements. After the flushing ceased and I finished the paper work, we all gathered around to observe the results. Thank goodness I didn't have anything left in my innards. Literally hundreds of those varmints scrambled around in that pestilent pot. I then ate a nourishing meal and went back to my unit that afternoon. Once again, Doctor, wherever you might be, you were a savior. I thanked Art Light at subsequent reunions. Ya know, several guys came around to congratulate me and offer apologies for what they had thought.

Mary Lou's Flag
Flying High above Campus of
Chamberlain-Hunt Military Academy,
Port Gibson, Mississippi

Chapter 11

Red, White, and Blue

Ya know, during my childhood the American Flag had only 48 stars in its field of blue along with 13 bars of red and white. During those formative years the US Flag held little meaning to me. I saw it simply as a piece of vari-colored cloth with a bunch of white stars and some red and white stripes on it. Heck, I didn't even know what those stars and stripes stood for. Well, in 1941, I got a profound lesson just what Old Glory means. Back in that year, patriotism and respect for our Flag seemed almost universal and most definitely in style. In Odessa, we celebrated the Fourth of July with a parade, lots of speeches and, of course, barbecue. I wasn't much into speeches, but I sure like the parades and the succulent, smoked brisket and ribs, the likes of which you find only in Texas. The parade started the day's festivities. Being the runt of the litter and short of stature, I needed to get downtown early so's to get a front row position to see and hear everything that passed in review. I always figured the front of Claude Foster's pool hall, popularly known as the Turf Club as the premier spot in town to see a parade . Sure 'nuff, I got there in plenty of time to place my skinny rump on the curb in front of the Turf Club.

Grant, the main street, filled rapidly with folks who loved a parade. A sidekick of mine came along and helped himself to a spot next to me. Being a hot July day, he sensibly left a ten-inch space between us for circulation – big mistake! It wasn't long 'til someone took that 10-inch void as an open invitation.

In no time, a big burly guy came to squeeze his fat butt between me and the kid next to me. Now, I took offense at this as the curbside always went to the urchins of the town who did not have a father's shoulders to sit on. At 95 pounds, I had no recourse but to tolerate this intrusion. It wasn't long 'til we heard the sounds of the Bronco Band coming from the north on Grant Street. The proud American flag led the parade. As the flag neared, I noted that all those seated stood to join the standees, and placed their hats or palms reverently over their hearts. I stood proudly to do the same and felt a thrill pass through me. While standing, I noted that Fat Butt neither stood nor placed his right hand over his heart. Quick–like, I heard a voice say, "Hey, fellow, that's the American flag. You stand for it."

To this the Butt replied, "I ain't standing for no pagan flag!"

I turned to see that the patriotic challenge had emanated from a slim cowboy who looked like he might weigh all of 150 lbs. In a rage, the cowboy bent over and grabbed the fat guy by the backside of his belt and jerked him to his feet. All in one motion, the cowboy turned, spinning like a discus thrower, and slung the poor bastard against the brick facing of the Turf Club. The fat one folded like a wet tortilla and ended up on his well-padded behind. The cheers and applause heaped on the seemingly embarrassed cowboy drowned out the Bronco Band.

Mr. Foster, who had stood in the open door of his club, called out, "The beer is on me after the parade and soda-pop for the young 'uns!" During the cheering, the Butt waddled down the sidewalk and turned the corner. Of course, when the parade ended, I hauled my skinny butt into the Turf Club and got served first. I opted for a legal Dr. Pepper.

In the late afternoon of that hot July 4th, the news spread through the Big O, like a California wildfire, that the police had arrested the cowboy. On hearing the news, I raced to the

197

courthouse to find that a large crowd had already amassed in and around the court building. Soon the county judge arrived and made his way through the noisy but disciplined crowd. He indicated that he intended to hold a hearing within the hour. Within that time, the courtroom opened and quickly filled, with most unable to get inside. I squirmed, wormed my way in, and claimed a front row seat. Seems the fat guy had rushed to the sheriff's office to file a complaint against the cowboy. They, the law, had no recourse but to bring him in. During the proceeding, the judge fined the cowhand $25.00 for disturbing the peace. About fifty men stepped forth to pay the fine. The judge settled the issue by accepting one buck from the first twenty five guys in line. The fat guy received a stern lecture about his lack of patriotism and respect for the flag of the USA. A lady stood up and said, "Judge, may I have your permission to lead this gathering in the Pledge of Allegiance and our National Anthem?"

"You certainly have my permission and thank you." That Fourth of July still stands as my most memorable Independence Day. I regret that the malady of time has erased the names of that cowboy and judge from my slate of memories.

The next deeply profound event that brought me even closer to our flag occurred several months later when I joined the Marine Corps. During the swearing-in ceremony, I held my hand high and proudly swore to uphold the Constitution and Flag of the United States of America. The oath moved me.

The officer in charge of the ritual added, "Fellows, you are now Marines and you have just sworn to serve and honor this flag and to uphold the Constitution of this country as other Marines have done for over one hundred and twenty-five years. You will soon be laying your life on the line for this flag and what it represents. Do it with honor."

Through misty eyes, my gaze remained riveted to the flag. This changed the course of my life. A devotion and love for our flag entered my heart, becoming an intrinsic part of my life. The oath engrained in me a deep sense of responsibility. I had found a home in the Marine Corps. I had a destiny to protect both the flag and the Constitution of the United States of America.

I followed the flag for a couple of years to the far reaches of the Earth. We, the Marines, planted it on many exotic islands and landfalls in the vast Pacific Ocean that I had never heard of. This odyssey of travel and adventure culminated for me on a very small volcanic island in the far reaches of that massive body of water called Iwo Jima. This term means Sulfur Island in the Japanese language. A vent in Satan's Hell itself spawned the elements that fabricated this isle of infamy so long ago. The volcano that belched forth the molten lava at Iwo bore the name Suribachi, truly hell's volcano. We gave a very appropriate code name to this island of terror: Hot Rocks.

Shaped like a pork chop, Iwo is only seven miles long and two and a half miles at its widest point. Thousands of Marines came ashore at the base of Suribachi. The 28th Marines turned south and headed up the sides of Suribachi. It took four days for the elements of the 28th Regiment to clear the hundreds of caves and pillboxes on Suribachi of enemy personnel. Until they secured the mount, the Japs used it as an observation post to direct devastating firepower from Iwo's big guns, heavy mortars, and small arms fire. Historians have labeled this the bloodiest battle of World War II. I concur. On that fourth day, a loud cheer went up like you hear when a team scores a touchdown. I turned to look toward that ominous peak of lava rock. There it waved in a brisk breeze, the American flag. Being high and faraway, it looked small and forlorn, but I thought it the grandest sight I had ever seen. With Old Glory standing sentry at our backs, I figured on a cakewalk going the rest of the way up the little isle to victory. Wrong! This battle lasted thirty-two more days at a cost of seven thousand lives. But, I didn't make it to the end. Several days later, on one of those terror-filled nights, my string ran out. As I told you earlier the enemy laid some real hurt on me. I've told you about my concern with my jump boots, now let me tell you another concern I had.

I find my memory of the events that followed a bit sketchy and vague. Not surprising since my brain marinated in morphine from the time I had been hit. During one of my infrequent lucid moments, I opened my eyes to find myself tethered to a bag of blood plasma. As I lay on my stomach, I twisted my head to find the flag. The Corpsman tending me cautioned me to lie still. "Is the flag still there? I want to see it."

"Hang on," he said. He took the bayoneted rifle supporting the plasma and moved it. He then took one end of the stretcher and pivoted it around so that I faced Suribachi. A light fog swaddled the peak. In the haze, I could barely see the flag as it waved in a gentle breeze.

Satisfied, I drifted back into a timeless oblivion. Time and place had lost their relevance.

Cold raindrops falling gently to my face wakened me from a deep, dreamless sleep. Before I could erase the cobwebs from my eyes I realized I laid on the open deck of a ship. I envisioned it a large ship due to the feel of roll and pitch in a choppy sea. (I found out later I was aboard the USS Ozark.) Since it did indeed sit high on the water's surface, I could see the far north of Iwo, though it was engulfed by scattered rain clouds. I searched vainly for Suribachi and its American flag. They were toward the front of the ship and hidden from my view.

Soon I felt a hand touch my head and a voice commanded, "Take this one now or we'll lose him."

I wasn't too concerned, as I felt pretty good. Stout hands lifted me from the deck and began to carry me toward the bow of the ship. As we moved forward along the starboard rail, the vessel pivoted suddenly on its anchor chain and came to a stop in a parallel position to the island. There it waved, in full view. The clouds had parted, giving a corridor for a radiant shaft of sunlight to reach down to mantle the mount and its flag of red, white and blue. The flag unfurled splendidly in a brisk breeze, showing proudly its brilliant array of color and loveliness, a sight of pristine serenity on high. The calm and untroubled flag seemed a cruel paradox, as it waved peacefully over a fan-shaped killing field. Below it, men locked in a deadly, desperate conflict to see that the flag remained there. Hell's volcano of Iwo Jima worked like an acoustical sounding board echoing the guns of battle. The distant sounds of war marched like rolling thunder across the open waves. The brutal calls of those engines of battle sent searing, white metal fragments into the bodies of my comrades, man's brutality toward man. My war was over, but Iwo was to be the island of my memories and what happened there shaped and fashioned my future.

I touched the hand of one of the stretcher crew and asked, "Mate, will you stop for a moment so that I might take one last look?" They stopped. I took a long, lingering look. I pulled my empty boots to my face to hide the tears that filled my eyes. That flag, what a beautiful sight. I have forever etched that view in my storehouse of memories. "I'm ready," I told them after a moment.

During the mid-60s when the Viet Nam war hit its zenith, patriotism and the love of Flag seemingly went out of style. This era with the so-called hippie culture burst in full bloom. During this period, I coached football at Eastwood High in El Paso, Texas. We had our share of this rebellious group. For the most part we chose to ignore them, their long hair, dirtiness, ragged clothing, and unsocial behavior. Parents had lost control at home and the malignancy spread into the public schools.

Out of this rebellious group stood one particular hard-core youngster named Danny. Now, Danny gave his teachers, administrators and other students hell. He spent most of his school time in the office or in the detention hall. If not in school, he sat at home, expelled. Danny could have made a football player had he stayed eligible scholastically. Sports and other extra-curricular activities might have helped him. One day he dropped by my office to report the principal had just expelled him. This came as no surprise.

I invited him in. "Sit down, Danny."

He complied as I continued, "You know, son, you're not hurting your teachers or the principal. All you're doing is hurting yourself. You're heading down a road that leads to a very troubled life."

I went on in this vein for several minutes and suddenly realized he actually had tuned into me. We talked for about an hour with his asking many meaningful questions. I answered all in the best way I knew how. Our conference ended when a bell sounded, alerting me I needed to get to the playing field for a PE class. Danny stood and proffered his hand for a shake. He held my hand tightly, at the same time thanking me in all earnestness. He walked with me to the field and thanked me once again. With a spring in his gait, he trotted off. I watched him as he made his way down the street, gaining speed as he faded away.

The next morning following a knock on my door, I found Danny standing, sporting this great big grin on his face. In a voice filled with excitement, he said, "Coach, my mom signed these papers and I've joined the Marine Corps, that is if I can pass the physical. The sergeant told me I could earn a GED while serving." He could hardly contain himself.

I shoved my hand forward for a shake and said, "Sit down and talk to me."

He did so, saying, "I can't stay long, as I have to get downtown for a physical exam."

"When did you make a decision to join up?"

"Yesterday after I left here, I asked my mom if I could join the Corps. At first, she didn't want me to go, but I convinced her that it would be best for her and for me to go in. She finally gave in and told me I could enlist. I called the recruiting office and they sent a car out to pick me up. The recruiter tried to talk me into staying in school until I graduated, but I told him that I was too far behind to ever get out of school. The sergeant told me how tough boot camp was and lots of other things."

"I was a Marine and I can tell you it is tough, but you can make it. I found a home when I went into the Corps and you may do the same. Just keep your nose clean. Listen to your sergeants and respect them. They are the backbone of the Marine Corps. Take care of yourself. You'll do well, Danny."

Several weeks later, Danny dropped in to see me. He had come home on a ten-day boot leave. He looked really great in his uniform. He emanated pride and self-assurance. I was happy for him. In time, he sent me a short note, informing me that he had arrived in Viet Nam. I beseeched God to look after him.

Many months later, I opened my morning newspaper to find that Danny Colgan had been killed in action. He died on Oct. 8, 1968, just twenty years old/young. I felt stunned and hurt, the same feeling of emptiness I had felt when I lost a comrade during my war. Danny now marches through my memories along side the many buddies I lost in WWII. God has blessed them.

Much later, Danny came home for interment in his family's burial plot. With his service set for a Friday morning, the traditional day of high school football games, it clashed with Eastwood's pre-game pep rally. I asked Bob Bradley, my boss, if I could pass on the rally to attend the funeral.

He said, "Coach, it's important that you attend Danny's burial to represent this school. Tell his mother we pray for her son. I plan to set the pep rally back two hours, giving you time enough to get back to take part." I found Danny's funeral service both impressive and touchingly sad.

I returned to the campus as the student body filed into the football stadium for the pep rally. The football team, band and coaches sat on the field. The band played loud and the cheerleaders worked at getting the crowd into a frenzy. I found my way to a seat among the other coaches. Usually I got really fired up at these feisty rallies, but not on this October day. Heavyhearted with sadness, my thoughts still on the rites of burial that I had just attended, I couldn't get fired up about the game. As I sat, my eyes wandered up into the upper row where the flower children of the hippie era usually sat during these rallies. I was reminded of a time when Danny had attended those rallies. He'd have sat on that top row with many of his friends, the anti-establishment culture. They sat there stoically, taking no part in the merriment going on below their perch on high.

When the student body settled into their seats, the head cheerleader stepped to the microphone. A hush fell on the group, "Will you please stand as we recite the 'Pledge of Allegiance' to our Flag."

Everyone stood with the exception of the top row who still did their thing. They showed no respect for the Flag of the United States of America. At the conclusion of the Pledge, the band broke into the playing of the "National Anthem," still no reaction from the top row. Everyone ignored them but me. The cheerleaders did several rollicking cheers and then the team captains came forth to tell all how the Troopers planned to whip up on the visiting team that night. Then, by tradition, they called on the coach to add fire to the already-boiling pot.

In bravado, I usually jumped up, trotted briskly to the mike and gave a short, fiery speech about the pending game, but this day I didn't have my heart in it. I rose to my feet and strolled slowly toward the mike, not knowing what to say to the waiting student body. As I passed the flag staff, on impulse I stopped and touched the furled flag, and suddenly I knew what I had to say.

In a choking, stammering voice I said, while pointing to the flag, "People, this morning I saw another flag. This one had just finished a long sad trip of seven thousand miles. Its journey of sadness began on the battle field of Viet Nam and ended here, draped over a silver coffin that contained the mortal remains of our own Danny Colgan." I had to pause here to clear my wits and wipe the uncontrollable tears from my eyes. "Danny paid the ultimate price; he gave his life defending and honoring our flag. I'm

204

heartbroken that there are among us those who will not even stand for that which Danny laid his life on the line." I raised my head and looked up into the top row. I then backed away from the mike and returned to my seat. Dead silence followed.

After a moment or so Patsy, God bless her, returned to the mike and said, "What can I say after that. Let us return to our classes."

I sat, bathed in emptiness and melancholia, as the stadium cleared and the band put away their instruments and left. When I rose to leave, I looked into that top row to see, to my surprise, many of those youngsters still sat there. As I strolled toward the end of the stadium, I noted that they, too, moved. I sensed that they might want to talk so I waited for them. When they gathered, one young lady asked, "Coach, where is Danny buried?" I gave them the location. They indicated that they planned to visit the cemetery that afternoon.

I said at that point, "It would be nice, too, that you go to Danny's home and offer his folks, especially his mother, your deepest condolences." The young lady gave me a hug and the young men each shook my hand as they departed. I felt better. Ya know, at the next pep rally that top row was empty.

In 1970, we moved from Texas to Littleton, Colorado where I accepted the football coaching position at the local high school. The Viet Nam War still raged and the anti-war movement heated up. One night as the family watched the late news on television, the camera visited the scene of an anti-war demonstration. There it focused on a group that had set fire to an American flag. As usual, I went into a controlled rage. My daughter, Mary Lou, and son, Chuck, sat on the deck in front of me. When this travesty played out, Mary Lou turned to me with eyes awash in tears and said, "Dad, why do people do that? It makes me unhappy to see our flag being treated in such a terrible way."

I knew I couldn't give her an appropriate answer, but I did say, "They do it because they are exercising their freedom of speech. Though I feel they are misguided, I know the made of mockery of that freedom. I fear most of them do it because the TV cameras are there. You can bet they'll all be in front of a TV set watching the evening news to see themselves do their thing. They can't gain attention any other way. They're losers."

Chuck added, "They should be put in jail!"

Late one night, a week or so after this incident, my wife and I heard a knock on our bedroom door. Mary Lou apparently had a question, "May I come in and talk to y'all?"

In answer I said, "Of course, you may. Come on in. We were not asleep." When she entered, she switched on the light and proceeded to come and sit on the edge of the bed.

Billie, my wife, opened with, "What's the matter honey, did you have another fight with your boyfriend?"

Mary Lou had enrolled in college and had dropped out after a semester, saying that we had wasted our money by sending her off to school. She said she'd grown tired of school and wanted to find a job. We didn't push her, but let her know that she could return to school anytime she wanted. She found a position as a cashier at a local restaurant. There she fell in with several other youngsters her own age. She stayed on the go with this bunch and seemed to enjoy life. After a short pause, as she sat on the bed, she took a deep breath and said, "You know, I have been running around with these other kids for several months now and we do the same things every night. We talk about the same things, the same people and the events of the day at our jobs. It has gotten to be a real drag."

At this I thought, "Golly, she's ready to go back to school". My wife told me later she had thought the same thing. Imagine our surprise when Mary Lou continued with, "May I have your permission to join the Marine Corps?"

After gulping down this surprising turn of events, my wife asked, "Why the Marine Corps? Why not return to school?"

"I haven't changed my thoughts on school. I still have no desire to go back to college."

"Why the Marine Corps, and when did you decide that you wanted to go into the service?"

"Remember the night we watched them burn the American flag? Well, I've been thinking about joining ever since. Dad, you have always told us how much you loved the Marine Corps and the men you served with. I've always thought that I might like to be a Marine. Also, you said that you had found a home when you joined. Maybe I will feel the same way."

I readily gave my blessing to this venture, filled with pride. Billie, however, wasn't quite so quick, but gave her approval after asking many questions. We talked way into the night. The more we talked, the more resolved she felt. Our little girl finally went off to bed in a gleeful mood. The next morning she headed for the recruiting office.

The Marines told her that she had to wait six weeks before another slot opened up in a recruit platoon. Disappointed, she perked up when the officer told her the Naval recruiters could take her within ten days. She then headed down the hall to talk to the USN people. Sure, they wanted her. She told them, "My dad was a Marine and may not let me go into the Navy. I'll go over to Littleton High School and ask him."

She found me on the football field. When she got my attention, she reluctantly said, "Dad, the Marines can't take me now, but the Navy can take me in ten days. What do you think? May I join the Navy?"

"What? You want to be a swabbie? No way!" When I saw her lips quiver, I smiled and said, "Honey, if you want to join the Navy, go for it."

She gave me a big hug with, "Thanks, Dad. I'll see you at supper." She hurried off to join the Navy to serve the Flag. Talk about a proud Marine dad.

A couple of years later while serving overseas, Mary met and married another sailor. Out of this marriage came three beautiful daughters, each in the image of their mother's loveliness, charm and sense of kindness to others, named Kerry, Katie and Kendra. A few years later, Mary Lou and her family moved to Fort Collins, Colorado. In time, she took a position in the Larimer County Department of Social Services. She loved working with and helping people.

Several years ago, I came out of retirement to coach football at a Christian/Military School in Mississippi. So happens, I called Mary Lou at least once each week. We talked and talked. On a Sunday afternoon in April 2001, we visited on the telephone for over an hour. As usual, Mary Lou signed off in high spirits and happy. That night she went to sleep and never woke up.

The news of her death hit me hard, shaking me to my very core. At times I still wake from a troubled sleep hearing myself calling out, "Lord, why her? Why not me?"

At her memorial service, Mary's daughters received an American flag in honor of their mother's Naval service. My granddaughters, in turn, asked me to take the flag back to Chamberlain-Hunt Military School to fly on its flagpole.

"Our mother would like that," they said.

Her flag did fly proudly above the campus of Chamberlain-Hunt Academy. The cadets marched under and around it while on parade. They saluted as they walked by the staff that held Old Glory on high. Each morning of a new day, I made it a point to pass and stop to look up and say a prayer in recall of that daughter of mine. Seemingly, each morning a gentle breeze gave it life to revel and cavort as if in elemental happiness.

On the day after 9/11, the day terrorists took the lives of over three thousand Americans, I rose from the bed that had held me captive through a long and sleepless night. Toughness and practicality come easily during the day but the night seems like another world. Daybreak came late with no sunshine to light the skies above. Instead, I faced a dark, dank morning with low-hanging clouds that ushered forth a light, drizzling rain. I dressed in rain gear and went out into the elements of the morning.

Subconsciously I headed to the flagpole. Without a hint of a breeze, the flag hung, limply furled around its staff. As the drizzle embraced the soft folds of the cloth, it formed into droplets. The drops then began to slide slowly downward like tears of sadness. I know that, way up beyond that flag in the Heavens above, Mary Lou shed tears for all the folks, especially the Americans, who lost their lives on 9/11.

Chapter 12

Lest We Forget

By tradition and custom, we retire an American flag after it flies for a year, after which we reverently burn it in a proper ceremony. This didn't happen with Mary Lou's flag. Instead, the school's Sergeant Major Chad Winsonr, an ex-Marine, took the flag down, laundered and pressed it. He then had his troops fold it in the traditional triangle. He then held it out to me and added, "Fred, take this to your granddaughters. It has served as your daughter served."

Is it any wonder that I shed a tear when I see the flag, hear the "Star Spangled Banner" or Pledge of Allegiance to it, our flag? God bless it.

In closing this chapter, I must tell you that I say a prayer each night for our troops, men and women who have followed our flag to the far off lands of Iraq and Afghanistan. I offer this poem written by Stevenson. I'm sorry I could not find his or her first name.

> *Dear Lord,*
> *Somewhere in far off Iraq or Afghanistan*
> *A young man or lady will die for me this day.*
> *As long as there be war*
> *Then I must ask and answer,*
> *Am I worth dying for?*

Chapter 13

Close Encounters
Some Famous, Others Infamous

During the late 30s and early 40s, I ran around with a redhead named J. D. Pinner. Between the two of us, we found more ways to get in trouble than any ten guys. We comprised the proverbial wrong crowd of Odessa, Texas. Our mischievous deeds earned us a certain notoriety in that West Texas town during the era mentioned above. Oh, nothing we did resulted in police involvement. We did, however, have a close encounter with the law that took the Governor of the state to get us out of the aggravation we caused.

Now, ol' Red had a Model A Ford touring automobile, a two-seater with a top that folded back like a convertible. Built about 1927, Red's Model A came out before manufacturers put metal tops on cars. Since we drove that thing around town, it too gained a reputation. I said we tooled around town, of course, only when we could come up with 15 cents for a gallon of gasoline. For you youngsters, yes, gas only cost 15 cents a gallon back in the good old days.

One day in the spring of '41, I think, the then Governor of Texas James Allred visited Odessa. Now, this stood as a big deal. That afternoon, the whole school turned out, as the town had arranged a parade. The parade included the Bronco band along with bands from Crane and Andrews. Red and I managed to come up with 15 cents. We had wheels. They blocked off main street with barriers at intersecting streets. We parked on one of those side streets near the start of the parade. We settled in to watch the Governor's parade from the comfort of Red's Model A Ford with the top folded down.

Directly, the Bronco band came marching, closely followed by the Governor in one of Carl Sewell's Lincoln convertibles. The honored VIP sat on the back of this grand automobile waving to the applauding crowd. As the Governor passed our vehicle, on a daring impulse, ol' J. D. started up the Model A, drove around the barrier and moved into the parade. His brazen move nearly scared the bleep outta me. In utter panic, I threw a leg over the side, ready to abandon the idiot and his Ford. Before I could bail out, I heard cheering and laughing. Moved by what I heard, the urge to jump quickly ebbed. Dang, I felt obliged to stick with the redhead. We had captured the imagination of the crowd, to heck with the consequences. What's so bad about feeling good? Pinner nudged me, indicating that I should crawl into the back. Good idea. So I got in the back and mimicked the Governor. I waved and threw kisses to an appreciative crowd. They loved it.

It wasn't long before a very disturbed motorcycle cop pulled along side. With a wave of an arm, he motioned Pinner to move out of the procession. Seeing this, the crowd began to boo. Also, we couldn't exit without running over people. So we stayed in for the long haul, although we had one aggravated lawman by our side. We had gone this far, so we stuck with it, to the delight of our fans. When the parade ended, the VIP auto pulled off on a side street. We had no choice but to follow. The Governor's car stopped, we stopped, and the policeman stopped beside us. He took out his note pad and proceeded to ask questions. To tell you the truth, I figured we'd get jail time. My spirits sank so low that I could have crawled under a snake's belly. Heck, I actually worried more about the hurt that Jessie might lay on my hiney.

At this point, Governor Allred got out of his car and walked over to intervene. "Officer," he said, "I wish you wouldn't give those boys a ticket. They were the best part of the parade. I got a big kick out of their show and so did the other folks." He added, "If your chief has any questions, I will take responsibility for their actions." He then turned to ask us for our names, shook our hands and patted us on the head.

By this time, a lot of people had gathered to see the action. They applauded him. Like any good politician, he went among them and shook a lot of hands. At that very moment, he had my vote for king of the land. We reluctantly went over to the policeman to offer apologies. He acted the good sport and told us to forget it.

When I joined the Marines, I had never shaved in my life. In fact, I spent a great deal of time inspecting my face to see if I could find a semblance of hair so that I could start shaving. I never found more than a little peach fuzz around the corners of my lips. Even then, I needed the light just right.

When I arrived at the Marine boot camp, they issued me a bucket. In this bucket, I found, among other things, a safety razor, a mug with a brush and a round soap bar. I didn't think much about this array of equipment as I didn't need it 'cause I didn't shave.

One day a DI (drill instructor) lined my platoon up for inspection. Now, the sun must have hit my face just right because Sergeant Hoeger found some of that elusive fuzz. He jumped in my face right quick–like, yelling, "Feather Merchant (the DI's name for us short runts in boot camp), did you shave this morning?"

"No, Sir!"

"Why not, Feather Merchant?"

"'Cause I don't shave yet, Sir."

"#%*%@! Who tells you that you don't have to shave?" He got so fired up by this time that he looked about as sour as clabbered milk. He got so close to my face that he slobbered on me. He scared me so much I nearly did him one better. I about peed in my dungarees.

"You're a foul up! This is a man's outfit and men shave! Now, you get your ass over to the head and shave! Ya hear? Ya got thirty

213

minutes to get back here!"

We stood about a half mile from my tent. At a track meet, that's 880 yards. With my rifle at port-arms, I lit a shuck. Had he timed me, I might possibly have set a world's record for that distance. At the tent, I grabbed a towel and shaving gear and, with my rifle still in hand, I lit out for the head. As I propped my rifle against the wall, I noted another guy about five basins down from me, shaving. I filled my mug about 3/4 full and stirred it like mad. While I stirred, I asked the guy, "Did you get in trouble for not shaving, too?"

"No, I did not get in trouble, but I did need to shave."

"Well, I got in big trouble. I've never shaved before."

When I applied the lather, it ran off my face like snot. I tried again with the same results. I looked down to the other guy and saw that his lather stood on his face like meringue on a good ol' lemon pie. He did a double take and realized I had no idea as to what I was trying to do. He then walked down to me, saying, "Having trouble, Mack?"

"Yes, Sir, this stuff will not stay on my face like yours."

"I think I see your problem."

He then took my mug and poured all the water out. He then said, "You're using too much water. You need just a little bit of hot water." He then whipped up a thick meringue and partially painted my face and then handed the brush to me. "Now try that." Satisfied, he turned and walked back to his basin.

As I shaved, I got to thinking, "I've seen that guy somewhere before." When he rinsed and put a towel to his face, I asked, "Are you from Odessa?"

"Where?"

"Odessa, Texas."

With a laugh he said, "Not hardly, never heard of Odessa."

"I'm sure that I've seen you somewhere before."

"Do you go to the movies? I do some acting."

"You're not Tyrone Power, are you?"

214

"Sure am."

"What are you doing here?"

"I'm a boot just like you, Mack. What's your name?"

"Fred Harvey, Sir. Gosh, you're my favorite actor."

"Thanks, Marine, but don't call me Sir. I'm just a private."

"Did your DI catch you not shaving like me?"

He laughed and replied, "No, I have to go on a War Bond tour today. You're lucky you don't have to shave very often. I have a heavy beard and have to shave two times on some busy days."

"Can I shake your hand?"

"Sure, it'll be an honor to shake your hand, Marine."

"Well, Fred Harvey from Odessa, Texas, take care and good luck to you."

"Thank you, Sir, and good luck to you." What a thrill for this Feather Merchant from Odessa, Texas.

A couple of weeks later on a Sunday morning, Sergeant Hoeger had us fall out. He then marched us down to the visitors' center. At the center, he brought us to a halt behind a Ford station wagon. That wood-sided wagon had so much weight in it that it looked like it sat on its axles. When the sergeant gave an at ease order, a beautiful lady got out and walked to the rear of the wagon. At this time, the sergeant brought us to attention. He said in a loud voice, "Troops, this is Annabelle. You have no doubt seen her in the movies. As you know by now, her husband, Tyrone Power, is a Marine, too. He told her that we were badly in need of clothes hangers. She raided her movie studio and has brought enough clothes hangers for every boot on this base. Give her a big hand."

We gave her a big hand along with a loud cheer. He then gave an order, "Line up in single file and walk by and you will receive two wire hangers."

Man, she had to have more than a couple of thousand of 'em in that wagon. Sergeant Hoeger stood next to her and handed her two hangers. She, in turn, handed them to us along with a handshake.

When I arrived, I said in a low voice, "Your husband taught me how to shave."

She smiled and said, "Really?"

"Yes, ma'am."

Several months later we invaded and captured an island called Vella Lavella in the Solomons. When we secured the island, I hung out at the airstrip when I got time off. I loved to watch the planes land and take off. I use' to sidle up to the pilots just to hear them talk. On one such visit, I sat in the Seabee chow hall when a Marine lieutenant walked in. I jumped to my feet and saluted Lieutenant Tyrone Power. He had earned his wings and flew as a pilot. He returned my salute.

I asked, "Remember me, Sir?"

While he was trying to remember, I added, "You showed me how to shave in boot camp."

"Yes, I remember now. How are things going for you?"

"Fine, Sir."

"Now, what's your name?"

I replied to his question.

"Well, Fred Harvey, I hope your luck holds out. I have to grab a bite to eat, as I have to take off in a few minutes." I wished him luck along with a salute. I saluted the man and his officer's rank.

While I attended the Camp Gillespie Parachute School, our platoon sergeant informed us that we had pulled special duty for the day. Our platoon caught the detail to set up a large, portable stage and seating in the base gymnasium for a star-studded USO show on base that day. Phil Silvers brought a group down from Hollywood. Now, this really generated some excitement among the troopers. It took about two hours for us to finish the job. As we went about this task, Phil Silvers and his entourage arrived. He had with him a band and a troupe of young ladies, all of them prettier than palominos in a clover patch. The group went immediately into the rest rooms behind the stage. When we finished our assignment, the platoon leader called for us to fall into formation.

He then told us, "Okay, troops, we did our act, so we're going to cash in. We are going to take the best seats in the house. You are dismissed." Now, I put my world-class speed to use and raced down the center aisle and claimed the center aisle seat on the front row.

The show didn't start for something like 40 minutes. No problem. As I sat twiddling my thumbs, Phil Silvers and his black horn rimmed glasses came to the restroom door. He did a come here gesture in my direction. Figuring he meant someone else, I made no move. But I looked around to see whom he might be waving to. When I looked back at him, he gave me a real impatient wave of the hand. I then thumbed my chest. With this, he gave me a yes nod. I told the guy next to me to save my seat. I then strolled to the back of the stage and he opened the door for me to enter. Inside, a tall, beautiful girl stood next to him.

He wrung my hand and said, "My name is Phil, (As if I didn't know.) and this is Rita. We want you to be part of our act."

"Really?" I stammered.

"Yes. Rita is going to sing a love song. About halfway through her song, she's going to look right at you. When she does, we want you to squirm in your chair. While she is still singing, she is going to walk slowly down those front steps toward you. Then you really start to squirm, big-time. Now, when she gets close, she is going to reach out to you. When she does this, you jump up and run like hell back up the aisle. Think you can handle this?"

"Yes, I think I can."

"Atta boy."

I can't remember much about the show as I sweated out my role in it. Sure enough, the young starlet came out and did her thing. My part came easy 'cause I didn't have to act. I actually was really, really scared and embarrassed, but it got a big laugh outta the crowd. When Phil beckoned me to return to my seat, I got a round of catcalls and boos. Marines don't run from women. When I got to my seat. Phil said, "Let's give that Marine a big hand. He has real talent." By the way, at the end of the show Phil Silvers introduced all the young starlets. I'm not real sure, but I think the singing Rita's name was Hayworth and she went on to big-time stardom.

While I remained at Camp Gillespie, another big-time star showed up to entertain the Paratroopers. Joan Blondell of stage, screen, and burlesque fame brought in a troupe of shapely singer/dancers and vaudevillian comics. Of course, Miss Blondell stood out as the shapeliest of this shapely group. Yeah, this lady had a super set of knockers, organically grown with no chemicals added, I'll bet. I think, however, her endowments might have been digitally enhanced. Why, she made most women look like boys. When she walked on stage, she wore dresses that showed a great deal of lush cleavage. I think she had blond hair. I say think because my attention loomed elsewhere.

After the show, the troupe was escorted to the indoctrination jump tower. Now, this tower reached two hundred and fifty feet into the sky. It had a parachute harnessed to several steel cables. The wires let the chute descend in a slow, straight drop. Inductees sat on a board similar to a playground swing. For safety's sake, the person wore a chest strap that buckled them in. When a recruit arrived in camp, he received an indoctrination hoist on this set-up to check to see if he really, really wanted to join the jumpers.

We followed the girls out to the tower like puppy dogs. Of course, I went right among them, the troopers, I mean. When the starlet troupe gathered at the simulated parachute, the captain asked if any of them wanted to go up. Miss Blondell volunteered to try the ride up and the drop down first. This took some nerve. I'm here to tell you, my first time on that rig really scared me. Heck, at the time I had never gone up in an airplane before. Being short of stature and brains, I had wormed my way right up to the front so that I could see. I stood at ringside to the action. With a big smile on her face, Miss Blondell took a seat on the board. She then took a strap in each hand and tried to snap the buckle across her well-endowed breasts. She made a big show of this. After a couple of bogus attempts to snap the buckles, she went to the crowd, "Will one of you nice Marines give a lady a hand?" With that, a guy behind me gave me a big push and I found myself nearly in her lap, not by design, of course. I swallowed hard and just stood there in utter fascination, not making a move. How could I possibly hook those straps without touching those things?

She challenged me, "Come on, Marine, give me a hand. I won't bite you." When I finally reached for the straps, she yelled, "Just the straps now!" Her reaction shocked me so that I jerked my hands back. This brought forth a loud burst of laughter.

At this point, a big sergeant stepped forward and said, "This is a man's job!" He easily snapped the buckle. She rewarded him with a hug. Dang. As she began her ascent, she threw a kiss in the troop's direction. I like to think she meant it for me.

When I returned to the States after my first tour of duty overseas, I joined the 26th Marines at Camp Pendleton, located between Los Angeles and San Diego. Now, just about every Marine and Sailor ever stationed in California lit a shuck for Hollywood on his first liberty. I conformed to this notion. Peter Adam, a buddy of mine, and I grabbed a train to LA on our first liberty together. In LA, we walked to the main avenue that led to Tinsel Town. We stepped into the gutter and threw up our thumbs. The second car going our way, a big convertible containing an attractive young lady, slid to a stop. She looked about 24 years of age.

"Hop in," she invited.

I called upon my quickness of feet to get myself into the front seat first. I slid across to leave room for Peter. I turned to say thank you, but instead, "Hey, ain't you Ida Lupino?" came out instead.

"I sure am. Who might you be?"

"I'm Fred Harvey and this is Peter, my buddy. We're Marines."

She laughed, "No kidding. I'll bet you're going to Hollywood and Vine."

"You bet. How did you know that?"

Again she laughed. "Just a wild guess. Where are you staying tonight?"

"We hadn't thought about that."

"I have a friend who likes to invite servicemen to stay at her home on weekends. She'd treat you like sons. Would you like to go over and meet her?"

In unison, "We sure would!"

As she drove, she carried on most of the conversation as both Peter and I tended toward shyness. However, I did venture to say, "Miss Lupino, you're my favorite actress."

"Why, thank you, Fred. I'm glad to hear that. I'll tell you what I'm going to do. I'll drive you through Hollywood and Vine, but don't be too disappointed because you're not going to see any movie stars. All you'll see is servicemen like yourselves."

What a big let down. I figured to see 'em all over the place. Of course, she knew.

She drove that convertible like a racecar. We didn't take long getting to her friend's home. She introduced us to Mrs. Miller. (I think her name was Miller. Unfortunately, time has robbed me of that recall.) Mrs. Miller proved a real genteel lady and treated Peter and me to a memorable twenty-four hours.

Meeting and sharing time with Ida Lupino stands as one the great events of my life. What a class act in all respects. Ya know, I think she married Louis Hayward, which certainly made him a lucky guy, in my estimation. Now, no one accused me of being a great dancer, but I did dance with Susan Hayward, the movie actress. It wasn't much. A bunch of us went to the Hollywood Canteen one night. During WWII, the Hollywood Canteen served as a USO club operated for servicemen. The one and only time I went there, I stood with the guys when Miss Hayward walked in with her escort. When she got near me, she stopped and her boyfriend took her fur coat.

Since I happened to be close to her, she grabbed my hand saying, "Let's dance." I guess I stumbled about two steps before someone cut in on me. I watched for a while, and two seconds seemed about the average time anyone got to dance with her. At this rate, she danced with nearly every guy in the club. After thirty minutes, her boyfriend draped the fur over her shoulders. With that, she turned to throw a kiss toward the gathering. She did leave a bunch of guys with a memory. The thing I remember most. She had a beautiful face enhanced with an abundance of cute freckles. That's about all I can say about this encounter.

In the fall of 1943, my unit, the 1st Paramarine Battalion, invaded the Japanese-held island, Vella Lavella. After we had secured enough of the island to build an airfield, we erected fortification to defend it. Doing so isolated the remaining Japs to hold and starve on the far end of the island. We only needed just enough land to build that airstrip. After we built the defensive perimeter, we sat back to wait for the Army to take over the job of protecting the strip.

One night we heard some action taking place far out to sea toward the Island of Kolombengara. We didn't find this at all unusual, as the Japs sent in ships to shell us nearly every night.

About an hour after the action afar, Lieutenant Ralph Hall woke me up with a question, "Harvey, are you up to going on a night patrol? This is strictly a voluntary detail. The Navy has lost a PT boat and they have asked us to send some people up the beach to search for possible survivors. You will be behind Jap lines all the way. Do you want to go?"

"Yes, Sir, I'll go. When do we start?"

He replied, "As soon as I find two other guys. I'll be back." Before long he came back with a corporal and another PFC. He instructed us, "Go up the beach four or five miles. You have about three hours before dawn, so get back here before daylight. If you run into any trouble, fall back while covering each other. Good luck."

Of course, the corporal ran the show. He moved us up the beach at the water's edge. I didn't like this at all, so I questioned him, "Hey, McCoy, why do you have us out here in plain sight in this moon light?"

His answer, "If there is any shooting we're going into the water and swimming!"

"Now, how in the hell are we going to swim with rifles and this ammo?"

"We will drop everything and run into the water and swim outta range."

"I'm not about to give up my weapon. That was the first thing I learned in boot camp."

"S_ _ _, Harvey, you ain't in boot camp now!"

I dropped to one knee to cut down on our silhouette. "Get down, let's talk this over. I say we stay in the shadows of those coconut palms where we can't be seen as readily. What do you think, Roy?"

Leon agreed, "I think you're right. Mac. I think we'd best stay in those coconuts like Harvey says."

McCoy retorted, "We do like I say, it's down by the water."

I turned and trotted toward the coconut grove, saying, "Let's go, Leon. Mac, you take the water route and we'll cover you from up there."

"Harvey, I'm putting you on report when I get back!"

"If you get back!" I answered.

We hadn't moved far when Roy said, "Look down there. I can see him plain as day."

"You go down and tell him about it. Maybe he'll listen to you. I'll cover you."

It didn't take long, as quick-like they both trotted up to join me. Without further delay, I volunteered to take the point. I took off at a trot, stopping only to listen and looking for any movement along the white sandy beach. I heard nothing but the usual night noise and the pounding of the restless waves on the shoreline.

After a while, McCoy called a halt, saying, "Fellows, I'd say we've come five or six miles and used about half our time. We better head back, else daylight is going to catch up with us." We all agreed on this point.

We had traveled about two miles on the way back to our lines, when Leon hissed, "What's that down on the beach?"

We dropped to our knees and studied an object about 30 yards down toward the water. One of the guys said, "It looks like some kind of trash to me."

McCoy said, "It could be junk from that PT boat."

I got up and said, "Y'all cover me. I'll run down and check it out." I found a battered wooden crate, half-buried in the sand. It contained a couple of gallon sized cans. They had to contain food. I slung my rifle across my back and took a can under my arm and hustled back. I whipped out my ol' K-Bar knife and anxiously made a surgical-like entry into the first can. Dang, a gallon of blood-red catsup. Leon had already started doing a job on the second can. Dang, this one turned out filled with blood-red beets. I'd never liked beets in normal times, but these weren't typical times. Half-starved, we each grabbed a beet and without hesitation dipped it into the catsup. We gorged on this combination 'til we'd emptied both tins. Today, when I eat beets or catsup, my thoughts go to that feast on the beach at Vella Lavella. Ya know, these things don't taste near as great as they did back in the year of '43.

Back at our lines, we reported that we'd found no survivors, encountered no enemies, but had rescued two shipwrecked cans of food and devoured same.

Some fifteen to twenty years later, I picked up a book entitled *PT 109*. I read about halfway through it when it dawned on me that we had spent that night looking for Lieutenant John F. Kennedy and his crew. What a coincidence, we'd searched for the future President of the United States. Why, if that bunch had made it to our beach and we had found them, ol' Jack might have made us Ambassadors of Podunk or some place like that. Unfortunately, , we only flirted with fame. Just another unrealized aspiration in the commentary of my life.

I'll throw the following yarn in the hopper and it might come out in the category of an infamous narrative. It does border on the scandalous side. If your memory spans back far enough, you might recall a Hollywood starlet who gained a degree of fame as a movie star by the name of Barbara Payton. Almost all of Barbara's fame came, not from her acting ability, but rather from the many scandals she provoked on the Hollywood scene. A beautiful blond of Nordic heritage, some might say that they coined the term dumb blond in her image.

In the post-WW II era, Barbara's star soared high and bright in Tinsel Town. But alas, it promptly fell into oblivion. The narrative of her rise and fall is very sad, indeed. Before she succumbed to an inevitable ending, she wrote a book entitled, "I Am Not Ashamed." Her candid story tells of her race with fame that led to an infamous drop into total depravation.

I first met and dated Barbara in the fall of 1941. In Odessa, high school football was king and with its popularity came the social event of the year. When the football season ended, the team got a festive, formal banquet, always a gala event for the squad and their dates. Why, some of the guys come out for football just for the opportunity to attend this affair. Many young belles of the town made sure they tied up with a player prior to the night of nights. For the girls, the banquet meant a time to dress formally in stunning evening gowns and all the pretty accessories that enhance innate loveliness. The young men, by tradition, decked out in suits, ties and shined shoes. For many of us, it represented the only time of the year when we dressed up.

The banquet featured great food, interesting speakers and the granting of awards. But the real entertainment took place after all the above formalities ended. Everyone headed for the Ace of Clubs, the honky-tonk of choice for the young set.

Of course, the whole group lacked legal age for such a

224

venture, but in a small, wild town like Odessa, authorities often overlooked or ignored such things. The Ace allowed the young to come in, as most did not imbibe anything except soft drinks and caused little or no trouble. In those days, the clubs couldn't sell anything stronger than beer, but they did serve set-ups which consisted of ice and mixers of choice. Adults brought their own liquor which they kept hidden discreetly under the table. The teenagers ordered the set-ups and danced to their hearts' content. Everyone was happy.

In 1941, as a junior and hot-to-trot, I let a friend, Gypsy Ann, fix me up with a pretty freshman named Barbara Redfield. Now, Barbara turned out a real knock-out in the looks department. I had only vaguely known her at school. So, she invited me to walk her home one afternoon, as her folks wanted to meet me. I found them a fine couple and got the opinion they were very protective of their young daughter. My sister Helen had suggested that I ask my date what color corsage she preferred. I took this meeting as an opportunity to ask this question. Mrs. Redfield suggested a small corsage of white carnations.

We planned to double date with my good buddy Jake Rhoades and his date. When I picked Barbara up, I found her dressed in a strapless pink evening gown and dainty pink shoes. Her blond hair seemed a halo, hovering above her angelic face. With a beautiful natural smile, Barbara's beauty exceeded my imagination. Dang! Her looks and that strapless dress stunned me so that I couldn't get up the nerve to pin on the corsage. Mrs. Redfield saw my dilemma and pinned the thing on Barbara's right waistline. Heck! I had thought that it went on the breast line, thus my reserve in pinning it.

When the banquet ended, just about all the athletes and their dates piled into cars and headed for the Ace on the outskirts of town. Ma Bargasser, the owner/manager of the club, had reserved two long tables. When we sat down, she commanded, "There will be no booze or beer consumed by you youngsters. And don't cause any trouble. If you do, I'll throw you out, ya hear?" We agreed.

We ordered set-ups that included Coke and Seven Up. Big Daddy Pat played the popular tunes of the era and we hit the dance floor jiving. Barbara and I danced up a storm. We did the slow, dreamy ones and jumped to the swing numbers. The jitterbug, popular at the time, involved fast dancing quickly drained your energy. We left the floor, only to rush to the table to gulp down large measures of soda pop. These trips grew more frequent as the night wore on.

Some of the older guys had smuggled in several bottles of vodka and had spiked the drinks. I had never drunk any alcoholic beverages before and, surely, the same went for Barbara. The vodka didn't alter the taste of the soft drinks enough for us to realize that our brains were being marinated in the hard stuff as the night went on. When the band took time off to rest, most of our crowd used the intermission to gather at the rear of the club to cool off. A lot of horseplay among the boys and giggling from the girls took place during the lull. I felt kind of unnecessary, as my head swam dizzily in circles. I laid the feeling to the jitterbugging. That I was stoned never entered my mind.

An evaporative air cooler cooled the club . This system leaked water and the excess formed a large puddle at the back of the building. The pond of water drew attention when someone called me by one of my nicknames.

"Hey, Arch! Bet you can't swim across this lake!"

Never one to let a dare go by and with very little command of myself, I ripped off my coat and did a skidding belly flop into the muddy mass. As I got to my knees, another person hit the puddle with a dull thud. When I rubbed my eyes clear, in shock, I saw Barbara in the mud with me. They took us into our respective restrooms and cleaned us up some, then they put us in Jake's car, there to pass out.

Now, Odessa High School had an outstanding running back named Otis McKelvy. In his junior year, his father transferred to another city. Otis remained in Odessa to work and live at the Rix Funeral Home. He drove their ambulance and lived in a garage apartment behind the place of business. Despite the fact the parking area of the garage held a showroom for caskets, Otis's small apartment served as a hangout for a bunch of the gang.

As I indicated, I passed out and did not awaken until early the next morning. A splitting headache brought me to. Waking up, I found myself on the floor of the coffin showroom. It took me a few minutes to orient my thoughts. Dang! What had happened to Barbara? In the room I found several guys in the same condition as myself. I went into the kitchen area and found more sleeping boys. In the bedroom, I found several girls, but no Barbara. When I checked the bathroom, I found her. She had up-chucked. What a mess! Half awake, she indicated that she had to pee. I helped her to the commode. As she did her thing, I went in search of Jake. When I found him, I shook him awake, a-saying, "Jake, Jake, I need to use your car! I have to get Barbara home right now!" He rolled over and wordlessly dug into a pocket and surrendered his keys. I returned to Barbara and found her back on the floor, asleep. I noted that she had no shoes on. In looking around, I found only one of them. I stuck it in my hip pocket.

Talk about a struggle! It took a lot of effort to get her into the car. As I drove across town, she slept. Although still dark, the gray streaks of dawn started to show in the eastern sky. About this time that the gravity of my situation hit me hard. I knew I headed for some real trouble!

When I came to a stop in front of her home, I jumped out and quickly ran around to the passenger side. In desperation, I implored her to wake up. I finally dragged her out the door and onto her feet to a degree. As I struggled up the sidewalk with her, I looked up to see her parents coming at us. I had thoughts of hitting the panic switch and running for dear life, but my fear kept me rooted there. They started giving me verbal hell the minute they came out the door. Mr. Redfield did help me get her to the porch where a chair awaited Barbara. She sat quietly, but did not go back to sleep.

I stood muted at attention as they fired questions faster than I could answer.

"Are you drunk?"

"I think so."

"You think so! Hell, boy, I know so! We could smell you halfway up the sidewalk!"

"How did you get so filthy? It looks like both of you have been rolling in a pig sty!"

Mrs. Redfield came across as one disturbed lady, and she had every right. I had no defense for my actions in that I did not take better care of her young daughter. She got right in my face asking question after question, but not giving me time to respond.

In time, Mr. Redfield interrupted, "Honey, let the young man answer some of my questions." This quieted his wife. "Well, Fred, we have been really concerned about you youngsters. We have been to the hospital, police station, and the Ace of Clubs, which was already closed. We called many of Barbara's friends and your mother. No one had any idea where you were. Son, we were really worried. Now, you tell me what happened and where you have been all night."

"I'm sorry, Mr. and Mrs. Redfield, that I have caused so much doubt and worry for you. It was all my fault and none of it Barbara's. After the banquet, we went dancing. We drank a lot of soda pop. Someone must have put something in our drinks while we were dancing. I have never had whiskey or anything like that before, so I think we both got a little drunk.

"How did you get so dirty?" they asked.

"We fell in a mud puddle behind the club. So friends took us inside and cleaned us up a little bit. Then they put us in a car and we went to sleep. When I woke up, I was in the casket room with many other guys. I felt real sick and went looking for Barbara. I found her in a bedroom where all the girls were sleeping."

"Casket room, what do you mean, casket room?"

"Sir, Otis McKelvy works and lives at the funeral home. He has an apartment in back of the garage where they keep all the new caskets. This is where many of the others went after the dance."

"That is some tale, but I've got to believe it because nobody could come up with a story like that."

Mrs. Redfield entered the conversation, "Young man, you have been with our daughter all night and she is very young. Did you touch her in any way?"

I thought for a moment, "Yes, I touched her when there was a slow dance and when I was getting her in and outta the car."

Mr. Redfield laughed and said, "I think what my wife wants to know is, did you get in her pants?"

I was taken aback and gulped an answer, "Oh! No, Mrs. Redfield, I never touched her like that! No, ma'am, never!"

Mr. Redfield asked, "Fred, you did say your last name is Harvey, didn't you?"

"Yes, Sir."

"Well, Fred Harvey, you have a lot of nerve and spunk. I doubt that I would have had the guts to bring a half-drunk girl home and to stay and face her irate parents. Hell, I probably would have pulled up long enough to put her out and speed away. In spite of it all, I've got to thank you for being man enough to see that she got home okay. Honey, I think these kids might be hungry. Fred, do you want to have a bite to eat before you go?"

"I certainly would, Sir, but I've got to get Jake's car back to him. I'm sorry that I caused y'all so much trouble and ruined Barbara's dress and made her get sick."

"You are forgiven."

Ya know, they let me date Barbara after all that, but working at two jobs and going to school set parameters on my social life. A real beauty, she attracted and dated others frequently. I remember the incident I had with her like a toothache. However, she has crossed my mind regularly ever since.

Barbara had about her an air of contentment, tranquil charm

and graceful élan. With these God given traits, she possessed visual delights and a vivid imagination. But in time, her airs of contentment, charm, and grace turned into more capricious manners. She went to Hollywood....

Chapter 14

A Day in a Korean Hospital

Bazooka: A portable military weapon consisting of a long, metal, smooth bore tube for firing armor-piercing, explosive rockets at short range.

After coaching for twenty-seven years in Texas and Colorado, I found myself doing my thing in the exotic land of Korea. The US Army hired me to coach and teach at the Taegu American High School. I had worked in country four months when the warmth of spring replaced the chill of winter, a time for spring sports. I announced to the student body the start of the co-ed track season on the following Monday. This call to arms netted a total of twenty-eight aspiring boys and girls who wanted to run, throw, jump, or hurdle.

Problems did exist. Now, the school's equipment for this sport proved in short supply. Point of fact we didn't have any. To add to our problems, the school had no oval track on which to work out. To say the least, my expectations for a premier season hovered in the area of nothingness. However, the kids' enthusiasm generated a measure of hope which bolstered my expectation of a quality coaching experience.

We scrounged around a long forgotten equipment room and found, among other things, a set of starting blocks, high jump standards plus a badly bent cross bar, an antiquated stopwatch, a huge bag of unmatched running shoes (some new, some well–

worn), stacks of nondescript sweat suits, and an array of shorts and tank tops. With all this, we felt ready to make our run for the gold. Undismayed by the lack of an oval track and related equipment, we went into our workouts with an enthusiastic fervor, with the thought that I could simply cancel those events for which we had no facilities. A couple of the boys wanted to run the hurdles. I tried to discourage them, since I had chucked hurdles due to a lack of basic equipment. I relented when we found a couple of repairable, beat-up hurdles in our junk pile. With these rescued barriers and a couple of hand tools, along with nuts and bolts, we put two serviceable hurdles into use.

The next day, after the team had finished their stretching and warm-up drills, I took the two would-be hurdlers over to the dilapidated, old hurdles and proceeded to indoctrinate them in the finer points and skills required of this event. Now, hurdling requires, above all, technique in getting over the barriers and the agility to maintain speed between each pass-over, a difficult skill to master. I walked through each phase and technique of hurdling skills several times.

When I reached a point where they understood what I meant, I said, "Stand back and watch the old coach show you how it's done."

Bad idea, very bad indeed. Now, this dumb old coach made it over that first barrier flawlessly, but as I soared, in full stride over the second one, I felt a sharp pain in the apex of my groin. Now, the agony of this pain felt akin to that of a red-hot poker touching that part of the anatomy where the sun doesn't ever shine, except maybe when mooning.

You will recall that while serving in the Marine Corps, back in '45, the Japs laid some hurt on the ol' coach in the aforementioned dark environs. This injury left a slab of scar tissue between the legs which tended to restrict a full stride. Since this old war memento had very little elasticity, it had simply snapped instead of stretching. All enthusiasm and eagerness went down the chutes with this turn of events. My coaching strategy from that point on consisted of do as I say, not as I do.

Anyway, during the next several days or so the fissured scar tissue secreted, slowly but unabated, a solution of blood and lymph fluid. During this time, I tried all the remedies that I could think of to induce healing in this sick spot, but with negative success. When the draining failed to terminate at the end of two weeks, I reckoned I needed to seek professional help.

I figured I just needed an application of silver nitrate to cauterize the opening or at the most, a couple of stitches to effect closure. So, surrendering my macho veneer, I waddled over to the base clinic. I do mean, waddled. I had the gait of an old duck out of water due to the restrictive nature of my delicate condition. Once in the clinic's waiting room, my keen sense of awareness led me to conclude that I had stumbled onto a convention of about-to-be mothers. Pregnancy abounded in the whole room. Seems I had, indeed, picked the day of the week set aside for prenatal visitations.

I eased my buns delicately into an idle seat next to a young expectant mother. When I had settled in, she leaned over and said with a twinkle in her eye, "How far along are you, Honey?"

"Two weeks," I groaned.

She patted my hand and added a toothy grin to highlight her mischievous eyes and teasingly said, "Two weeks! Why, Honey, you're not even showing. Come back in a month."

I endured a two-hour wait embellished with small talk about imminent birthing, motherhood and the qualities and spirit of being a military wife. I can say this, without reservation: I'm very glad pregnancy is one experience from which I enjoy a lifetime exemption. I did, however, have empathy for those ladies as I gave birth to a kidney stone once. Throwing a stone, they say, approaches, to a degree, the agony and misery of birthing a baby. When I gave genesis to my procreation, a pea-sized stone, I carried on like a real wimp. So, to all mothers, I have a deep propensity for compassion and understanding.

At long last, they called my name just as the last expectant mom tottered out of the doctor's office. As I waddled past her in a manner akin to her gait, she grew incensed and enraged. She verbalized Bastard, thinking most assuredly, that I was mimicking her serious shuffle. I felt pangs of regret. The inept apology that I offered fell on deaf ears. So, I continued on in my own stilted walk.

Now, in peacetime, the military establishment has a very hard time providing enough doctors to man the many stations where our flag flies worldwide. Korea proved no exception. To cope with this shortage, the Department of Defense, out of necessity, engages available host-nation physicians. My doctor happened to be one of these local hires.

On entering the office, the seated doctor, with a garbled mumble, directed me to sit. He didn't bother to look up from his paperwork. The nicotine-stained fingers of his left hand clutched a cigarette that he offered to his lips from time to time in a slow, practiced manner. After each drag, he exhaled, and the ensuing smoke drifted slowly upward where it joined a dirty, amber-hued cloud. This beclouded accumulation hung in the room like a dreaded Los Angeles smog.

After six puffs, by count, he directed his attention to me and asked in halting, pidgin English, "What problem today you have?"

I responded to his query by standing. Pointing toward my crotch, I said, "Doctor, I have a drainage problem down here." I unhitched my belt buckle with the intention of exposing my dilemma.

He flagged me off with a negating gesture of his cigarette, saying in Pidgin English, "Not necessary, I understand problem."

Reluctantly, I hitched my belt buckle, questioning his call with, "Hey, don't you need to examine me?" Where upon his cigarette made an irascible jab in my direction and, with annoyance, he spouted what I took as a malediction in his native tongue. Right now, with blithe indifference, he scribbled on his note pad, ripped the top sheet off and thrust it toward me. He seemed more than a bit troubled to me. Perhaps he had cause since he had just wended his way through a dozen or more expectant mothers with their crush of agony and misery. By comparison, my aggravation and woe appeared lightweight. Understandably, he had little compassion left for what he thought ailed me.

With indignant bewilderment, I tramped out of his office with paper in hand. Down the hall, I presented my prescription to a pharmacist behind a cage-like opening. I fully expected to receive a tube of oily ointment similar to what I had already applied to my sick spot, without cure, for two weeks. He returned shortly and handed me a sizeable bottle of pills. I asked, as I read the directions, "How are these going to heal an oozing lesion?"

He replied with a knowing smirk, "Hey, man, those pills are what we give to everyone who comes down with a case of clap (slang term for gonorrhea). Take 'em and you'll be ready to go again in about a week, but use these next time." At the same time, he tossed me a packet of GI issue condoms. The shit-eating grin that dominated his face turned to one of astonishment when I dropped my britches and ceremoniously dumped half of the antibiotics in my jockey shorts. I hitched up my pants and ambled down the hallway, dropping penicillin capsules with each step I took. From the cage, I distinctly heard the words, "I'll be damned. I ain't never seen the likes of that a-fore." Of course, the story of this incident did not remain secreted in the clinic. My thoughtless act of idiocy went through the base like small-town gossip. By the next day, many in the base community made me the butt of derision and general amusement. For the next few days, the good-natured ribbing from friends and colleagues rattled me, but I did, however, cash in on the incident. In the base clubs, along with the needling, I received several martinis including a double from the pharmacist who laid the pills on me.

Not one to give up readily, I asked around the school the next day for the name of the best civilian hospital in town I could find someone who could speak English. Several people recommended the Presbyterian Hospital. I resolved to go there the next day.

The following afternoon, I found my way downtown to the recommended hospital. Once inside, I located an English-speaking secretary who escorted me to a doctor to whom I could express myself. I met Doctor Kim, a physician educated at New York City University. His rapport impressed me. After taking my temperature and blood pressure, he had me strip. He pondered my plight for just a moment, saying, "You do have a problem, but I think we can fix you up." He then went to a side door and beckoned a nurse to come in. I tried desperately to get my trousers back on.

I failed.

She entered.

I blushed.

She didn't seem embarrassed. She nodded acknowledgement to instructions that Doc Kim relayed to her. She went to the door and with a dainty hand, waved goodbye to me.

I waved back to her, whereupon Doc Kim gave me a lesson in Korean customs, "Mr. Harvey, that gesture in Korea signifies follow me, not good-bye as in America."

Whereupon I complied. I tried, without success, to find out where we were headed, but she either didn't understand or else she ignored me. After walking down several teeming hallways, we arrived at an unmarked door which we entered.

Behind the door lay a small, cold, nondescript room with only a few pieces of medical equipment hanging on one wall. A washbasin with a single water faucet emanating above it occupied the adjacent wall. Also, I noted two doors in this room, the one that we had just entered and another in the opposite wall. The only warmth or cheer that imbued this sterile, drab room came from three females; two with golden-hued skin, significantly pretty, and very young sat with note pads in their laps and wearing uniforms. I figured them for student nurses.

An older woman, short in stature, with a face that played host to a stern aura that said, "I'm in charge," rounded out the threesome. My escort babbled something to the boss nurse, then gave me an impish smile and departed. Little did I suspect that within the next few moments I'd be subjected to a very disagreeable experience.

Now, this veteran nurse had a look in her eyes kindred to that of an African lioness. Her almond-shaped eyes had a steely, vexatious look about them. She eyed me much in the same manner that a boxer eyes his opponent from across a boxing ring. I found this unnerving, to say the least. She had psyched me out. It worked! I felt intimidated. The premonition of a confrontation welled from within me. Although a petite bantam weight, her presence dominated the room. She delivered a sharp command, whereupon a pair of giggles emanated from the pixie-like faces of the girls. Let the circus begin!

In wild anticipation, they jumped up and pushed a chair toward the wall that supported the above-mentioned medical gear. The Boss Lady, with the grace of a ballet dancer, sprang upon the chair and selected a contraption made of a thick, clear plastic that looked like the mother of all bicycle pumps. Man! I'm here to tell you, that piece of ordnance stood nearly as big as her and looked just as ominous.

I wondered out loud and to no one in particular, "What the heck is that thing?"

In a more detailed description, the plastic cylinder was about two inches in diameter and about two feet in length, with a ramrod on one end and a nozzle on the other. She walked over to the faucet, unscrewed the nozzle end and proceeded to fill it with water. At that very moment I realized what that hideous contraption was.

Hell, they planned to lay a purge upon the bowels of the ol' coach. Enema! I abhorred this abomination to the human body. When just a lad, my mom used to visit this repugnancy upon me.

She called this demeaning act a belly-full. She saw it as a panacea for all ailments. I hated it then, and the thought of it repulsed me even more at this point in my life. As this tragi-comedy began to unfold, a gut-wrenching panic permeated my whole body. I wanted no part of this impending assault upon my body.

When the boss finished loading that assault weapon, she did an about-face and, behold, that bicycle pump now looked like a menacing bazooka. Whoa! Reader, do you recall the descriptive paragraph at the onset of this composition? If not, read it once again so that you will get the feel for the full sense of urgency that permeated my very soul at that moment. With that device at port arms, she began to stalk me, like a combat veteran in the heat of battle. With a passionate insistence, I tried to reason with her that I did not need this type of treatment for what ailed me. My plea and whining fell on heedless ears. She had her orders and, like a good soldier, she intended to carry them out. As she continued her advance, a sense of exigency compelled me to back-pedal toward the door. She anticipated this contingent move and beat me to the door. This failed retreat and subsequent maneuver by the Dragon Lady evoked cloned giggles from the Gold Dust Twins.

Having trapped me, she now moved in for the kill. With her bazooka presently cradled in her left arm, she straightaway made a downward motion with her extended right hand. When I did not respond to this gestured command, she pointed to my belt buckle, followed with the same downward motion of the hand. Again, I failed to react. She closed in on me, backing me to the wall. She then jerked at my belt and, at the same time, with a sense of demand, stamped a size-three foot. This sent reverberations off those acoustically barren walls. I saw something in her black, flashing eyes and grimacing jaws that seemed to say, "Yield, or suffer the consequences 'cause I ain't gonna give you no quarter in this clash." I surrendered.

With utter resignation, I tugged at my belt buckle in compliance with the Boss Lady's demanding wishes. Then, to my dismay, the two almost-nurses moved into a flanking position on either side of the Boss, giving them a frontal view. Out of embarrassment, I balked, pointing at the door and then at them, hoping they'd get the message. This only brought more giggles and another stamp of that size-three foot. What the hell! I then did an about-face. I lowered my britches and held them at knee level, knowing that I needed to move expeditiously when my time came. I ceremoniously presented my bare buttocks in a sacrificial mode and awaited the inevitable. Then more chuckles. I blushed. The novice nurses, devoid of embarrassment, displayed not a hint of discomfort at my partial nudity. I learned, in time, that the Korean people lack the modesty inherent in Americans. However, they do have an insatiable curiosity and an innate inquisitiveness, which I don't mean as a criticism.

In this complying stance, I stood ready to bite the proverbial bullet when the old adage what goes up must come down hit me like a thunderbolt. With stark anxiety I realized I had not seen a toilet in the room. Of course, all of this raced through my mind in milliseconds.

Standing erect and showing visible concern, I gasped, "Benjo?"

This they understood. Benjo is the word for toilet in the Korean idiom. The Boss pointed to the other door in the room. Satisfied that a toilet lay beyond. A place in which I could make an urgent deposit, that of the anal ingest. I stood ready.

I bent over and spread my cheeks with both hands. A big mistake! My britches and underwear fell to the deck Where they shackled my ankles. More chuckles from the audience of two. I bit the bullet. Once again, I was ready. Without benefit of lubrication, she then viciously inserted the nozzle into my anal orifice. I flinched, the brief pain was only a harbinger to a shaft of icy cold, cold water that hammered my stomach via the colon. Spasms of excruciating pain engulfed my total entity. If you will, just imagine a long, cold, cold icicle being rammed up your.... You get the gist.

For what seemed an eternity, the frigid pelting continued. My sense of reasoning hit the panic switch. An unheard-voice commanded me to void this malady right now! I grabbed my shackles with frenzied ado, with no thought of buckling or zipping. I tried to stand, to no avail. Severe, excruciating stomach cramps prevented my standing erect. With bent body and left hand clutching my pants, I shuffled, with marked urgency, toward the benjo. The little nurse, sensing my stress, dropped the bazooka, took my hand and led me. With her free hand, she pushed open the door. Lo and behold, it was not a benjo! We had entered a hallway that doubled as an elongated waiting room, filled to capacity with both ambulant and seated folks. This crowd looked at us in reserved amazement and hushed wonder. Talk about embarrassment. Abashment stood as only one concern as my humiliation appeared about to fall victim to the laws of gravity. I felt myself about to lose it. Here we went, down the hall, in procession. The young ladies took the point and moved forward, hub-to-hub, leading interference aggressively. They shouldered and shoved the startled crowd with the gusto of two football players, blocking up-field on a power sweep. They could have made my ball club. This, I appreciated. The Boss Lady followed her blockers with a vise-like grasp on my wrist and manhandled, with a well-placed forearm, any strays that got by the Gold Dust Twins.

The convoy made an abrupt right turn and, to my relief, there loomed a door with markings indicating that a benjo lay beyond. The Twins blasted the door open with all-out effort. Still in tow, they pulled me through the open door. My initial state of elation, thinking myself about to get relief, quickly turned to dismay as I found this room also occupied to capacity. Now, Korean public restrooms accommodate both sexes. Women outnumbered the men folk in this crowded cubical at the time. These arrangements always made me feel uneasy. Heck, I'm an old boy from West Texas where a man could get hung for sharing a public restroom with a lady. Of course, this sharing only added to my anxiety. However, right then, in my dired state, I would have shared with Mrs. Devil herself.

On one side, men stood three to four deep, awaiting their shot at one of six thirsty urinals. On the other wall, a row of doors enclosed stalls where the female gender did their thing. With me still in tow, the Boss Lady preceded me down this row of doors, opening each in search of a vacancy. Talk about some startled and terrified women! Finally, she opened a door on a shocked young man astraddle an oval slit in the floor that served as a repository. Now, I don't know in what stage of disbursement he was in, but in any case, she terminated his use of that hole in the floor. With a yank of his coat sleeve, out the door he came. She then unceremoniously propelled me into this poor guy's spot. With an urgent sense of demand, I assumed the position over the slot and blew my bowels. A wave of surging relief ran through my total being. Hey! You know the feeling. Unfortunately, as I squatted there, savoring the moment, I noticed that all my bombs had not hit their target. Dang, I would have needed a Norden Bomb Sight to get that load of ordnances on that target.

About this time, another troubling concern presented itself. Korea had an acute shortage of paper products. Therefore, many public privies did not furnish toilet tissue. So, it behooves a traveler to carry his own. Of course, I arrived empty-handed and had no intension of leaving until I'd finished the paper work.

Hopefully, I called out, "Mamasan."

The door opened and, with hand simulations and pidgin English, I made her understand what I needed. She had anticipated this and handed me a folded sheet of newsprint. I did the best I could, what with the poor man's Charmin I had to work with. When I stepped out of my sanctuary, all activity came to a standstill. A reserved hush prevailed. All eyes watched this out-of-control and visibly soiled American. In a full blush and total embarrassment, I sheepishly walked out, flanked by my three escorts.

They ushered me into a room where a shower stall awaited me. They handed me handed a towel and signaled with hand gestures to undress and shower. Fortunately, the ladies moved behind a barrier screen so that I might bathe in privacy. In the stall, I found only one tap and knew I had to shower in the same water whence the she loaded the bazooka. It goes without saying, I took a very quick shower. When I exited the shower and dried off, I noticed my clothing had disappeared. I wrapped the towel around my waist, shivered and waited.

One of the girls eventually handed me a flannel gown. Catch this: their hospital gowns open at the back, too. Did we copy this from them? Now, it seems to me that in their twenty-five-hundred-year run, they could have improved on this abomination. America has an excuse. We've had only two hundred and some odd years. Give us two more centuries and we'll, with our ingenuity, improve on this horrible contrivance. Then again, they might have copied it from us. In any case, I extended my arms and stepped into the proffered gown. I clutched the backside and felt promptly stimulated by the warmth it offered.

Soon they escorted me down the same hallway again, with the same eyes looking on. We entered a door into what I took for a medical examining room. The sloe-eyed medics and I waited for several minutes. Doctor Kim entered the room with an entourage of three men in long, white, linen coats, indicating they too served as disciples of Hippocrates. Doctor Kim instructed me to climb upon a table that sported a pair of contraptions that looked like little saddle stirrups. He told me to lie on my back and place a foot in each stirrup. I did as instructed and you can well imagine the posturing that my body assumed. I tried to keep the gown between my legs, but to no avail. The good doctor hoisted the gown to expose the most personal parts of my anatomy.

My attention centered on scowl and her two grins. Looking at Doctor Kim, I pointed and asked, "Do they need to be here?"

He spoke, "Sure, they're a part of our staff. They're used to this sort of thing."

I replied, "But, I'm not."

He laughed and in his idiom said something that brought forth guffaws from the doctors and, of course, giggles from the youngsters. Again, what the hell, for those student nurses my situation just meant a lesson in the human anatomy, the likes of which they'd never get from a textbook. In resignation, I gave them a great, big West Texas smile. In unison, their pert lips parted in wide-mouth gapes and I do believe their golden-hued skin took on a blushingly red tint. They ceased to dismay me.

As one, the four men of medicine drew closer, forming a semicircle at my protracted feet. In the seams, betwixt the gathering docs, there they stood, the pixie-faced neophyte Florence Nightingales. A pictorial countenance of student nurses studying the integral parts of the human male replaced their previous smiles.

After an indeterminate time of musing and deliberation, the doctors huddled about a chalkboard, whereupon one of them sketched an outline of my lower extremities. Each of them had an opinion and expressed it with chalked lines, arrows and slashes. After a period of arm waving and verbalizing, they came to some sort of agreement.

Turning, they regrouped at my feet. As spokesman, Doctor Kim stepped forward and announced, "Tomorrow we operate."

Operate? This got my attention. My feet came out of those stirrups and I sat bolt upright. "Hey, I don't need an operation. All I want or need is a couple of stitches!"

The good doctor then countered with, "Stitches would only cover up the underlying problem. We need to get at the basis of your difficulty and clear it up, once and for all, or else it will be a recurring thing."

I didn't want to appear crass so I merely nodded my head in acceptance. I guess they wrongly figured me for a real dummy.

I needed some time to think. How could I get out of this

gracefully without hurting the feelings of these gentle folks. Losing face is a big thing to Orientals, with nothing more devastating than losing face to a visitor to their country. Also, I didn't want to appear the Ugly American in their eyes, but on the other hand, I did not want them whittling around on this old body either, especially for something no more grievous than this minor annoyance.

Doctor Kim then addressed the Boss Lady, which brought her to a ramrod-like attention. He voiced an extensive set of orders and dismissed her with a detached hand gesture. I fully expected her to give him a hand salute. She then barked an order to the young ladies that sent them off in a scurry. I didn't understand a word any of them said, as it filtered down the chain of command, but I knew enough to know that it revolved around me and my sick spot. I knew, for sure, I couldn't let this operation happen. The Boss Lady then motioned for me to follow her. I did so obediently.

As we journeyed up two flights of stairs and down two darkened hallways, my only thoughts centered on flight. But how? I didn't even have my clothes which held the car keys and my wallet. Our travels, to my consternation, ended at a patient ward. Although still late afternoon, the winter's short day had begun to bathe the ward in a half-light. The sick and their visitors filled the long, narrow chamber chock-full. Visitors far outnumbered the ailing and unwell in gowns. I don't think Korean hospitals have a period set aside for visiting. Seems people visited at all hours, day and night.

The Boss Lady still held my hand in the guise of ushering me to my destination but, in truth, I think this little lady realized that I planned a get-away. So she held on, sensing that I might bolt at any moment. How to exit this mess that I had gotten myself into dominated my thoughts. However, without my clothes, I didn't see anyway of going nowhere right soon-like. Apparently, the ol' coach just had to bide his time for a while.

My escort released her vise-like grip and, trusting me to stay put, entered a room that I presumed a storeroom. She left the door ajar, so I tried to look inside to see if my clothing might hang in there. I saw nothing. When she returned she carried a yo and a block of wood. Now, the block of wood needs no explanation, but the yo does. It serves as a mattress of sorts. It consists of textile woven to a thickness of an inch. Man, seeing this only amplified the need for a panic-inspired breakout.

By custom, Koreans don't sleep on beds, but rather on the floor, utilizing the marginal mattress mentioned above. And believe it or not, a block of wood serves as a pillow. Really. You can't dream dreams at night with your head resting on a block of hard wood. It's no wonder they have not put a man on the moon in their 2500-year history. Man's gotta have a dream. But, they deserve some credit, they did produce *kimchi*.

I had already experienced this technique of self-torture. The pad, I could handle, but the block of wood, no way. I needed a real pillow of sorts. She handed me the pillow but retained the *yo*. With the block of wood in my left hand, she took my right hand with which I had held the slotted gown together. Once again, she led me still deeper into the confines of the ward. Now, if you recall without being held closed, the gown left my buns for all to view and contemplate. So they did, but at this point in time and circumstance, I couldn't have cared less.

Here again, I entered into mixed company, as men, women, and even some kids occupied this ward. My keen sense of observation led me to believe that here too, the numbers not in gowns about equaled the numbers of the sick. Those same powers of observation told me that those folks in street clothes planned to remain overnight. Yes, these visitors intended to spend the night with spouses or their children, whichever case fit. These overnighters had brought bags, parcels, bundles, and, of course, yos. I foresaw a long night since this ward already sounded like a zoo. This really, really kindled my need to break out.

In Korea, as in many countries, the hospitals don't have a

responsibility to feed their patients. So, they have to depend upon their kinfolks or friends to get food to them. They follow the same policy in the country's jails and prisons. When you do the time, you pay to dine. We, in America, ought to adopt this policy. It could possibly serve as a deterrent to our ever-increasing crime problem. But, I'll get off my soapbox now and get on with the problems confronting me at the time.

My nurse moved some yos and bodies around to make room for me. This done, she tossed my mat down and motioned for me to settle in. I dropped the block of wood on the yo and wearily sat with my back against the wall. At that moment, my low spirits could've passed under a snake's belly.

I looked up. There she stood with hands on hips contemplating me. Dang! For the first time this long day, her stern countenance had softened profoundly with just a hint of a smile highlighting her circular face. This smile came from a sensitive woman's heart. Suddenly it seemed to me her demeanor actually stood in harmony with that of her calling. My spirits rose slightly. My lips unconsciously projected a smile. Without words, we had come to an understanding. A smile is a universal, wordless language, understood the world over.

She turned her head and said something, I know not what, to several of the visiting ladies squatting about the area. With a bustle and laughter, they opened and rummaged their pouches and bags. One produced a large bowl which another ladled half-full of rice. To this others added *kimchi*, an assortment of other veggies and bits of marinated meat. They handed this to the still-smiling nurse along with a pair of chopsticks.

She, in turn, bowed and presented it to me and simply said, "*Be-bim-bop.*"

My favorite Korean dish! In fact, *be-bim-bop* was the first phrase I had learned in this exotic land.

I thanked them whole-heartedly in English. They all knew what I felt and meant. The little nurse sat on the end of my yo with her legs crossed and joined with the others watching me eat. They laughed at my obvious lack of skill with the chopsticks. I ate with visible gusto. I had not eaten since breakfast and, added to that of the stomach purge, I found myself ravenous with hunger.

When I finished this succulent dish, I graciously burped loud and clear to show appreciation and place compliments on the donors of this fine meal. Now, don't lay any infamy on me for my lack of decorum or manners in this distasteful act. In Korea, it's perfectly acceptable and a highly complimentary act. Along with belching, Koreans accept both slurping and smacking as acceptable manners and propriety at the dining table. Hey! It's their culture. Who is to say it's wrong? I know that if cooks in the US had accepted such compliments, my mom might not have swatted or spanked me so often. To complete the rite of showing my appreciation, I stood, clutched my slit gown, and bowed to the ladies. To my little nurse, I bowed dramatically with a flair and embellished it with a great big grin. Her smiling face glowed with appreciation.

Soon the Gold Dust Twins returned and proudly presented to me my cleaned and neatly pressed clothes along with my shoes. I thanked them with a smile and a pat on their respective heads. The Boss took my clothes from me and, to my dismay, entered the storeroom and left them there. To my relief, she did not lock the door. She returned to stand between the two girls. They said something to me and all three bowed and then slowly backed away from me. I stepped forward and gave each of them a big hug. Gosh, looking at their beaming faces, you'd have thought they had just discovered teeth. They departed. I watched them as they walked the length of the long ward. At the door they stopped, turned, and curtsied. It made me sad, considering how I'd first viewed them.

I sat down on my *yo* to ponder my next move. It grew dark in the ward. The lights came on and seemed like a signal for the visitors to open their bags and bundles in preparation for dining. I was glad because it diverted attention from me. However, several people offered me more food. I declined. My stomach felt as full as a tick at a boy scout camp. As I prepared to go into the storeroom and dress in my street wear, the English-speaking nurse came in.

We swapped pleasantries, then she explained what they had planned for me for the next day. I nodded agreement, but paid no attention to what she said. My thoughts stayed on that door, all the while hoping that no one came to lock it up. When she left, I sat down to wait. After a while, two new nurses came in and began to work their way toward me. When they arrived at my *yo*, they tried to tell me something, but gave up when they realized I could not understand them. One of the ladies read from her notebook. She then took two pills from her kit and indicated by sign language that I had to take them by mouth at bedtime. They moved on.

I walked the length of the ward, and turned at the exit door to slowly pace back. As I ambled, I kept my eyes on the two nurses, who by now worked the far end of the ward. When I got to the storeroom, I opened the door and slid inside. Darn! Not a speck of light inside, so I lost time trying to find a light switch. After finding it, I located my clothes easily on a shelf near the door. I put on my britches first, took off the gown and switched off the lights. I finished dressing nervously, but quickly.

When dressed, I eased the door open a couple of inches and peeked out. To my relief, the two nurses continued about their duties, oblivious to my actions. I opened the door quickly and stepped through and made my way toward the exit, not looking right or left and assuredly not behind me. I made it to the door without incident, as I heard nothing. I found the main hallway dimly lit, which cut down on the possibility of anyone recognizing me. Initially, I got lost in the maze of hallways, but after a time I found an outside door which I exited.

I found my auto and drove to the gate and noticed many employees heading toward the same gate. Heck! Quitting time.

Fortunately, no one recognized me. I got to the gate and the guards waved me through.

Like a thief, I had slipped away into the night. I felt badly about the whole incident, especially the way I faded out. But, I had no plans of letting them talk me into getting on that operating table.

Dog tired after this long, eventful day, despite the fairly early hour when I arrived at my quarters on base, I undressed and promptly drifted into a deep sleep. I dreamed of the Dragon Lady and the Gold Dust Twins. Surprisingly, a pleasant dream, not a nightmare

In the end, I had to take a year's leave and returned Stateside to resolve my problem. I checked into the VA hospital in San Antonio where I underwent several operations and skin graphs. Subsequently, I had no more problems in that area, thanks to the VA hospital. My memories of my day in a Korean hospital linger.

Chapter 15

Life with Sou Nee

After roughly two weeks in Korea, I discovered the Officer's Club on base featured a nightly poker game. Some nights two tables hosted the action, but at least one held a game every night. This arena of gaming captured my fancy and imagination right off. This gaming table in the round usually attracted several helicopter pilots and two to three Korean gamblers each evening. The military had policy of inviting a number of host country citizens to join the clubs as a public relations endeavor. These invitees tended, more often than not, to have substantial wealth. In addition to the club privileges, they received access to the base golf links and similar morale and welfare venues.

Now, I grew up on poker. Heck! I learned to play stud poker before I got on to my ABCs. This experience paid off for me right quick. Within a week's time, I got on to the Koreans' strategy, which was basically no strategy at all. I also found it difficult to bluff or buy a pot from them because of their view of the whole thing.

To them, with their bucks, these games constituted penny ante stuff. For my meager bankroll, I saw it as high stakes poker. Money had little or no meaning to them, with their losses mere pocket change to them. They played only for winning's sake. They simply wanted to beat Americans at their own game.

This ol' American boy played out of greed. I wanted their

money for money's sake. I built my game plan on finesse. I found that the Koreans never gave up on a dealt hand, good or bad. They kept throwing money in until all the cards hit the table. We played mostly seven-card stud. If I didn't have favorable prospects after three cards, I simply threw in my hand. As a snot-nosed kid, I had learned when to hold and when to fold. 'Til the dealer dealt the next hand, I merely twiddled my thumbs to pass the time. When I had a sure winning hand, I threw money in the pot to the limit. With this strategy, I took home, on the average, fifty to seventy-five bucks every night. With these numbers, I came close to equaling my coaching pay.

After a while, I found something more interesting to occupy thought and mind than thumb twiddling. A wispy maiden of innate Oriental beauty captured my attentive curiosity. My! She made the Dragon Lady of the old Terry and Pirates comic pages look frumpy in comparison. As a cocktail waitress, she moved like a butterfly on the wing, flitting about the room laying down drinks to one and all. She went by the name of Sou Nee. Her movements constituted a study in sensual motion. Her decorative qualities and her graceful attributes blended without contradiction. Many pairs of yearning eyes and hungering hearts followed her every move. Many lonely soldiers who followed the flag to this Oriental post tried to date her; none scored. She rejected all bids with a smile and a motherly touch to the shoulder. Some might have mistaken her innate charm for seductive flirting, but they missed the mark. She loved people and her work. At times, however, young bucks, out of frustration, resorted to overt acts to attract her attention.

One such incident occurred when a young man patted her fanny. Her jet black eyes flashed with rage. Out of this fury, she dashed his drink fully into his face. This cooled his impulsive yearning right quick. A stunned silence engulfed the whole room. The laughter of his amused buddies quickly broke the hush. She glared at the laughing heads, then wiped the man's embarrassed face. Out of this gracious act, his abashment ebbed quickly away.

A week or so later I inadvertently became involved in one such encounter. This event defined, altered and shaped my life.

It started as a typical night at the club. The perennial poker game was in full swing. The usual bunch hovered at the bar, nursing their favorite beverages. Those who came seeking (and found) the best pizza in all of Korea filled all the dining tables. Of course, the pizza proved best when washed down with scads of beer. At the dining table adjacent to the poker game sat five young pilots, gorging themselves on pizza like they'd just discovered teeth. Gallons of beer escorted the pizza to their bellies. The beer's alcohol content soon marinated their young brains. This pickling process turned the gathering into a festive occasion. The party turned into an orgy of drunken revelry, a normal payday event. Soon, laughter, song and shouts of "Sou Neeeee, Sou Neeeee" highlighted the merriment.

Sou Nee stood up to the call. At a half-run gait, she moved about the room with a restless air. With abundant energy, she cavorted among the tables and customers with the grace of a ballerina intensified with the zest of a fiery flamenco dancer. Her movements carried the essence of grace and vitality.

My poker game reached high gear, impervious to the din and clamor of the gaiety nearby. I gave all my attention to an ongoing hand when a sudden silence engulfed the assemblage. I looked up to see that a burly pilot, known as Big Mike, seemingly out of frustration, had pinned Sou Nee's arm to a table. A veil of silence engulfed the room, broken only by the soft whimpering of the young lady in obvious pain. No one moved as the scene played out. Next to me stood an empty, heavily upholstered captain's chair. On impulse, I put my foot to it and thrust it with all my might. Like a missile, it barreled a short distance to bang forcibly into big Mike's chair. This got his attention.

Harshly, I said, "Turn her loose, Mike!"

Now, this really got consideration. He snorted maledictions, but released the young lady. He put both hands to the table and pushed himself to a standing position. In doing so, he knocked over his chair. He turned and kicked the other chair out of his way. Then, like an omen, he lumbered toward me. I chose to remain seated. He loomed over me with clenched fists. In a rage, he came out with, "Stand up. Let's take this outside!"

Knowing myself no match for him, I opted to use diplomacy. Clearly, one of my better decisions. Without moving, I looked up at him and calmly said, "Mike, you have put yourself in a no-win situation. If I go outside and you batter me around, all you have done is beat up on a little old man. (pause) Then, on the other hand, I just might whip your drunken ass. Now think about that."

He thought for a couple of seconds and evidently saw logic in my lecture. He sort of sagged, mumbled something 'bout my ancestry, turned and kicked that hapless chair once again and strode out of the door. Much to my relief.

I heard "Way to go, Coach," from several places. Cold Dr. Peppers appeared along with lots of pats on my back. I collected all this unsolicited adulation with embarrassment. One of the ladies had taken Sou Nee outside and possibly home, as I did not see her again that night. Quite an unnerving event for both of us, to say the least.

The next night the usual crowd showed up at the club. As I bent over my poker chips, studying a so-so hand, the bell over the bar rang out. I turned to see Big Mike ringing for attention.

When the peal got everyone's ear, he declared, "I'm buying drinks for the house!" This brought forth cheers. He then signaled for quiet. And added, "Also, I'm here to apologize before Miss Sou and Coach for making an ass of myself last night."

I arose, threw in my hand and went to the bar to accept his sincere apology. He then walked over to Sou Nee and handed her a package. She opened it to find a beautiful bracelet. She graciously rewarded him with a hug. All was forgiven and good cheer reigned.

For a couple of nights after the incident, Sou Nee seemed to avoid the poker table, letting the other waitress handle it. Although at times our eyes met, she always turned quickly to avert steady eye contact. I didn't see even a hint of a smile about her lips. The lack of a grin on her face led me to think my interfering in her strife with Mike might have upset her somehow.

Several nights later, I entered the club to take dinner and the gaming table. As I ate, Mr. Che pointed to a vacant chair indicating he's saved it for me. I nodded. After sipping down a glass of Chardonnay, I sauntered over and bought into the game. I had played for a time when I realized I hadn't seen Sou Nee about. I figured it must be her night off.

I had played for about an hour when Mr. Che reached over and took a stack of my chips and counted them. When he took a second stack I asked in wonder, "What are you doing?"

Wordlessly, he continued to count. When finished, he moved the stacks to his pile leaving me agape. Still in silence, he handed me the equivalent in cash. He then pointed in the direction behind me. I turned. There she stood, just as beautiful as flowers.

She beckoned me to follow. I followed. At the door, she took my hand and led me into the blue veil of night. Quiet prevailed as she led me to the grassy quadrangle between the BOQ buildings. We walked in the balmy autumn evening with a three-quarter moon glowing softly above. She released my hand, kicked off her shoes and settled into the moist grass. She beckoned me to join her. I contentedly let her show play out. In the moon glow, her beautiful face had an aura of dreaminess about it.

She spoke in Pidgin English, "Fred Harvey, (I was surprised she knew my name) you have not girlfriend. I be your friend."

As I looked into her almond-eyed face, I saw something real, something certain. Her words shocked me. In giving serious thought to her offer and talking slowly, so she could understand my every word, I asked, "Sou Nee, how old are you?"

"I be two-three years."

"You mean twenty-three?"

"Yes, me two-three. You maybe four-two, I think."

"Miss Yi …."

"Fred Harvey, you call me Sou Nee maybe."

"Okay, Sou Nee, I'm fifty–five. Five, five. Two times your age."

"Really?" She moved closer to study my face in the moonlight and in candor said, "No matter, Fred Harvey."

"You realize I'm probably older than your father."

"No problem. He dead many years. I be your girlfriend only."

"Maybe I do not need a girlfriend."

"Mer'can man like girlfriend, I think."

Even in Pidgin English, she proved an engaging conversationalist. I dropped the reins and let her run with the dialogue. As she spoke tenderly, quiet engulfed me. I listened. The resonant qualities of her voice flowed like a melody out of the moonlit night. Her eyes, shimmering with faint tears, mirrored distant lights, giving them a starry, heavenly aura. She at times touched my cheeks or lips tenderly with her velvety fingers. Each contact sent responsive thrills though my every nerve. Far from immune to her charm and loveliness, Sou Nee's earnestness moved me deeply.

A void had developed in my life and like a wind-driven tumbleweed, I drifted along. This made me vulnerable. Normally, I tended to stay apart, but at that moment, I opened my heart. She stepped in to fill the emptiness. This comely young lady of the Orient expelled the loneliness within me. No way I wanted her to come into my life only to pass into its shadows like so many others. We came to an understanding on that meaningful Indian summer night.

This initial meeting ended all to quickly, as the nightly midnight curfew called on us to end our fulfilling moments. South Korea observed a nightly curfew from midnight to six a.m. I drove her home that night, which soon turned into a nightly thing. At the gate of her home, I had to bid a hasty goodnight, since I had to get back to base before the bewitching hour of 12 a.m.

She did take time to ask me a parting question, "Fred Harvey, you really, really my boyfriend, yes?"

"Yes...." I sought her lips. She proffered a cheek. With this, she hopped out of the car and skipped blissfully toward her home. At the gate, she turned to wave and then to disappear into the darkness of the night. Since that night of so long ago, memories or thoughts of her have stayed forever with me.

Out of the rendezvous on that magical night there developed a torrid romance. We lived together in a trial marriage of sorts. A bittersweet union in truth and reality. Being a realist, I could see the distinct possibility of heartaches coming from this relationship. Did she see in me the father she lost at seven years of age? Her big concern appeared to involve the cultural abyss that lay between us. My only doubt lay in the age thing, she could've been my daughter. As for our respective cultures, she gave and I gave which melded into a one-ness. In the beginning her family posed a problem with her status as the youngest member of a very proud family. That she lived with a man, an American at that, did not sit well with her family.

We had not lived together for very long when, in the deep of night, the soft fall of tears on my neck awoke me. When the veil of sleep cleared from my eyes, I found her head resting on my chest. The full moon's glow streamed through an open window. Tears in her ebony dark eyes glistened in the moonbeams.

"What's wrong, Honey?"

After a pause in Pidgin English, she said, "Fred Harvey, we make baby."

"Sou Nee, remember in the beginning, I told you that I could not make babies."

"But you make love okay."

"I know but I can't make enough sperm because I lost one testicle in the big war."

"What is sperm?"

"Sperm are little animals that live in love juice. When sperm meets up with your egg, they join up and the egg is fertilized. Do you understand?"

"Yes, I understand. I know. But you make two babies before."

"No, I did not make babies. My wife and I adopted a boy and girl when they were very young. Would you like to adopt a baby?" She ended the conversation, turned over and softly sobbed. I put my arms around her and held her wordlessly until she fell into a troubled sleep. We talked about adoption many times. She opted only for a full-blooded Korean, but it seemed none needed adoption. Had she chosen to take an Amerasian, (a baby of American/Asian birth) we could have readily adopted a baby with these bloodlines. After a year or so, the subject of adoption drifted into oblivion. But I knew she always had a need and longing for children in her life. I was truly sorry. This caused some of the bitterness that lingered throughout our marriage.

Soon after Sou moved in with me, we found that our respective jobs curtailed the amount of time that we spent together. She worked at night and I, of course, taught and coached during the day. To alleviate this conflict, she opted to return to the company where she previously worked as an office manager. Her old boss, president of a textile company, happily welcomed her back. This worked out very well. She and I both worked at the same time, then on the weekends, we shared in the fun and games.

I found Sou Nee a wonderful companion. One of our favorite pastimes involved traveling the back roads of her small nation. She loved her country, its culture and heritage. On these trips, she invariably turned to songs sung in her native tongue to express her feelings. The lyrics I did not understand, but the melody, her eyes and lips portrayed her mood. Her songs of heart unveiled life's sadnesses, passions, desires, and loves. I congratulated myself each day that this living, vivid person had come into my life.

During this period of time, the country of South Korea fell under the leadership of Park Chung Hee. Park ruled as a repressive dictator and resentment grew to the point where people openly demonstrated against him and his government. The spirit of rebellion and revolt emanated from among the colleges and universities of the country. Some thought communist-leaning professors in these schools fueled some, if not all, of this chaos. On one eventful day, one of these chaotic demonstrations engulfed me quite suddenly and unnervingly.

Each day, I drove across town to fetch Sou Nee when she finished work. Taegu is a large metropolis with many broad avenues and boulevards that traverse its limits. I usually drove one of these routes, which took me past two universities. One day as I entered an intersection near one of these institutions, I ran into a tidal wave of college-aged youths. As they ran, some stopped to throw rocks back in the direction from whence they came. Of course, this halted my forward movement. Stuck, I couldn't move my car in any direction. Then, all of a sudden, a wave of riot police in full battle gear waded into the mass. They wielded clubs, pushing, shoving and really laying some hurt on those kids. En masse, the kids surged in, backed off, and then again surged into their outnumbered protagonists. The police dropped back and whipped out and donned gas masks. With their masks secured, a whistle sounded, bringing a downpour of tear-gas grenades. Closed windows offered but little protection against the noxious gas. Gasping for breath and with tears flooding my eyes, I got out of the car, only to stumble blindly to my knees. Hands grabbed each arm and pulled me to my feet. Two unseen benefactors led me down a side street out of harm's way. They stopped at a gate and punched a button that alerted someone beyond the wall. They shouted something in Korean. A buzzer sounded, signaling the opening of the gate. A little lady dashed out of the house with towels and led us to the well beside the house. She pumped water on the towels and handed one to each of us. Man, did that wet piece of cloth feel good when applied to my burning eyes. When my eyes cleared, I found that my rescuers were a young man and a girl. They had used wet handkerchiefs to cover their faces, which had given them a semblance of protection from the gas.

The lady of the house invited us to go inside with her. She served each of us a cup of barley tea which eased the sting in our throats somewhat. The young man introduced himself as Mr. Kim and his girlfriend Yong Lee. Mr. Kim spoke almost flawless English. When we finished our tea, he said, "We had better get back to your car or the police might take it away." I had forgotten all about the car. I expressed my anxiety to get back to it, expecting damages. We thanked the lady of the house exuberantly.

We then moved quickly back to the car. The melee of the streets still sounded in the distance. When we got to the intersection where the car sat, the place looked like a war zone. Debris cluttered the pavement. Litter and the gaseous haze that hung over the intersection emphasized the havoc that had taken place a short time ago. At least a dozen bloodied youngsters lay on the pavement, receiving aid from medics and nurses. Other students with lesser injuries offered comfort and aid to their less-fortunate friends. When I got to my car, the driver-side door sat open with the engine idling. In my haste, I had failed to turn the motor off.

A policeman came over to command us to leave the area. I insisted that Kim and his girlfriend leave with me. They complied readily. As we moved across town, Kim answered my many questions about the events that had just transpired in the streets of Taegu. At Sou Nee's office building, we found her waiting at the curb. When we pulled up, Kim relinquished the front seat and moved in beside his girlfriend. Sou Nee climbed in next to me with a quizzical look on her face. Before she could say anything, I introduced them. I then deferred to Kim to tell her in his vernacular the events that had befallen us. Sou listened intently and asked many questions as I threaded my way through the traffic. During the conversation, she turned to me, asking, "May I invite them to have dinner at the Officers Club, okay?"

I replied, "Sure, I wanted to treat them for saving me today." They accepted, so we went directly to the club. Steaks were the order of the day.

During the course of the evening, I engaged Kim in lots of questions as to what the students hoped to bring about through rioting. In essence, I found that the people of Korea wanted a form of government fashioned along the lines that we enjoy in America. "What about reunification with Communist North Korea?" I asked at one point.

He replied, "That is our dream, but not a Communist government."

"Do you think the leaders up north or your own Park Chung Hee would ever consent to a democratic form of government?"

"I do not know."

"Do you think the Communists might be behind these demonstrations that you and others are putting on?"

The question visibly shook him. His answered "yes," with only a hint of a smile. In further questioning, I found that he and his cohorts planned to do their thing again the following day. He filled in the details as to time and place.

The next day I returned and parked on a side street several blocks from the college. I walked to the campus with my loaded camera slung over my shoulder. Once on the campus, I noticed the soccer playing field occupied by several hundred students divided into groups of about one hundred persons in each cluster. In each of these groups a leader lectured and demonstrated the tactics they wanted exercised that day. Older and more mature than most of the students, the leaders looked like professors or maybe outsiders. I walked among the groups, freely taking snapshots. My presence, however, did not go unnoticed, as I received cheers and thumbs-up gestures from the different groups.

After a time, all the groups formed up in ranks about thirty deep at one end of the playing field. They then marched en masse out the campus gate and halted near the street. Runners then went into the wide boulevard to stop the heavy flow of traffic. This brought on a blare of sounding horns and screeching tires. Despite the shouts and curses from hundreds of teed-off motorists, the runners stood their ground. When all traffic had stopped, a shouted command moved the mass of humanity into the void between the runners. In the roadway, the student body extended from curb to curb and about fifty yards wide. On command, the whole group then sat quietly down. Nothing moved. A hush fell among the blaring horns and shouts of the blockaded motorists. The students had put a peaceful demonstration into play. Unfortunately, things changed quickly.

I looked up the avenue to see ominous brown-clad riot police in full battle gear. I figured standing behind those troops would be the prudent spot from which to watch the action. So I took off down a side street and came up behind the law. With camera tethered to my wrist, I set about taking snapshots of the impending action. I had just reloaded my camera when, all of sudden, a hand reached and yanked the camera out of my hands. It didn't go far, since I had it secured to my wrist.

It felt as if my arm might come off. I jerked it out of his hand. The man reacted with a drawn pistol. He shouted, jumped up and down and slobbered at the mouth. In other words, one enraged, hotheaded, little man stood before me. I couldn't understand a word he yelled, but the pistol let me know he wanted my camera. I surrendered it readily. His jumping continued but on my Pentax. He laid some real waste to it. At that very moment, all hell broke loose with startling suddenness. A shrill police whistle sounded, announcing the onset of chaos. The whistle detonated a thousand voices, shouting slogans and battle cries, accentuated by the blazon sounds of tear-gas grenades launching. These noxious missiles fell amidst the hapless students. They countered with rocks and bottles. The brown-clad troops, protected with shields and gas masks, moved through the mob and beat the tar out of those kids with their billy clubs. This clamor and subsequent pandemonium served me well, as it distracted my adversary just long enough for me to fade outta there. I followed the action as it played out from an adjacent street that ran parallel to the avenue of engagement. This all-inclusive scene repeated the hectic events that had taken place the day before.

Sou Nee and I met up with Kim and Yong Lee at a prearranged café that evening. As we dined, Kim and Yong Lee talked excitedly about their activities on the streets of Taegu that afternoon. Sou Nee joined in with many questions. The three talked rabidly in their native tongue, so I sat as a spectator. As the evening played out, Sou Nee seemed more and more caught up in the game. The excitement generated by our new found friends galvanized her. She asked questions and the answers she received only led to more questions. I sensed that she wanted to join in the action and that concerned me.

As we motored home, she queried me on the possibility of our joining the students' drive for a new government. I answered, "Sou Nee, as a visitor to this country, there is no way that I can become a part of a revolt against its government."

She lingered on this for a few minutes and asked, "Is it all right if I help them?"

"Sou Nee, you don't have the time to work with them."

"I could help them on some nights after work."

"You know this movement can become very dangerous. The police can start using bullets instead of tear gas and clubs. This is not kids' games that Kim and Yong Lee are into. And it could lead to some jail time."

"I do not think the police will do that."

"The government and their police mean business. You should have seen the way they beat up on those students yesterday and today. They could have easily killed some of them."

"Is it okay if I go to some of their meetings, but not fight the police?"

"Sou Nee, I can't prevent you from going to those meetings,

but I strongly advise you not to get involved."

The next day I received a call to go the principal's office where I met two police officials. Without hesitation or preamble, one of them said, "Mr. Harvey, you were seen and were seemingly involved at a student demonstration yesterday. If you attend another one you will be deported from the country. Do you understand this?"

"Yes, sir, I understand."

They abruptly left the office.

The principal asked me about all that had happened. I gave him all the facts. He listened intently. When I finished, he said, "Fred, these people mean business. If you get caught again, you stand alone. Neither the school nor I can become a part of any of this. Keep your nose clean. I don't want to lose you."

"I understand and I will not attend any more of the demonstrations. Thanks for going to bat for me today."

I saw Kim and Yong Lee from time to time, but Sou Nee met with them once or twice a week. I did not ask questions. I let her know my position on the matter, which she understood. In a stern warning, I pointed out that she and her friends could get into big, big trouble over their involvement in this unrest. She promised to exercise great care. My concerns and doubts persisted.

Several weeks had passed when one day I picked her up after work and she announced that she had resigned her position with the textile firm. "Do you know what you're doing, Sou Nee?" I asked.

"Yes," she replied, "I like to help students make country better."

"But I have told you many times that this is serious business. I beg you not to get involved in this mess."

"It's something I must do, Fred Harvey. Okay, Fred Harvey?"

"But I love you...."

I quickly saw the futility of going further with my plea. I had learned she was a very headstrong young lady and I could say nothing to change her resolve. "I wish I could help you, but you understand, I can't."

"I understand, Fred Harvey. I will live with my brother. When I get my things from apartment, will you drive me to brother's home?'

"Sure, but you might get brother in big trouble."

"No problem."

I continued to the apartment in silence. As she packed, I felt a deep sense of finality and loss.

As I drove her across town, I talked in a stammering voice. "Sou Nee, you will come back to me when this is all over. If you ever need me, I will come to you. Money is always here when you need it. You be very careful and use your head at all times."

"Thank you, Fred Harvey."

When we arrived at her brother's home, she hesitated, then turned to throw her arms about me. A streetlight showed that her eyes and face glistened with melancholy tears. A kiss savored those droplets of sadness. She grabbed her bag and raced through the gate.

I could not leave, but instead put my head to the steering wheel to say a prayer for her. In an utter state of tear-jerking aloneness, I realized how deeply I loved this young Oriental lady. The void she left pierced my heart. I remained there for an indeterminate length of time. Out of the darkness, she opened the car door and slipped in beside me. "Fred Harvey, be not sad. I will come back to you. Now you go home and be happy for me." She then embraced me hungrily and kissed me passionately. She then slipped into the night once again.

I cranked the engine, loneliness moved into the seat beside me, to return to a home filled with emptiness. The sunshine had gone out of my life.

In May of that eventful year of 1980, she phoned me, "Fred Harvey, this is Sou Nee. I'm at Apsin Park. Will you come here?"

"Yes, I will drive up there right now." Elated, I drove to the park. When I arrived at the park, I found her at the gate along with Kim and Yong Lee. My elation ebbed quickly and disappointment set in at seeing her friends with her. They each carried a backpack. I parked at the curb and opened the trunk. They tossed their packs in. We all piled into the car. She laid a quick kiss on my cheek that led to a request, "Fred Harvey, can you drive us to Kwangju?"

"Kwangju! Are you kidding?"

"No, not kidding."

"Do you know that Kwangju is over one hundred kilometers from Taegu?"

"No problem for you, Fred Harvey."

"Why do y'all need to go to Kwangju?"

"Business."

Looking at Kim, "Is this demonstration business?"

He replied, "Maybe so, but no problem for you. We leave you before we get to Kwangju."

"What t'a heck, show me the way!" Now they had me caught up in the intrigue. I needed the excitement. I knew both the area and the city we headed to stood as a hotbed of discontent with the dictatorial leadership and martial law that gripped the country.

We drove south for a time, then turned in a westerly direction. Everyone seemed in a festive mood as they feasted on cuttlefish washed down with sips of beer. Since I drove, I opted for Coke with my cuttlefish.

In time, we headed into a setting sun as it dropped to a waiting horizon. Like the setting sun, the frivolous demeanor of my passengers began to fade. Sou Nee unbuckled her seat belt to move closer to me. I felt a shiver pass through her body. This prompted a whisper from me, "Why not go back to Taegu with me?" She did not answer, but snuggled even closer to me. My concern grew. What did these young folks have planned?

The road we traveled, actually more of a lane than a road, tunneled its way through a tree-lined right-of-way. Beyond the trees lay rice paddies and occasional farm homes. We saw no other cars. As we began to climb a short incline, Mr. Kim tapped me on the shoulder and hoarsely said, "Stop here, please." I complied, stopping in the middle of the road, since I saw no place to pull off. Everyone got out and I led the way to the trunk of the vehicle. They each grabbed a backpack. In total silence, I adjusted the pack on Sou Nee's back. Mr. Kim thanked me and took Yong Lee's hand and headed slowly up the rise.

I then drew Sou Nee to me and kissed her hungrily. We both shed bitter tears.

My parting words were, "If you need me, just call and I'll come."

She ventured a hint of a smile, turned and trod slowly up the slope. I watched and waited, silently begging her to return to me, but to no avail. With each step, a part of me went out to her. By the time she reached the ridge of the low hill, the sun had dropped partly behind the yearning horizon. At the crest, the sun's last rays silhouetted her. The silhouette turned to face me. For a long moment, she stood unmoving, then waved and turned to drop below the scalloped fringe of a dusky sky.

I lingered for a long spell. The wait lasted 'til the gray skies turned to darkness. The stay was not rewarded. In total sadness and utter aloneness, I drove to the top of that hill and looked down on Kwangju, a city of glimmering lights that now embraced Sou Nee and my longings. I then drove, with a heavy heart, back to Taegu. I arrived at my apartment just before the 12 o'clock curfew set in. I went to bed, but sleep did not come. The night seemed endless.

The following days ran long and the nights empty, with loneliness my constant companion. Seclusion and its helpmate, despair, took hold of my heart to make it sting as if touched with a red, hot poker. At night, I found myself walking the peopled avenues. I looked into the face of each passerby, hoping to find her. When the night called upon the folks of Taegu to sleep, I walked their streets of silence in hopes of hearing her call my name. Each night, the curfew compelled me to return to an empty apartment where I found no peace for a tormented heart.

One Saturday morning, about two weeks after I had dropped the threesome off at Kwangju, I went for a drive. My route took me along Taegu's Naktong River. Along the river's flood plain, the poor had built shanties. In some areas, several of these shanties connected to one another to form one long structure. Built of scrap lumber, rusting tin and tarpaper, these makeshift abodes were primitive and desolate, but they were homes. As I passed over a bridge that spanned the Naktong, I looked down to see one of the elongated, multi-family shacks afire. The door of the end shanty spewed forth flames and smoke. And what looked like an elderly woman kneeled down, waggling her arms wildly. I gunned the engine to get me off the bridge as quickly as possible. I parked on the side of the embankment and raced down to check on the now prostrate woman. She wasn't hurt, but I couldn't get into her room to save any of her belongings,, so I ran to the second compartment to alert anyone who might be inside. I found the door open and a woman quietly sitting inside, showing no concern for her already-smoking wall. I pulled the bewildered woman to her feet and shoved her out the door. I then began to grab anything I could get my hands on and threw it out the door. The woman stood agape, not making any effort to help.

When the fire broke through the smoking wall, I moved to the next unit. I opened the closed door and yelled "fire" loudly. A man inside did not understand fire as he, too, did not make a move to save or help himself. I began to shuck housewares out the door. I realized that I couldn't keep ahead of the flames at this rate, so I raced ahead and banged on the side walls and doors of the six remaining abodes. By this time, there a big crowd formed, just watching. I motioned and pleaded for help. Ya know, not one person stepped forth. I went into undamaged rooms and began to haul stuff to the outside. Even then, some owners resisted, only to regret it when the flames consumed everything. Still no help from the crowd which now numbered in the hundreds.

At one point, I struggled to pull a large, heavy trunk through an open door. It was a tight fit. As I heaved and pulled, someone pushed me in the back and urgently said in a familiar voice, "You push, I pull!" I vaulted over the trunk and pivoted. There she was.

Together we got that trunk out that door. I paused to say something, but she pushed and followed me back into the hovel. We worked hard, however, she paused several times to berate the still-gathering crowd. I knew she shouted maledictions in Korean. Her pleas did not move one person to step forth to help. While we worked, I asked her, "Why does the crowd not help these poor people who are losing everything they own? In America everybody would have jumped in to help."

"In my country it is not Korean custom to help."

"But you helped. Why?"

"Because you needed me."

During all this, I heard the sirens of several fire trucks. Not one of them got close enough to put one drop of water on the fire. Why? Because that damned crowd refused to move to let the trucks in or the firemen to move through them with their hoses.

When it ended, the crowd drifted away. A pall of smoke hung over the smoldering ashes. The bewildered losers gathered their few belongings. Sou Nee went over to them and they closed ranks about her. She spoke to them and when she finished they hugged and kissed her. The women touched me and the men shook my hand. Dog-tired and dirty, we climbed the embankment to the car. I tried to open a conversation. She slid close to me and offered her lips for a kiss. She said, "Not talk now, later." My heart swelled with joy to have her back.

When we got to the apartment, she got out and said, "Fred, you go to commissary and buy much all kinds of food. And cash check for maybe one hundred dollars. Come back in hurry."

Without question, I drove over to the base commissary and accomplished all that she requested. When I got back to the apartment, she waited for me amid a pile of clothing and an assortment of kitchen gear. Back at the disaster scene, twelve people waited for us. She distributed the food, clothing, and money which she had changed into Won (local currency). We hung around for a while. When we got into the car, she laid her head on my shoulder and promptly drifted into blissful sleep. I had noticed before she closed her eyes a dark, hollow sadness about them. Her lips did not have the perennial hint of a smile that normally dominated her copper-toned face.

At home, I drew a warm bath and she lay in its warmth only to succumb to sleep once again. She remained there 'til the cold water wakened her. I then bathed. In the bedroom, I found her asleep. I quietly moved into the bed and lay beside her. Without waking, she put her arm over me and snuggled closer. She slept around the clock. She never offered a single word as to what had happened in Kwangju. I never asked. The secrets of her adventure and what happened there remains locked in her storehouse of memories.

Three days after her return, the news came out of Kwangju that the Korean Army had massacred over two hundred citizens during a riot. Out of this heinous action, dictatorial rule soon came to an end in South Korea.

During her absence, I had looked deeply within myself to find how much I loved and needed her. She was not just another woman who had come into my life only to pass into the dark recesses of my heart. Without any control over my heart, I asked her to marry me. She accepted, but with reservations. She worried a great deal about my family stateside. I, too, harbored doubts and uncertainties. This proved to be the most sobering decision I have ever made.

In time, we moved into an animated lifestyle that centered on a wonderful companionship. We joined a poker club, swam, danced, hiked, and camped. Our travels took us on space A (available) flights to the Philippines, Japan, the Republic of China, Hawaii, and Okinawa.

She loved to dance, so we danced often at the NCO Club,

Officers' Club and Korean nightclubs. On the dance floor, she threw herself fiercely and joyously into dancing with an elemental frenzy. To watch her felt like witnessing the birth of a small tornado lending tension and excitement to her every movement.

I taught her to swim and she really took to the sport of snorkeling. With her mask, fins, and breathing tube, she spent a great deal of time in the waters wherever we went. I asked for a transfer from Korea to the warm tropical Island of Okinawa. There, we spent most of our leisure time among the coral reefs that abound in its warm coastal waters. When we heard about the great diving in Turkey, we opted to go there. The Mediterranean waters held many, many artifacts of the varied cultures that developed in the Middle East. She treated every dive as a great adventure.

She passionately took up snow skiing on the slopes of Turkey. Within two years, she surpassed me in that she possessed more daring and grace than I could ever muster on the slopes.

One summer we spent forty days in the campgrounds throughout Europe. We traveled with no fixed plans or concern over where we ended up at sundown. Without benefit of hostelry, we spent our nights in a tent. We cooked most of our meals on a camp stove. To illustrate what a great sport she was, I have to tell this story about her.

We developed a routine based on amusement and organization. When we were ready to leave a campground, we packed at a leisurely pace and hit the road by 9 a.m. At noon, we usually stopped for a short lunch break along the roadside. Without time and distance as factors, we made frequent stops to shop, take pictures and to visit with locals. Why hurry? We had the whole summer to do our thing.

About 4 p.m. each day we began to look for an ideal place to spend a night or two. Once we selected a campground, we pulled up to the office. Here Sou Nee hopped out with our passports, signed us in and selected a tent site. Once at our assigned spot, we got on with it. The tent, always the first chore, took about ten minutes. She then moved our bags into the tent while I set up the cook stove and folding chairs. I put a bucket of water at her disposal. She then put rice on to boil. While the rice cooked, we relaxed and sipped wine. By this time, twilight set in, our favorite time of the day.

We had spent several days traveling through the heart of Macedonia and up the coastal byways of Yugoslavia. When we neared the northern parts of Yugoslavia, we figured to spend one more night in that country before crossing the border into Italy. Our maps indicated the coastal city of Pula offered a campground located on the shores of the Adriatic Sea. We figured there we could snorkel and spear a fish or two for the frying pan. Life was great.

We pulled into the camp. Sou Nee hopped out and did her office thing. When she got back in the car, I asked, "Did the man give us a good spot?"

"He said that we could take any spot we liked, no numbers. Over there." She pointed to a large grass-covered meadow dotted with many large trees. Having arrived early, we had our pick with only a few other campers around. We selected a lush, grassy spot under a large tree. After we finished the set-up routine, Sou Nee got on with the cooking.

As we entered the campground, I noted a bathhouse about one hundred yards from our selected site. Feeling an urge, I excused myself and headed up the path that led to the bathhouse. I had gone about half way, when I came face to face with a buxom blonde. She wore only a set of Walkman headphones. I'm here to tell you, she was buck naked, with the earphones covering only her ears. You notice, I said face to face, and I did not let my eyes stray. Poise took over. I did not look back nor cop a peek. Damn! When I opened the bathhouse door, I found myself mooned by seven or eight people standing at lavatories on two of the four walls. Here I got some attention. I had on clothes. Thank goodness, the commodes sat behind doors. I did my thing and got outta there.

Heck, I didn't tarry long enough to wash my hands.

As I ambled back to our digs, I looked around and, sure enough, folks in the buff occupied all the other campsites I could see. With my inherent powers of deduction, I figured we'd landed in a nudist camp. As I looked further I realized the folly in our Constitution's statement "... that all men are created equal." And that goes for the women folks too.

When I got back to our site, I found Sou Nee busily peeling potatoes. Not far from us sat a group of several tents with about a dozen men, women and children, all showing full skin. She had, evidently, not paid any attention to them. I stepped up beside her and pointed, "Sou Nee, look at our neighbors over there." She glanced up and did a classic double take. On that second look, she let forth a muffled scream, dropped the potato and knife and made a headlong dash to the tent. Luckily, the flap was open.

Inside, she gasped, "What are those people doing? They don't have any clothes on. Fred Harvey, you don't look, you get in here. What's happening?"

I laughed and said, "You lodged us in a nudist colony."

"Nudist colony, what is nudist colony?"

"Nudists are people who prefer to spend their vacations in the nude. They love nature's sunshine. They wait until they get here to take off their clothes. We have nudists in America. No problem. "

"You pack up, we are going now!"

"It's too late to leave now. Come on out and fix supper. The rice is done."

"No, I'm not coming out, you do cooking."

She then thought better of this proposal which compelled her to come out. Ya know, she cooked the whole meal wordlessly with head down and not looking up one time. I teased her by giving her a play-by-play account of our neighbors. After her third request to hush, I let up. At meal's end, I volunteered to do the dishes. Wordlessly she got up and went quietly into the tent. However, she did request a towel, water and a urinal which I supplied. Well after dark, I went in to join her.

She opened up finally and the pillow talk lasted deep into the night. She wanted to know all about the strange people who found joy in the nude. I tried to convince her it had nothing to do with sex or eroticism, but she didn't buy into that at all. Just before she dropped into a troubled sleep, she requested that we leave early the next morning. I agreed to do so. I'd never seen this facet of her personality. Was she a prude?

The next morning at dawn I got up, took off my PJs and reached for my daytime wear. I paused and said, "What the heck, when in Rome do as the Romans do!" I stepped out of the tent wearing only a big grin.

This move brought on some real movement from the voice box of the Oriental lady. "Fred Harvey," She cried, "you get back in here and put your clothes on right now!"

This brought on a laugh and an invitation. "Come on out, Miss Sou. This is great. You'll like it."

She rewarded me with some real maledictions shouted in her native language. I took this as a signal that she was really hot in the heart. I went about fixing some hot chocolate. This brought on the universal urge to visit the bathroom. By this time, I'd really gotten into this skin thing. With bravado, I took soap and towel in hand and headed to the bathhouse. Now, this really brought on the verbalization in rapid staccato, some of which related to my ancestry. At this point, I did a smart thing. I took the car keys with me. When I got back, I received still more criticism for crass behavior.

As I ate breakfast, quiet and peace prevailed within the tent. As I read a camp guide, I heard the zipper slowly open the door flap. Out she stepped, wearing a beach hat with a huge floppy brim. Over her shoulder she draped a large beach towel that concealed most of her body. She wore pink panties. I gaped in utter amazement and then bit my lip to keep from laughing. She could not see my face, nor could I see hers, because of the brim.

Wordlessly, she slipped into a chair to let the towel cover most of her body. I kept my face in the book. I did not say a word, too amazed to speak. Heck, I didn't want the wrath of God to come down on me.

The standoff lasted about twenty minutes when, of a sudden, she picked up her make-up kit and headed up the trail. I watched her all the way into the bathhouse. She came out in about ten minutes. She then selected one of the doorless shower stalls located on the outer wall of the bathhouse. She kicked off her slippers, dropped her bag to the deck and then hung her hat and towel on a hook. At this point, I made a silent bet, "She'll never take off those pink panties." I lost the bet. Then she went about doing the shower thing. Directly, a couple came by, saw her, paused for a moment and then proceeded into the bathhouse. Then out they came followed by six or seven other nudies and they all stood and watched her shower. Most of them had never seen an Oriental lady before, much less one in the buff. She went about her bath with the graceful poise of a go-go dancer, seemingly oblivious to those watching. Dang, I think she enjoyed it. She had gotten with the program. As she toweled off, I grabbed my camera and hid behind a bush beside the trail. Here she came, wearing nothing but the floppy hat. When she got near, I jumped out and snapped a picture. She howled and threw her bag at me. I ran. She showed fury, but then laughed. She called for a dozen prints. She opted to remain long enough to go for a swim. She hurried through her breakfast. We had planned to stay overnight. We spent three days. We wanted to see everything. Heck, we didn't figured on the canals of Venice drying up before we got there.

We found the camp had attractions other than the obvious and swimming. We could work on our tans. In fact, we filled in all the white spots. Also, we held laundering to a bare minimum.

We spent two wonderful months touring Europe which included ten countries. For forty days and forty nights (Now where have I heard this phrase before?) we crisscrossed the many lands of the Old World. Would you believe it, we did it all on just $16.75 per day. This included fuel, food and camp fees. Ya ought to try it some time. Of course, having our own car made it possible for us.

While living in Turkey, we met and made friends with many Turkish families. One day we went to a garage to have some work done on our car. Our dentist friend, Doctor Ercan (when pronounced it sounds like John) Ates, went along to interpret the language for us. We had not sat there long when a Turk drove in. He drove a big Mercedes-Benz, the luxury auto of choice of the rich in that part of the world. Ercan knew him well and went about the formality of introducing him as Ali Bey, or something like that. I soon realized he seemed quite taken with Sou Nee. Of course, this didn't bother me in the least since I'd grown used to fellows showing interest in her. It's not in my nature to suffer jealousy. Sou Nee paid him no heed, as she talked to the children of the garage owner. In time, Mr. Bey went to his car and opened the trunk to take out several big, luscious oranges. He then whipped out his pocketknife and peeled one and offered it to her. He offered Ercan and me one but did not offer to peel them.

He now had Sou Nee's attention and between them, they carried on a lively conversation through Ercan. He asked for and exchanged telephone numbers with her. Before we left, he put two burlap bags in our car, one filled with grapefruit and the other with oranges. Several nights later, I answered a ringing telephone. A Turkish voice asked in poor English, "Can I speak to your wife? I'm calling for Mr. Ali Bey."

"Sure, hang on."

I called her to the phone. Right off, I knew she had trouble understanding the guy. Finally, she put her hand over the mouthpiece and asked, "Who is this guy?"

"He is a guy speaking for Mr. Bey. You know, the orange man."

Her side of the conversation went something like this, "No, I have already eaten. No, I will not come out to meet him. No, I will not meet him tomorrow or anytime without my husband." She grew tired of this and slammed down the phone. I told her not to worry about it as he obviously was just a guy on the make.

Several days later, as I sat at home for lunch when that big ol' Mercedes drove up. A Turkish lieutenant came to the door and knocked. I answered. He asked, "Sir, are you Mr. Harvey?"

"Yes."

"I have a Mr. Bey here to see you and your wife. May we come in?"

"Sure, bring him in." He made a motion to the car and Mr. Bey and a very pretty young lady got out. Sou Nee joined me at the door and we watched as they approached. The pair entered with the officer and accepted an offer of seats.

Once seated, the young lady, about 22 years of age, spoke up. "My name is Ahbu;

I'm his daughter. I speak English rather well and father brought me along to speak for him." We made some small talk for a while, then I had to excuse myself to return to work. When I got home two hours later, Sou Nee informed me that they had just left. She showed me a couple more bags of fruit and veggies along with a big bag of pistachio nuts. She had made friends with Ahbu. As it turned out, Ahbu currently attended her third year of college. Before they left, Ahbu had given Sou Nee a map showing the town in which they lived. They insisted that we come to visit them in the near future.

A couple of months after the visit, Sou Nee and I went out for a Sunday afternoon drive and I happened to see a road sign with an arrow pointing to the town where the Beys lived. We drove through the town, but we did not have their address with us. So we just continued through the town. When we had gone a couple of miles on a dusty, dirt road, I saw a great cloud of dust bearing down on us. Figuring the driver might not see very well, I pulled off the road. When the dust settled, I pulled back on the road to continue. I had not gone far when I looked into the rear-view

276

mirror to see that cloud of dust attacking from the rear. When I heard a horn blaring, I pulled off the road again. The car pulled along side and stopped. Mr. Bey hopped out of the car and came over and welcomed us and indicated that we should follow him. We followed. He led us farther into the countryside. He drove through the gates of what looked like a large resort-type motel.

He led us into an ornate dining room. There he motioned us to have a seat. We complied as he ordered tea for us. When the tea arrived, he stood and pointed to himself. Then he pointed toward town, and mentioned Ahbu's name. I gave him a knowing nod and he hurried out. The way he drove, he returned in no time at all with Ahbu in tow.

Ahbu gave Sou Nee a warm hug. She explained, "My father would be honored if you would remain here and have dinner with us. It is now 5 o'clock, but we can't dine until the sun goes down. It is Ramadan, you know, the holiest month of the year for Moslems. This month of fasting is one of the Five Pillars of Islam, when adult Muslims refrain from drinking, eating, smoking, and conjugal relations from dawn until dusk."

I readily accepted the invitation.

She continued, "We have two hours before dinner. If you like, we can take you up to look at the animals in our zoo."

This certainly impressed Sou Nee. "Do you own this hotel and a zoo, also?"

"Yes, this belongs to my family. My father says that you are welcome to come and stay any time you please. At no cost. Please come."

We then drove up a short way to the animal pens and cages. For a private zoo, it had a lot to offer.

As the sun sank low in the western sky, Mr. Bey left and returned with the rest of his family. Ahbu introduced her mother, her sister and brother. The children looked about twelve and thirteen years of age. By the time the dinner bell rang, about twenty men, women and children had gathered in the room. Ahbu introduced each as they arrived, both kinfolk and close friends. Mr. Bey went about, placing each person at a seat at the long, narrow table. I found myself assigned to a seat next to Mrs. Bey and the youngsters at the far end of the table. Mr. Bey, of course, sat at the head of the table with Sou Nee on his right and Ahbu on his left. With everyone seated, we waited in silence. A cannon sounded in the distance. At this signal, the kitchen staff arrived in succeeding waves with a formal seven-course meal.

I enjoyed every course, unhampered by idle talk, as I had drawn a blank. No one spoke near me. The threesome at the head of the table stayed in an on-going conversation throughout the meal. Mr. Bey figured that Sou Nee didn't know how to use a knife, as he cut all her meat servings into bite-sized pieces. I didn't mind that, but did he have to fork the pieces into her mouth? Thank goodness, I didn't take offense to this 'cause it might have spoiled my appetite.

By the time the formal seven-course meal ended, the hour had grown late and we had a long drive back to the base. They insisted that we spend the night, but I feared that Mr. Bey might take the liberty of assigning beds. When we headed to the car, the whole gathering walked out with us. At the waiting car Ahbu, speaking for her father, insisted that we promise to come back the following Sunday. I promised to return after asking Sou Nee her opinion. Mr. Bey set the time at 9 o'clock, as he had planned a picnic at the zoo. On the trip home, I offered a few opinions on Mr. Bey. She answered, "He asked too many questions about our life and if I was happy living in Turkey. I didn't like him to feed me like a little baby. I like Ahbu very much. She wants me to visit her at her college some day. Is that okay?"

"Yes, that's fine with me."

The next Sunday we kept our promise. When we arrived, we found Mrs. Bey lying on a board on a hearth at the fireplace.

Ahbu explained, "My mother has a back problem and has to lie on a board for three hours each day. She has a present for you,

Sou Nee."

When Sou Nee accepted the present, she bent over and gave the donor a kiss on the cheek and a lingering hug. Sou Nee had received a traditional pant-like garment worn by all women in Turkey. Mrs.Bey had made it herself.

Sou Nee then got into a conversation with the children who could speak a little English. They moved to a far corner of the room. Mr. Bey then moved three chairs near Mrs. Bey and invited me to sit. Ahbu sat between us and opened the conversation with these words, "Mr. Harvey, in Turkey a man can legally have four wives."

"Yes, I have heard of this. Also, I have heard that many have more than four."

"That is true. My father, as you might know, has only my mother. We all feel that he should have two wives."

"What does your mother think of this?"

She then asked her mother a question which her father answered. "He says they have talked it over many times and they both agree that it is time to have another wife."

Naive me, I had no idea where they were heading with this and wondered why they talked to me, a stranger, about a family matter. I soon found out and it struck me like a bombshell.

Back to Ahbu. "My father and mother wish Sou Nee to be wife number two."

"You've got to be kidding! She is married to me!" I took this all in as a big joke and laughed at their comments.

She then said something to her father and he replied and she translated. "He says he will pay much money for her."

"She is not for sale. American men do not sell their wives because it is illegal."

"He will pay you much money and send her to any school in the world that she wants to attend, but she will have to be Islamic in religion."

"She would never do that. Besides, she is taking college

studies at the air base."

He spoke and she relayed, "He says we should ask her about this."

"No, we will not ask her, it is out of the question." I could sense Papa Bey becoming irritated by the answers I gave him. I heard him mention liras. She quickly scribbled some numbers on a note pad.

Then she said, "He is willing to pay you $45,000 American money for her."

"I told you she was not for sale at any price!" By this time, we were both hot under the collar. But he persisted. I paused and collected my thoughts.

I looked the young translator straight in the eyes and slowly and deliberately said, "You tell your father that I will sell my wife for $45,000, but that I want you, Ahbu, for myself in the deal." At this, she let out an audible gasp. She then collected her wits. She repeated what I had said and in the same way that I had said it. This brought Papa to his feet and Mama off her board. Ahbu screamed something and calmed her irate parents. He sat down and the mother, with a deep groan, lay back on her board.

Again, Ahbu, "You have insulted my parents."

"I have come to your house and you have insulted me and my wife. We will leave at this time. I'm sorry."

She relayed this to her parents. The mother sat up quickly saying, "No, No!"

She then said something to Ahbu, who in turn said, "My parents do not want you to go, please stay for the picnic."

I accepted their invitation to remain, but added, "I do not want to hear any more about the buying and selling of wives." Sou Nee stared in wonder as she had heard me say something about big-time money and a deal about Ahbu.

We went up to the zoo and all seemed back to normal except for Papa Bey, who remained quietly subdued. I noted that his eyes went to Sou Nee often. When the day came to a close, the group moved back to the house. Papa had to insult me once more. He took great delight in trying to aggravate me, but I just laughed at his asinine attempt to needle me.

As we prepared to go, Mr. Bey assembled everyone in the vestibule, an area walled with glass-enclosed bookcases and whatnot shelves. He shouted a command toward the kitchen and a maid promptly brought out two wine glasses. He put them on a table near-by and turned and opened one of the glass doors. I saw three beautiful cut-glass wine bottles inside. I could not read the labels but I did see 1932 stamped on a label. I did a quick mental calculation and came up with fifty years, at least. Man! I thought myself about to sip some really fine wine. Ali opened one of the decanters and filled the two glasses. I wondered why he wasn't drinking with us. He then presented a glass to Sou Nee and took the other and raised it to her and then hooked her arm with his and they sipped on that fifty-year-old wine. While they drank, I looked across at Ahbu, and she stood agape. When she saw me looking at her, she shook her head in the negative. I smiled and winked. She said something with silent lips. On our way out, she moved close to say, "I'm sorry."

I touched her arm and said, "I'm sorry that you were caught in the middle of what happened."

"I don't think my father will give up."

"No problem, don't you worry."

I will add a postscript to this tale. Several years later when we returned stateside, we had a little spat one day. I said, "Pack your bags!"

"Why, where are we going?"

"We are going to Turkey."

"Goody. I love Turkey. When are we going?"

"I'm going to buy two tickets, mine will be a round-trip ticket and yours will be one-way. I will be coming back $45,000 richer."

After that, when she made me angry, she'd simply smile and say, "Shall I pack a bag?" I could only laugh.

You should know that Sou Nee had a hair trigger temper, to say the least. Many times the Dragon Lady's rage made me the target. In anger mode, she projected a hundred and one pounds of lithesome fury, virtually the wrath of God. Of course, I brought most of this aggravation on myself. But a good many times she turned this indignation to the boiling point in my defense. I'll tell you about one such incident.

On a football Friday night, my team had its hands full. It seems a couple of drunks thought they could do a better job of coaching than I. They came down to the fence in back of the bench and shouted a few cuss words at me. Now, I have a rather thick skin and I paid them very little heed. But they made the mistake of directing their maledictions at the players. Now, this got my attention. Aggravated by this behavior, I headed to the fence. Several of the players grabbed me before I could climb over the barrier. As they pulled me toward the bench, I looked back to see that the Dragon Lady had answered the call-to-arms.

She raged into the middle of them, kicking, ripping, and pulling hair. She really laid some hurt on those poor devils. The team restrained me again. A security policeman got there quick-like and pulled them apart. Ya know, she got a big round of cheers and applause. This really fired up the team and they went on to win the hard-fought game. The squad dedicated the game ball to her. After the game, I went over to the policeman to thank him for taking care of her.

"Hell, Coach, I didn't go over to save her. I went over to save those two drunks!" She was like that. She added lots of excitement to life.

Sou Nee also had a dark side to her character. Jealousy and its helpmate, a suspicious temperament, lay deeply rooted within her character. She generally directed her unfounded suspicions toward me. This quirk in her character came to a real boiling point when we lived overseas. At the time, I coached where we lived on base at Incirlik Air Base near Adana, Turkey.

I had the habit of hopping on my bicycle and peddling home for lunch each day. One such day I came in and Sou Nee, as usual, had a nice meal prepared for me. We talked as I ate.

Without preamble, she stated, "You love your children more than you love me, don't you?"

Taken aback by her question, I answered, "No, I do not love them more than I love you."

"Oh, yes, you do. I know!"

"I love them just as much as I love you. It's natural. They are my children and I love them with all my heart, just as I love you with all my heart. It's a different kind of love."

She turned noticeably belligerent. "You lie, you love them more!"

She just wouldn't let-up. I pushed my plate back and got up. I had learned that the best and only way to fight her was with my cap. I put it on and hopped aboard my bike and left. Usually she cooled off in a short while and returned to her sweet loving self. I planned to play golf after work. When I returned home to change into my golf togs, I walked into the house, but she didn't greet me at the door as usual. So, I walked into the bedroom and found her in the middle of the bed with a sheet pulled up about her. She had a malicious look in her ebony dark eyes. This wild, menacing look sent a cold shiver through me.

As I drew near the foot of the high-poster brass bed, she threw back the sheet and produced two quart-sized jars filled with jet fuel. In one fell swoop, she dashed it on me, soaking me head to toes. She then reached for a flaming candle on a bedside table. In milliseconds, terror and free-flowing adrenaline fueled my reaction. I did a headlong dive over the footboard of the bed and slapped the candle out of her hand. No ignition, thank God.

I rolled off the bed yelling, "That's it! I've had it with you. I'm calling the APs!"

Before I could clear the bedroom, she leaped on my back like a wildcat, doing the things that wildcats do. She pulled out a wad of hair, ripped the shirt off my back, scratched my face and bloodied my nose. This all took place as I tried to get to the telephone located in the kitchen. I couldn't dial the Air Police because of the frenzied attack. So I put her on the floor and sat on her.

We lived in a duplex with a carport dividing the units. I knew my neighbor was at home, so I yelled, "Frank, call the police!" Bloodied and sick at heart, I waited.

Within less than a minute, I heard sirens blaring from all directions. When the wildcat heard them, she went limp in utter surrender. Four police cars and two fire trucks responded. They rushed in and sized up the situation. It did not take them long to see who received and who gave in the donnybrook. A police lady slapped a pair of cuffs on her wrists.

In a whimper, she begged, "Don't let them take me, Fred. Please, don't let them take me from you. I love you. I'm sorry!"

The lady cop interrupted to say, "Mrs. Harvey, he no longer has a say in this. You're in our custody. You'll be locked up for your own safety and the safety of others."

Sou Nee began to sob uncontrollably. My heart went out to her. At this point Marie, a friend and neighbor, stepped forth and asked if she could accompany her.

The arresting officer replied, "That's a good idea, as she's going to need someone other than her husband at this time."

I put my hand on her shoulder and walked with her to a waiting police car. When they closed the door, a cold shiver ran through my body. As the car pulled slowly away, she looked back at me, so helpless and forlorn.

I thought, "Will the future be harsh on her or me? Will we be able to free ourselves of our yesterdays?" Even today, I can still feel the sense of loss and emptiness that pervaded my soul that fateful day.

As I returned to the house, the firemen and police waited for me. In the bedroom, noxious fumes hung heavily in the air. Only then did I see the damage she had laid on the furnishings in the room. All of the furniture and trappings that I had brought into the marriage lay damaged beyond repair. Why, she had taken a heavy meat cleaver from the kitchen and turned a desk, two chairs, dresser, bookcase, and a bedside table into kindling. She had cleaved three slits into a two-drawer metal file cabinet eighteen inches deep. One of the policemen declared, "Hell, Coach, with that much power she could have opened you up from the top of your head down to your navel!"

My school principal and great friend, Milt Alexander, arrived on the scene about the same time as the police. When all the excitement died down and the base officials had left, Milt stayed to help me clean up the mess. While we worked, he offered comfort and sage advice. He had served with the Department of Defense schools for a long time and he told me what to expect. He added, "Sou Nee needs to be put into the care of a psychologist. I'm sure she will be unable to remain on base." He proved a Godsend that evening and in the days that followed. Later in the night, Marie called from the base hospital to say that Sou Nee wanted to see me. I went over to find her in a cell/room. We had a long sorrowful visit. I told her to expect the worst and pray for the best.

At the hearing at the JAG office the following morning, the lawyers told us we had several choices to consider, none of them good. Basically, I could send her to the States while I remained in Turkey, we could divorce, or I could press charges against her for attempts on my life.

She and I talked it over and we agreed that for her, divorce worked best. Already a citizen, she planned to live in the States, but she wanted to spend a couple of months in Korea before she settled stateside. I opted to remain in Turkey and seek a Turkish divorce. All this took place in April of 1988.

Soon after my divorce became final, I received a phone call from my sister, Patty, loaded with devastating news. My buddy, Cobber Dortsch, had suffered a debilitating stroke. He lived with his mother in Clyde, North Carolina, at the time. I made a snap decision.

"Get word to Cobber and his family. I'll take retirement in a couple of weeks and will be there as soon as possible."

When I arrived in Clyde, I found a lot to do. Happily, I had the ability to do most of it. Caring for Cob was a 24-hour-a-day job. His mother, although a remarkable lady at 100 years of age, had limited capabilities to care for him. So I took over. I worked night and day and soon reached the point where I was about to run out of gas. Then one day, just at my wit's end, I heard a knock on the door and there she stood. I had not told her of Cobber's stroke, or that I had retired and left Turkey, or even where I lived. I don't know to this day how she found me and she has refused to tell me who gave her the information. She had arrived by taxi.

I reacted quickly and yelled at the cab driver not to leave. In a stern voice I said, "Sou Nee, you get right back in that cab and leave. You have no business being here."

She only smiled.

Then I reiterated, "Leave now. You're big-time trouble and I don't need more at this time!"

Mrs. Dortsch came to the door and greeted Sou Nee warmly. With her, I figured I had some back up. "Mom, tell her she must leave now."

"I will do no such thing. She's welcome here. She's like another daughter to me. She'll stay."

"But, there are only three bedrooms, so where is she going to sleep?"

This line of rhetoric only brought a smile to lips that said, "As far as I'm concerned, I don't believe in divorce, so she can sleep in the same room with you."

"But...." That's as far as I got with my rebuttal. She took Sou Nee's hand and led her past me.

Then, to add insult to injury, the Dragon Lady said with grinning lips, "Fred, will you pay the driver and bring in my bags?

Don't forget to tip him." Very, very angry at this turn of events, I sulked for a day or so.

She moved in and took over. This, in itself, proved a Godsend. Her presence cut my workload to less than half. I slept at night and regained my sanity. Here we were, back like married folk, but without benefit of clergy.

After a couple of months we settled into a routine. Each morning we held council at the breakfast table where we planned an agenda for the day. Cobber's sister Helen usually joined us for breakfast. She's a remarkable lady who owns and operates an antiques business and teaches ballroom dancing at night.

One fall morning, as we talked it over, Helen asked, "What are y'all planning to do today?"

Cobber spoke right up a-saying, "I would like to drive through the mountains and enjoy the colorful leaves of autumn." When it came to me, I opted for the drive through the mountains.

When Sou Nee's turn came up, she said, "I've got to do some grocery shopping."

Then all our attention turned to Mom. She looked first at me, then at Sou Nee and said, "I'd love to see you two kids drive over to Tennessee and get married today." That received four yea votes and one abstention. I worried that I might be letting myself back into a world of torture. Reluctantly, I made it a unanimous vote. We indeed drove over to Tennessee and remarried that day. Cobber acted the role of Best Man. When she moved into my bed that night, Sou Nee once again buffered my loneliness.

When we finished our work in North Carolina, we moved back to Austin. Sou Nee needed to enroll in college so she could finish work toward a degree. She majored in math and wanted to go into a math-related profession. We purchased a condominium that brought intense happiness into her life. At long last, she had a home of her very own. She studied hard and long at her schoolwork. I spent my time golfing, canoeing, and writing. We were extremely happy for a couple of years.

Unfortunately, the tyranny of fate came between us once again. The shadow of jealousy and suspicion crept back into our world. To cope with this omen of darkness, she turned to a cult of Holy Rollers. Before long, those people had her believing that she was the second coming of Christ. She spoke in tongues, whatever that means. She had almost nightly visits with the Holy Ghost. She prevailed upon me to attend her church. One Sunday morning I reluctantly accompanied her, a big mistake. I sat both amazed and appalled at the rabid extreme to which those folks took their religion.

I let Sou Nee know that I respected her beliefs, but I could never join her in that type of worship. With this, she said in all seriousness, "Fred Harvey, if you do not belong to my church you will never get to heaven."

Now, I never argue religion. But I did say, "I will stick with my religious beliefs and take my chances on getting to Heaven." Tranquility walked out the door that day never to return.

Every day seemed a constant hassle with hate, jealousy, and religion the basis of the discontent. I couldn't reason with her. Again, taking to my cap appeared as the only way I could contend with her. One night at the supper table, I said a blessing which she found fault with. "Don't ever pray again. You do not mean what you say!"

I only shook my head in disbelief and said, "As you wish."

With this, she stood and got in my face and declared, "I will see that you never get to Heaven! God does not want you there!"

"You mean that you will have a say in my salvation?"

"Yes, I speak to God and he has told me that you can't come to Heaven unless you join my church! My preacher told me this, too." She spouted all this with revulsion akin to fanaticism.

"You mean to say that you will be standing next to Saint Peter when I come to the Pearly Gates and that you will tell me to go to hell?"

"That's right!"

I stood and said in a cool, deliberate tone, "I will go to Heaven in spite of you and your church."

"How do you know?"

"Sou Nee, I'll certainly go to Heaven when I die because I've spent my time in hell with you!" With that, I picked up my laptop computer and hat and walked out.

However, I did return the next morning after she had left for school and loaded my pick-up with my belongings. I then stopped at my lawyer's office and then headed west. Yep, I ran away from home, but not for the last time. Since I'm a slow learner, it took a third marriage for me to wise up. I'm a slow learner, very slow

Chapter 16

Return to Iwo Jima

During the early 1980s, while working for the Department of Defense in the Far East, I got a seat on a Naval aircraft in Japan that took a weekly trip to Iwo Jima. At that time, the island remained under US control. About the only thing that we maintained there at the time was a weather station. With the plane scheduled for an overnight stay, I had lots of time to roam about the island.

Due to the compactness of the islet and the fact that the battle lasted only six or seven days for me, I found myself able to retrace just about every step I had taken while there. I say six or seven days because I'm not sure how long I actually fought there. Time had no meaning, only the dark of night and light of day had any relevance. During the war, our short days quickly filled with a multitude of activity. In contrast, the nights seemed endless and filled with terror and loneliness. The rise and fall of the sun melded into oneness, like a circle, no beginning and no ending.

As I strolled about the quieted arena of combat, each step brought forth a memory. I made notes of those memories. The profound events that took place there so long ago came back to me in a rush. As I studied these notes to write of my experiences, I found it hard to put them into story form. I figured, what the heck. Below, I have simply transcribed my notes as I wrote them.

Put yourself in my place and develop your own account of

what I might have felt while there in the winter of '45. You will find incomplete sentences and dangling participles. (I think that's what you call those things that dangle.) I've given little thought to punctuation marks. I paid no heed to spelling, as I spell poorly. So here goes. I hope you get the essence of my feelings on my return to Iwo.

As my plane circles high above this little islet, I'm struck by the vastness of the Pacific Ocean....

Iwo is but a mere dot in its magnitude....as we descend to land I feel a strangeness and wonder.....

a sense of dread pervades me as we draw closer....

....As I stepped from the plane, I was met by loneliness and its companion, sadness....they remained with me....

This little isle has met with defiance the raging seas for eons of time....there is no contradiction in its turbulent past....history and the defiant, raging defenders that were here to defy us, the Marines, who stormed ashore in the winter of '45....As I stand on the landing beach looking out to sea, I recall the mad dash our landing crafts made to this very shore....I remember all too well the thundering sounds of artillery fire that came marching across the open span of pounding surf to meet us....On the rapidly nearing beach could be seen the tell-tale puffs of black smoke indicating the impacting area among the Marines of the first two assault waves. I knew then that many men were going to die on this day and the days to follow....

We took our appointed positions on the beach and, in quick order, our own gunfire from the many ships lying off shore laid down a withering barrage just beyond our lines. As our own black puffs began to move up and away from the beach, we, the Marines, followed in close pursuit. The enemies' black puffs continued to fall amongst us as ours fell among their caves and bunkers....I confess, tears are forming in my eyes....

If a single word could describe this place and what took place here, it would be simply, Hell.

Even now, long after all the participants have departed these shores, I can, seemingly, feel that phantom others are about....

For days and nights there was a continual flow of action....at no time was my stomach constant....

Only the crashing waves break the ghostly silence....

Will the peoples of this world once again be engulfed in a war that will ravage mankind still further?

Time has tempered the remembrances of this little island....

....fierce fragments, white with torrid heat, slammed their way into the flesh.

The silence, in memoriam, holds the echoing crash of cannon fire.... the quietness gives up the crescendo of a mean, impatient Jap Nambu machine gun....cries of human suffering....the sounds of war come echoing back to me in vivid remembrances....

The dull, sickening sound of metal impacting flesh that turns bright eyes to a look of terror....Death then gives them a vacant, peaceful gaze as if looking into eternity....

....his face emitted a soft cry and then tears....

A poor, sad mother's heart is broken....utter grief....

The Angel of Death collected many a soul from battle-torn, ravaged bodies....

The human unit reduced to its integral parts....souls in amazement, others raged in silence to their last mortal breath, but most passed on in a peaceful serenity....but, for all, the world's madness was over for them.

I remember well in my mind the broken bodies of fellow Marines, their anatomies reduced to their integral parts....withered and strewn

I have been a spectator in our recent wars and wallow in depths of guilt-ridden inaction....wars that our country has been involved in since WWII have left their mark on me in an almost....in a way....

I stand muted, swallowed by emotions that bring floods of tears to my eyes. I have not sobbed so....since I stood on these very sands so long ago.

Silence welds the spirits and camaraderie of the fallen of this historical little spot....the message that carnage and death wrote of this place has been lost in time....there still be wars.

With a feeling of guilt, I have lived in the freedom that these men purchased at so high a price. Will there always be men who will be willing to pay the price for future generations' freedom?

It is hard to believe that this somnolent little island is the prime depository for the life's blood of those thousands, both the dead and the wounded, American and Japanese fighting men.

The broken and torn bodies of the dead have been taken to their final resting place at home but their life's blood that ebbed from their bodies to flow into the insatiable volcanic ash of Iwo remains. Along with their blood, their spirits must surely remain to march into eternity in league with their comrades. The silence gives the eerie feeling that spirits of the warrior enemies still linger here, enemies who once pointed their brutality toward each other.....now their ghostly spirits march together into eternity.

They must ask, "Why?" Maybe God has given them the answer.... As their physical strength ebbed into Eternity....spiritual strength took hold at the transition.

My sorrow is unbearable....Fever of excitement....the days, weeks, months, and then the years, the chronology of time has wiped away most of the visual aspects of the battle fought here, but time will never wipe away the memories....

My chest is bathed by the teardrops that well into my eyes....the rage to live....before my ravaged body gives out....

I remember climbing these steep, unyielding, fluid-like terraces of volcanic ash....with a sense of immediacy and urgency, as the Japs had the whole beach area zeroed in with heavy artillery and mortar fire. We, the Marines, were mantled in a thick pall of smoke that seared our throats and lungs like a red-hot poker. The acrid smell of spent cordite mingled with the sulfuric acid fumes that were emitted unceasingly from the bowels of the island....

itself made breathing an excruciating struggle.

As I tread this lonely bit of ground, each step brings bitter tears welling into my eyes....my heart and soul cry out for the fallen buddies who were left here, oh, so long ago.

The tears flow in memory of those fallen comrades ....Iwo Jima had its moment in history....the stream of life and time has passed it by....in all probability it will never be more than a lonely spot on geographers' charts and maps.

What happened here during those killing days, so long ago, will fade from memory with the passing of the last Marine and Sailor who fought here.

The chronology of time, seemingly, has vanquished....I still feel the intensity, I remember....

The Earth's new day begins here each twenty-four hours, but the stream of life on this desolate spot, like a circle, has no endings.

.....where life, spirit, and the human entity were reduced to a myriad of fragments....disenchanted with war....There was no contradiction between the carnage that took place here and its diverse faceted surface....

....as I walk its volcanic sands, this little island holds me in utter fascination.... With total being marinated in adrenaline, I raced across this open space with shells falling like rain drops....though there were hundreds about me, I felt as if I were all alone....

Here, it was easy to be tough and practical during the day, but the nights were a different thing, another world....life and death and their maddening contradictions....echoes of history reverberate as I walk this desolate little island of my memories....the mist of splashing waves mingles about and on me as I stand looking east....beyond the horizon lay home. I looked in that direction many a time during the heat of battle to wonder if I....So stirring and vivid are my memories and visions of this place that they cause uncontrollable tremors to take hold of my body to....

As I stand here in vivid recall of that which took place here with fear, heartache, pain and human waste, I wonder in awe why the specter of the events that took place here do not come to me in the shadows of my nights....nightmares of this place have never been a part of my dreams....I dream of my buddies but only in joyous circumstances and shared jest....I thank....

The setting sun and the play of declining light cast grim shadows of black on gray over the terrain giving it a ghostly....

Bob, (I penned this note about the spot where Robert Clark met his end. He was from Odessa, my hometown. I worked for his father. His body is now interred there, along with his grandfather, father, and mother.) there was no poetry in your death, only honor....your heart's blood has found its depository among the lava sands of this....The lava sand of this island is the storehouse of your blood and that of the enemy....to remain here forever visited only by the ghostly spirits of you who drew your last breaths here....you are with God....You died for me so long ago.... Seeing Bob's broken, dispersed body lying on the grimy sands of this alien, desolate land, my thoughts and heart went immediately to his mother in far-away Texas. Mrs. Clark, a gentle loving woman, would have her heart broken in just a few short hours when a cryptic message of death would be placed in her trembling hands. At that very moment, my world darkened, never to be the same again.

The day is calm with only trembling heat waves moving....

I marveled at the bravery of my comrades. Their deeds made me a better Marine....The loose, volcanic ash of Iwo Jima hungrily ingested life's blood that ran so freely from the broken, shattered bodies of Marines and Naval Corpsmen during those hellion days and nights. The ebony, black sands of Iwo Jima will remain a depository for the blood of thousands of Americans for eternity.

I see this little island in its three-dimensional sense, but as I walk ....the eerie quietude of silence, seemingly, gave it another dimension, a spectral zone where the spirits of those who perished here so long ago must march together in eternal camaraderie with enemies who, at one time, pointed their brutality toward each other....there is a marked contradiction between this visit and the first time I set foot on its beaches 38 years ago....the voluntary excesses that men visited on each other....the intense, surging, immediacy of the action punctuated by the compactness of the island....the incompatibility of the invading Marines and the defending Japs and the very nature of this little island could be likened to hell as depicted in the verses of the "Inferno." Read this lucid, stark descriptive narrative by the poet Dante. This master wordsmith could have, very easily, been writing about Iwo Jima.

It was near this spot that this had its occurrence: A mortar shell impacted near-by sending white-hot shards of metal ripping through the air. I heard a repugnant thud. A searing fragment had found its mark. I watched as a fellow Marine sank slowly to his knees, his head turned slightly to stare across the vast Pacific, traces of tears formed and glistened in vacant eyes, his trembling lips softly formed the word "Mother." His lifeless body pitched forward, burying his face in volcanic ash, sealing forever his quivering lips and unseeing eyes....

The vernacular of battle sounds no more; only a deathly silence mantles this islet of desolation....why have I been spared the nightmares?...The shelling, when it began, came down like crescendo-ing pelting rain....

There were no concessions on the evils of destruction and death....in their angriest moods. There was a fever of excitement, stress, and of course, fear....most were able to control this fear....

...her guns were shouting a tirade of maledictions against a backdrop of deep-throated cannons belching forth vociferous bursts....the dogs of war were about to be unleashed on a well-entrenched, determined enemy....a lot of good men were to die that day and the long bloody days and nights that were to follow.

It was a soul-depleting moment ingrained in my memories seeing his fragmented body lying there encrusted with the volcanic grit of Iwo. Bitter tears welled in my eyes as my thoughts went to a mother I knew so well.... she too was soon to shed emotional tears of anguish and hurt that only a loving mother can experience. At that very moment the war ....

Iwo is to me hallowed, blessed, spiritual, sacred, pure ground.

If the spirits of the dead could speak, what would they be saying to me? ...Count off, Marines and Sailors, you of the vanquished dead. When your number reaches 7,000, we will know that you are present and accounted for in this, your eternal duty station.... Serve well....

....your ranks are growing each passing day as some of us, your mates in war, are coming to join you....

Those endless hours of terrifying nights....The carnage, devastation, and pain turned hope into despair....

....the remnants of formerly dynamic human bodies that carried hearts filled with dreams of peace, home, and loved ones....

....after the rush of battle, my eyes became heavy with tears; my body trembled with rage as I looked upon the broken bodies....the searing invasion of human flesh....aftermath of war....an elemental, suffocating fear....through and through my very soul....

The rattling peal of gunfire.... involuntary excesses that these men visited on each other lives only in the memories of those who survived....there is a marked contradiction between this visit and my visit of 38 years ago....

....the intensely surging immediacy of the action was aggravated ....no place to hide....

There was not only an incompatibility between the Marines and the defending Japs, but the very nature of this morbid little island....

Will the bugles and drums be answered when our security is threatened?

Will these 30 some-odd years that you bought and paid for

with your lives be in vain? What are 30 years, when you think in terms of eternity?

Its notoriety was written with blood that flowed from the carnage....

The sounds of battle, which were intensified by the human voice, with all its emotions, are absent today.

The moral revulsion that took place here, so many years ago, has been forgotten, except by those who fought here and survived and those who lost loved ones here.

.... indignations and vulgarity were unleashed on its defenders....

As I fought and watched the ebb and flow of life in this arena of carnage I thought, "How can anyone hold a belief that there exists an all-knowing God". (At the time of the battle for Iwo, I believed myself a full-blown atheist. I did not abide in God's Grace until fifteen years later. My conversion is detailed in the chapter *I Fought The Lord and The Lord Won.*)

....I remember looking toward the east each morning and thinking, "This, my blazing sunrise is my mother's fiery sunset...." The gap of time has not muffled or vanquished the intensity with which I feel and remember....

Iwo had its moment in history.... the stream of life

....surely, God has consecrated this little island, as He used it as the gateway to His Heaven for so many souls....

With tears in my eyes, I walk this lonely bit of land....disenchanted with war.

So stirring are the memories and the visions of this place....

The crashing waves of the sea break the ghostly silence....

The setting sun casts grim shadows.... to be absorbed in black volcanic soil....

Bob, the Clark Ranch that awaited you in the Panhandle of Oklahoma could hold hundreds of Iwos....I'm sure that you noted that there were a great many similarities between this island and the topography of the ranch; they both were born of volcanic action....

The play of light....Iwo, you touched my life so very long ago in a way that I can never forget....the memories stayed with me to the point of haunting me....as I walk, memories are set in motion....On that night I felt the reality of death.

Some passed with gaping wounds while others slipped into eternal sleep with seemingly unmarred bodies. Does God determine how a man goes?

The noise, the din, the wild disorder and the terror would give way to moments of eerie silence. The bang, the sounds of battle would rend the air once again.

For each and every wave that has crashed upon these shores since those days so long ago, a mother has shed a tear for a son who fought and died here. Many of those mothers, at this time, have gone to be with their sons....

Here, pride took over; you screamed loudly and ran straight ahead.... Its notoriety was written in blood and courage.

Absent are the sounds of battle that emphasized the human voice in all its emotions against a backdrop of roaring cannons and small arms fire.

The engines of war are silent now....

Iwo Jima today offers an innocuous view in stark contrast to what took place here in the winter of '45. The hurtful and injurious qualities that it supported those days, so long ago, no longer are in evidence. Yes, the engines of war are silent here, but man has cranked them up many times since, in other lands....

Iwo today still offers a landscape that features a rugged coarseness. Everything that took place on this spot emphasized strength, power and courage. Time and its helpmates, wind and rain, have erased the scars of war on the landscape but still it presents a paradox with a rugged beauty about it. Time, on the contrary, has not healed the scars left on the hearts and bodies of those who fought here.

There's nothing so brutal when men point their brutality

toward each other....My plane is rising to take me back to Japan....I look down on Iwo as a new day is having its beginning....loneliness and sadness have crept aboard....my heart holds many unsaid words, as I can't put into words the fragments of my thoughts and feelings....Thoughts and feeling that I can't ignore....a pain of unreasoning desolation....

I'm engulfed by a gray veil of sadness....

....I leave with mixed emotions. I'm glad that I came while regretting the return....though great distances separate me from this island, the thought of it is always just a heartbeat away....I'm determined not to ever forget the men I marched among....all my tears will not ever wash away the memories....

Now in my twilight years, all I've got are my yesterdays and a whole arsenal of memories—and Hell yes, I'd do it all again.

ONCE A MARINE, ALWAYS A MARINE

The Cob and I

T. Fred Harvey (the author) and Lee E. Dortsch

Our faces are bathed in sadness. We had just been medically discharged from the Marine Corps. The Corps which had been our home, was now just a memory. We loved the Marines and thought we'd always serve the flag. But circumstances intervened and left us homeless. We now faced an uncertain future. However, it didn't mark the end of the friendship that had been forged and nurtured by war. Like brothers, we have remained close ever since.

1st Assault Squad
Company C 26th Marines
1944
From left to right
Peter Adam, William F. Herold, Robert D. Hastings,
T. Fred Harvey (the author), Richard H. Skinner

Liberty Call Hawaii
1944
From top left: T. Fred Harvey, William E. Herold, Willard A Cross
From bottom left: Carl Hammett, Lee E. Dortsch, Peter J. Adam

Sergeant Ott Farris
He saved my life one dark night.

1ˢᵗ, 2ⁿᵈ, 3ʳᵈ Assault Squads
Company C 26ᵗʰ Marines
1944

1. Myran E. Teeters, 2. William R. Ryan, 3. Wiley C. Crook, 4.
Charles Irvin, 5. William E. Herold, 6. William S. Vernam, 7.
Peter J. Adam, 8. Robert D. Hastings, 9. Carl D. Hammett, 10.
Richard H. Skinner, 11. Euel Renfroe, 12. Raymond H. Thacker,
13. T. Fred Harvey

To order additional copies of
Hell, Yes, I'd Do it All Again

Name _____

Address _____

_____

_____

$18.95 x _____ copies = _____

Sales Tax _____
(Texas residents add 8.25% sales tax)

Please add $3.50 postage and handling _____

Total amount due: _____

Please send check or money order for books to:

Special Delivery Books
WordWright Business Park
46561 SH 118
Alpine, TX 79830

For a complete catalog of books,
visit our site at
http://www.SpecialDeliveryBooks.com

CPSIA information can be obtained
at www.ICGtesting.com
Printed in the USA
FSOW01n0957031216
28131FS